From the Edge of the Sky

Also by Maurice Shadbolt

FICTION
The New Zealanders
Summer Fires and Winter Country
Among the Cinders
The Presence of Music
This Summer's Dolphin
An Ear of the Dragon
Strangers and Journeys
A Touch of Clay
Danger Zone
Figures in Light
The Lovelock Version
Season of the Jew
Monday's Warriors
The House of Strife
Dove on the Waters
Selected Stories

MEMOIR
One of Ben's

DRAMA
Once on Chunuk Bair

NON FICTION
New Zealand: Gift of the Sea (with Brian Brake)
The Shell Guide to New Zealand
Love and Legend
The Reader's Digest Guide to New Zealand (with Brian Brake)
Voices of Gallipoli

From the
Edge of
the Sky

A Memoir

MAURICE
SHADBOLT

An annotated list of works by Maurice Shadbolt
appears on pages 230-238

David Ling Publishing Limited
PO Box 34601, Birkenhead
Auckland 10, New Zealand

From the Edge of the Sky
First Edition

ISBN 0-908990-59-6

First Published 1999

The cover shows a detail from *Titirangi* (1994) by Lois McIvor.
Reproduced by permission of the artist.

Photograph of Maurice Shadbolt by courtesy of
The Waikato Times

Typeset by Express Communications Limited
Printed in Australia

Author's Note

Alert readers of my earlier memoir, *One of Ben's*, may detect occasional repetition and overlapping in these pages. In my defence I can only plead that my life has been irritatingly rich in repetition: ask any of my female friends or former wives. As for overlaps, they creep into manuscripts on furtive feet and retire as stealthily; in the realm of the memoir, as distinct from that of the painstaking autobiographer, they tend to go with the territory. Nor do I feel obliged to account for the unsought and other-worldly events which may now and then undermine the reader's generous suspension of disbelief. Though frequently tempted, I have refused to refashion such events in the interests of plausibility. Memory is sometimes better left to its own arcane devices.

I should add that names and identifying details have sometimes been changed for the peace of mind of old friends and nervous relatives. It may be helpful to remind them, as I did in *One of Ben's*, that a novelist is at work in these pages. Finally, I acknowledge use of lines written for me by Piet Hein, versemaker, scientist and Nobel prizewinner, while we sailed the fiords of Norway in the long days of a Scandinavian summer.

Giving in is no defeat
Passing on is no retreat
Selves are made to rise above
We shall live in what we love

Maurice Shadbolt

For my grandchildren
Winston and Amelia, Maggie and Finn.

The story so far

The year is 1845. Benjamin Shadbolt, a 20-year-old English rural labourer and part-time thief, a married man with one child, commits one felony too many in his native Hertfordshire. This wins him a fifteen-year term in the chain gangs of Britain's antipodean penal colonies. It seems certain that the rest of his life is to be lived in the shadow of the gallows and in earshot of the lash.

Correctly assessing his prospects as dim, and his survival as unlikely, Benjamin marries bigamously into an otherwise wholesome Australian family named Perham. The Perhams have been mourning the loss of their household head, Thomas Perham, a much-loved husband and father. Thomas had been felled by a bushranger's bullet in an outback ambush. Benjamin's timely arrival, with his ill-concealed desire to better himself, is therefore a reason for rejoicing. There is now a sturdy man in the house, one with the muscle to see off wrongdoers of every stripe. Unable to return to England and envisaging a more lucrative future in the neighbouring non-convict colony of New Zealand, Benjamin marries seventeen-year-old Elizabeth Perham, fathers the first of their sixteen children, ships off to New Zealand and almost instantly begins to prosper. By the time 1861 rolled into view he was a respected citizen of New Zealand. He was an affluent farmer, a prosperous sawmiller, a well-heeled storekeeper, butcher and publican, proprietor of a billiard saloon, promoter of worthy causes, owner of a smithy and stables, owner and breeder of fast racehorses, and not least a dedicated churchman. Benjamin did nothing by halves. The Shadbolt living room boasted two pianos. The family carriages were regal, the homestead palatial. Life-sized paintings of the family hung on the walls. On his demise in 1882 Benjamin would be mourned as a model colonist. In fate's

7

most piquant twist he had even become the beefy arm of the law in his locality. Sworn in as a constable, he dutifully helped magistrates keep the peace. It was kept. Benjamin's formidable knowledge of crime and criminals was seen as an asset to the colony.

His children, however hard they strived to equal their ebullient parent, remained lesser beings. As farmers they were often unhappy and frequently bankrupt. Womenfolk tended to devote themselves to polishing and playing the piano when not buffing up the family name. Convict ancestry was seldom claimed by its owners. It would be another century before descendants of the South Pacific's scarred founding fathers were socially acceptable. These days people no longer back away from their lawbreaking forbears. They boast of them. Some even invent them.

The most conspicuous Shadbolt of the next generation, and the nearest approximation to his Falstaffian father, was Ernest Francis Shadbolt. The most robust of Benjamin's sons, he was a boxer, footballer, runner, oarsman and marksman. Possibly spurred by Benjamin's difficulties, Ernest began interesting himself obsessively in matters legal; he became, for most of his life, New Zealand's most notorious litigant, leaving magistrates suicidal and politicians in life-threatening disarray. He was also a conspicuous member of the Canterbury Yeoman Cavalry, selected to serve as a bodyguard for England's future monarch, George V, when that worthy toured New Zealand as Duke of York in 1901. Did Britain's king-in-waiting exchange pleasantries with the son of a convict riding at his side? Did the future monarch learn at length of Ernest's extravagent legal woes? It is an intriguing possibility. Ernest never passed up a chance to advance his affairs. That meeting with royalty may have been the loftiest moment in Ernest's life. It was then all downhill, with dozens of dizzying court cases (some even successful) and a punitive prison sentence or two for rowdy contempt of court.

Like his father, Ernest proved a successful breeder, and not just of horses. He sired ten children before being counted out by the Great Referee. Though some had problems with the land their parents pioneered, most lived circumspect lives. By far the most distinguished was Renee Shadbolt, known by near relatives as Aunt Sis, a disciple of Tolstoy and Krishnamurti, a compassionate nurse who in the 1930s sailed off to Spain to tend the wounded and dying of that country's civil war. Another afflicted by politics in that highly political era was Frank Shadbolt, Ernest's eldest son. Early in the same decade Frank and his brother-in-law Joe Kearon joined the Communist Party. They were on hand, fortunate not to be flung into a police cell, when unemployed rioters rampaged through Auckland city in April 1932. Less than a fortnight later Frank's first son, Maurice, was born. In other words, me. Encouraged by the women in his life, especially by his loved and childless Aunt Sis, Maurice for a time mixed literature with politics. This wasn't successful. Disillusion with Marxism moved in, accelerated by travel in Eastern Europe and the Soviet Union. Literature won. With his first book published, he and his wife farewelled England and set off to New Zealand.

Should all this matter? It does. If I can manage it this is where this memoir will start. Guesswork at this juncture may be useful. For my purposes I need to imagine Benjamin living and breathing, not just as a cluster of words on the page. Like this, say.

This is Benjamin Shadbolt reporting from six feet under, though I suspect the lackadaisical grave digger didn't dig half as deep as he was hired to. As for my great-grandson, I might have known that I'd be landed with someone like him.

I first sighted him on a fair day with a touch of autumn in the air. Downhill Akaroa's harbour was bright. Uphill there was just a little cloud patching the tops. I watched the young fellow climbing the hill road, opening the creaky cemetery gate, pushing through the high weeds, and stopping to squint at the headstones. It struck me that he might be more sprightly for a man of his youthful years.

Perhaps a shade fearful, he was slow finding my present location. For a while, as he circled the cemetery, blind as a bat, it seemed he might miss me altogether. Though I willed him to take care he stumbled here and staggered there and ignored my urging. Finally, with an evil burst of obscenity, he shinned himself on my headstone. Good. That woke the young sod up. He stopped and rubbed away lichen to read the words hidden beneath. Not before time; he was at least three score years late. I took a deep breath, something helpful in this subterranean address. (I had more elbow room when I was tossed into Norfolk Island's dummy to think on the error of my ways.) I'd seen enough Shadbolts – sons, daughters, grandsons, granddaughters, now great grandchildren too – come and go for more than a hundred years. I'd seen them come juvenile; I'd seen them return senile. They stood here dumb. Some had flowers. Most didn't. Some yawned. One or two prayed. Not that it was easy to tell the difference. As a character-building exercise, visits to my grave were a fiasco; most merely gossiped. Since I can't help eavesdropping, I have to suffer their maudlin muttering and makeshift tears. The fact of the matter is that they don't know what they are looking for. This Johnny-come-lately didn't either, not yet. What he knew about me, that April day, wouldn't fill a thimble.

It was some time before I saw that he might have some use. For one thing he was the first in the family to make himself handy with pen and ink. That day in the cemetery – April 17, 1960 in the land of the living – he was just back from London and full of his own importance. Having published his first book there he was reckoning to write more on home ground. If anyone was going to winkle out my story, he seemed the likeliest bet in a field of fidgety nags. Phantoms can't be fussy. That was more than thirty years ago; it isn't more than a hiccup hereabouts. One result of that rendezvous, among graveyard weeds and wild roses, was a book called One of Ben's. *I found it disappointing. Who wouldn't? For a start there was bugger-all about me and much too much about my half-baked descendant. Let him shed his own tears, grieve his own griefs, if he must. Then there were the things he laboured long and hard to get wrong. I daresay he meant well. Dissecting my relative serves no useful purpose. Though I wouldn't put money on it, he might improve with practice.*

One

Much of my life, possibly too much, has been lived in a studio set above a serene New Zealand estuary. This hermit hideout, where I write now, is fringed with spindly mangroves, wreathed with rainforest, and always under siege from loudmouthed birds. My nearest dictionary defines an estuary as a breach in the land where local tides blend with global currents. That bears some similarity to my situation. With one foot in Oceania, the other in Europe, my life has been a miscellany of the near and the far, the native and the exotic, the insular and the cosmopolitan. As a New Zealander I belong as much to the societies bordering the North Sea as to those fringing the South Pacific. The new righteous might denounce this suggestion as a sell-out. Europe, especially in this locality, has lately and mysteriously become a dirty word. What will they pick on next? And who? Me, for example? I suspect my proletarian credentials might not count for much when the politically correct take to the streets on the Day of Judgement. Even my impeccably luckless ancestors may not guarantee me a box seat above the mayhem. In the long view, the short too, I remain indelicately waspish, a reluctantly card-carrying white Anglo Saxon Protestant. (With the Protestant part optional.)

Other than in storm, my situation is seldom less than agreeable. In a lively letter about my first book of stories, *The New Zealanders*, the Australian novelist Patrick White likened New Zealand to Norway with a dash of Greece thrown in. White could have cast his net wider. The view from my windows in moist weather is often mistily Japanese in character. Framed with palm and fern, the outlook can also be surprisingly equatorial. Something resembling a snowless Scandinavian fiord drops sharply from my back door. I greedily wish Greece nearer too.

It is a grey and humid summer day. Ignoring the world beyond my window, I have been drifting back and forward, looking for a way into this book; a book which, according to the best information at hand, may be my last. I riffle through faded fragments of manuscript, puzzle over scraps of paper with indecipherable messages addressed to myself. Most fall into my wastebasket with never a murmur of protest. There is too little time to resurrect them now.

With few modifications, and an occasional lick of paint, this cliff-hanging bivouac, all but buried in greenery, has been a sanctuary for more than thirty years, roughly half my adult life: three hundred square feet where I dwell with my fancies and fantasies. In this modest space I have seen soldiers and warriors roaring recklessly into war; strikers battling bloodily with baton-swinging police; mariners hoisting sail to brave the world's waters; pioneers toppling trees, torching scrub and putting the earth to the plough. Other, sweeter scenarios have been enacted here. As an intrigued voyeur I have heard lovers exchanging passionate endearments, sometimes en flagrante on my couch. There has been birth and death. There has been flood, fire and earthquake. Most of my dozen novels, and more than a score of stories beside, have taken form under this roof. My studio – call it a cabin or office if you wish something less fancy – sits among the sea-filled foothills of the Waitakere ranges, overlooking the vast Manukau harbour, one of the world's largest. The Maori tribesmen of the region believed a sacred land lay under these waters, an extinct Atlantis. The community now embowered here goes under the name of Titirangi. Translated from Maori, Titirangi means 'the edge of the sky'. Further, the short and winding cul de sac in which I reside is named Arapito Road. Arapito translates as 'the end the track'. For more than three decades, then, I have been content with my situation at the end of the track at the edge of the sky. The place needs a poet. Not a novelist. Nevertheless, though it may be thought second best, I keep notes. Notes, that is, from the edge of the sky.

Auckland, New Zealand's biggest city, is a dozen miles to the east, though most of the time I don't make a point of acknowledging its existence. From my perch I glimpse silverings of sea through foliage and hear the tide rustling over rocks. Birds – obese wood pigeon, white-throated tui, darting kingfishers, diminutive fantails and colourful rosellas – prosper in this neck of the woods. A few months ago

12

we had unfamiliar visitors – two circling skua on vacation from the Antarctic. The estuary emptied of its customary creatures when these predators shadowed the shore. A swirl of white wings heralded their arrival. Quite suddenly no gull was to be seen, nor any seabird on commonplace errand. For a few minutes trees alone were lording it over the land, especially the kauri, the dinosaur of the vegetable world. Save for California's sequoia, these spellbinding columns of wood are the greatest of their kind in the world. Even the most modest seedling, as its apprentice years pass, may climb more than sixty metres and live two thousand years. It is what we have in place of the Parthenon. Which is not to see it as a poor relation.

My window-dressing is almost done. What, then, of homo sapiens, the most ubiquitous arrival here? Aside from tiny bats, New Zealand lacks indigenous mammals. Creation's strategy made no provision for two-legged interlopers. One might surmise that it had more than enough on its mind. Such as creatures winged and finned and trees too tall to be true.

Fish and shellfish remain abundant. This morning I set a net, hauled in several mullet, and smoked them for a fish pie tonight. Towards dusk two of my sons, holidaying with me, arrived in with an entrée of fat scallops. We dined with the knowledge that life has much to be said for it in this vicinity.

My boys, my girls too, would like to take over the place when I relinquish my role here. No thought gladdens me more.

There is history here, of a highly coloured sort. Two centuries ago the tide-lapped terrain below my windows was the setting for genocidal slaughter when Maori of the northern Ngati Whatua tribe wrested these ranges from the seemingly peaceful Kawerau people; the tide reddened with the gore of the slain. Then it was the turn of the Ngati Whatua to perish in anguished fashion. Arming his tribesmen with muskets, gifts from Britain's monarch, a Maori Napoleon named Hongi Hika pitilessly levelled the inhabitants of the Auckland isthmus, the young and the old and the middling. In keeping with battlefield custom, feast followed slaughter, perhaps with cooking fires smoky along the rocky shore I walked this morning. Apart from eroded hilltop fortresses, there is little left to tell of generations of terror. There are few vestiges of the pre-European Maori anywhere in this locality: middens here and there, and rock paths meandering among mudbank and mangrove and along which canoes were portaged by men now centuries dead. When putting out my net on a misty morning, wading slowly through cool water, I sometimes imagine I hear faint voices, whispers not of my time. Others hear sounds more robust. It seems the noise of ancient strife persists here longer than it decently should.

Men of my colour made their debut when muskets had harvested local tribesmen in sufficient number. These raucous arrivals were interested in timber for tall vessels, flax for reliable cordage, and the fossilised residue of the kauri tree, much esteemed in the making of marine varnish. The British navy was an enthusiastic buyer of New Zealand timber; the skippers of merchant ships found it enriching too. I often encounter their debris: rusted chains, sea-worn bricks, rum bottles encrusted with barnacles, an iron kettle. Nothing survives of the industrious missionaries who toiled to tame warrior souls in this neighbourhood. The flogging cleric Samuel Marsden – loathed by English convicts, revered by Maori converts – was no believer in sparing the rod. More to my point, he became the first European to marvel at the great sheet of sea which races away from my feet into sunlit distance. He may not rate high as a humanitarian; he was no journeyman explorer.

Contemplating my past, I am all but buried under the detritus of a writer's life: pencils, pens and paper clips, manuscripts, notebooks, an extinct typewriter, reference books, a prematurely senile word processor. There are also wholly sentimental mementos. They don't necessarily relate to each other, though I look for connections. There is a lump of cooled lava lifted from the volcanic heart of the Icelandic island of Surtsey after it burst from the bowels of our planet in 1966. With Danish botanists and geologists I climbed on to the island soon after it began cooling. There was already a lone daisy resident in the crater. I was tempted to pick it. At the last moment I faltered. I saved it for science.

Less romantically, there is a collection of flattened bullets and grenade fragments gathered on the Gallipoli peninsula, remnants of the suicidal campaign waged there in 1915, and where the bones of three thousand of my fellow countrymen, victims of the elegant lunatics of the British high command, still litter the Turk landscape. With a book, a stage play, a documentary film, a radio reconstruction and a movie too, I have laboured lengthily to persuade Gallipoli to give up its forgotten New Zealand dead. Little by little it has begun to. I see this as missionary work. I find nothing wrong in writing for the record. It is where we all began, Homer too.

Still meandering about my studio, and lusting after magic, I idly pick up and rub a Roman coin I found in Troy's rubble. It happened to be the day I was re-reading the *Iliad* beside the wine-dark waters of Homer's Agean. Was our distinguished forerunner using the coin to signal that he was ready to discuss the film rights? Unlike that daisy, the coin might be considered legitimate loot.

Elsewhere in my studio, among discarded scraps of indigenous warfare, is a Maori carving salvaged from a defunct tribal village. It does much to remind me where I belong. It certainly has a link with my novel *Season of the Jew*. Te Kooti, the Jew of the title, an aggrieved Maori warrior who took inspiration from the Old Testament, lived his last years in the village from which my carving came. Skilled in dismembering his fellows, his hands may also have worked the wood for my carving. More personally, in this mini-museum of mine, there is an impressive lump of native greenstone, pounamu or New Zealand jade. Half of it survives in its early rough form; the rest is ground smooth to a high polish. It seems to be saying something about the craft of fiction. Actually it was a gift from a woman I might have married. Instead, for reasons unclear to me, I married four others. Time and chance allowed us just one summer. Again our timing was poor. When she was free, I was not. When I was free, she was elsewhere. We now seldom see each other from one year to the next. She continues to believe that we will finish together. Past experience leaves me unconvinced. Nevertheless no item in my workplace is more eloquent than that greenstone. Love makes children of us all. Fools of us too.

Two

Pinned to my walls are photographs and faded newspaper clippings. My five lively children and four grandchildren are on show there. So too are many of my more eminent contemporaries, not least the stocky and drawling poet James K. Baxter: my generous and eloquent mentor. When I first led Jim into leafy Titirangi his talent for word-spinning leapt into top gear. He took fewer than fifteen minutes to produce a poem of celebration. Then as always, Jim literally oozed verse; his pockets daily filled with first drafts and fine versions. For my hideaway there was this:

> The arms of old man manuka
> Reach up toward low cloud
> At Titirangi – so quiet a harbour
> Promises peace – Coves of green water hide
> The chugging of a launch, and always out beyond
> Bank and breast of land
> There is the open sea,
> The raging mother in whose abyss
> Man and boat are lost – but I prefer
> To look at the shallows, smoke, drink coffee
> And talk with you, old friend.

As always, when I read these lines, my eyes begin to blur. Jim, also known by the Maori name of Hemi, was dead soon after writing that poem. There will always be a gap in my life where he should be.

Barbara, once lawfully my wife, now my affectionate companion, appears at the door of the studio. She has been weeding the garden. She looks about the studio with a puzzled air.

16

'Did I hear you talking to someone?' she asks.

'You did,' I admit.

She is rightly mystified. 'Like who?'

'Old friends,' I explain.

Old friends, then. The larrikin New Zealand novelist Ronald Hugh Morrieson is resident in my rogue's gallery too. Despite my best efforts, his life ended in a maze of alcoholic misery, too late for him to hear applause for his racy novels ringing around or ever to see the movies made from his breakneck yarns. 'I hope I'm not another one of those poor buggers who gets discovered when he's dead,' he told me. The fear was justified. When the world finally discovered him he already had one foot in death's door. Here too, another of those buggers, is the equally uncelebrated American novelist Stephen Becker who praised my first novel thirty years ago and has used it as a text for his student writers ever since. The English novelist Colin McInnes, another stoic foot soldier in the empire of literature is to be seen, bottle in hand, ducking the camera. The celebrated photographer Brian Brake with whom I collaborated for much of his life, continues, dead, to smile down on me. There are documents recording awards and prizes. There are poems, prints and paintings, gifts from companions who have allowed me to look into their life's journey.

Perhaps because they are less charged with envy, I have always felt more at home with painters and sculptors than novelists and poets. Most conspicuous among them has been Colin McCahon, now widely thought to be the most powerful painter the Southern Hemisphere has produced. Though he might have been seen so earlier, he was no longer a lone figure at the time of his death. I think of visionaries at large on the land like Michael Smither and Eric Lee-Johnson. Alive or dead, these chroniclers of my country are seldom far from me here. It has been my good fortune that my dead decline to die in a hurry.

Nor do my weathered ancestors. I have been slow to name them because I have been slow to claim them. Until ten years ago I knew little of their existence. They had been buried deep by grave diggers who took pride in their workmanship.

I could go on. I could name others. More than a few lived with exuberance on the wrong side of the law. So far overlooked in this narrative, there is a worn calf-skin rug on the floor of my studio.

George Wilder, a frequently convicted criminal, a prison escaper par excellence, presented me with the rug the day after his one legitimate departure from prison. I had negotiated with the authorities and had something to do with securing his release. Thus the rug: a reward from New Zealand's most celebrated rascal.

There is one maverick among my local memorabilia, another rank outsider, in his way an escape merchant too. It is a painting of John Kasmin as seen by the British artist David Hockney. Once a colourful if half-starved citizen of New Zealand's bohemia – usually posing as a Polish count – Kasmin is no longer an aspirant poet but an affluent art dealer in London, widely known as the man who discovered Hockney and set Francis Bacon on the road to success. Before fleeing New Zealand for more remunerative shores, Gillian and I used to nourish him with potato soup; Kas now treats his old friends to caviar. Life isn't without happy endings.

Books. Of course books are here in bulk. As year follows year more and more spill from my shelves. What writer's den can do without them? An author needs not only his own work but also the visible toil of others to reassure himself of his vocation. Among those currently on show there are several novels by the once eminent English author C.S. Forester. I have been making his acquaintance. It is said by American reviewers that my 19th century novels owe much to his. Mystified, I am now reading Forester for the first time, forty years late, to see where and how he has influenced me. I have not been successful in the search. At least it makes a change. For my first two decades as a writer English reviewers held Katherine Mansfield responsible for my shortcomings. Until well into the 20th century she was the one New Zealand writer of whom outsiders spoke, if seldom knowledgeably. Poor Katherine. Her compatriots continue to bedevil her posthumous existence. She may have abandoned New Zealand. On present showing New Zealand, however, has no intention of abandoning her. This morning I even found myself wondering whether her name shouldn't have a niche in the final title of this manuscript. *On the Run from Katherine* perhaps? Or *Making it with Katherine*? To settle my longstanding account with her I recently made a pilgrimage to Menton, in southern France, where she wrote several of her most memorable stories. It was a dour day, with bone-chilling rain and snow misting the Alpes Maritime. It was no place for a tubercular waif from New Zealand in 1922.

Nor was it especially healthy for an author nearing his three score and ten in 1998. A basement room meant to be a memorial to New Zealand's most illustrious writer, now reeked suffocatingly of dust, mould and neglect. One of Stalin's cultural commissars might have seen merit in the location as a place of exile for troublesome writers. Otherwise it was difficult to see who it might serve. God knew what I might catch there. Malignant bacilli left behind by coughing Katherine might be the least of my woes. I didn't linger long enough to learn.

My gaze roams again. It comes to rest on Bulgarian peasant pottery gathered from remote Slavic villages. Then on delicately inlaid boxes from Croatia and Soviet Georgia. These innocent souvenirs talk of the time when I was footloose in Stalinist Eastern Europe with subversive volumes by Orwell, Koestler and Pasternak in my hitch-hiker's pack. Walls have fallen. Frontiers are sundered. Those dangerous days have gone. But they weren't a frolic. Did I help bring down a little of Berlin's wall? I shall continue to believe it possible.

Three

My eyes move to a paperweight with a distinctive character. It is an almost fully formed Maori adze, quarried and fashioned from rock of the South Island's wild shore. I found it while taking a beachcomber's stroll along uninhabited coast, a bitter wind off Antarctica freezing my face. Why was it discarded? It still looked useful to me. Had the stone age craftsman gone fishing and been swept off the rocks, leaving his wife and children bereft? Or was it that iron and steel had suddenly, in the hands of enemies, become more deadly than stone?

I rummage among the other objects, hoping for something which might set my manuscript in motion. Carvings from Borneo, from Tonga, from the highlands of Malaya. Scraps of marble from the Athens of Pericles. None offer a way into this narrative. It must have a beginning. How did I get here? What am I doing here? It puzzled Bruce Chatwin, possibly the most emblematic writer of my time; it certainly mystifies me. 'The 21st century is going to be wonderful with people like you and me around,' he told me on our last encounter. I wasn't sure what he meant and it is too late to ask. He didn't make the millenium. I am not sure I shall.

The morning mail came to my rescue. There was a typescript of a recent interview with a fellow called Francis Richards, whoever he may be. I began to recall a rather desperate young pipe smoker in trouble with his tape recorder. When that baffled him sufficiently he began trying to rescue his pipe from oblivion. Among far too many other things he wanted to know whether it was my intention to write a second memoir, a sequel to *One of Ben's*. It became clear that he didn't mean to leave the wretched subject alone. I was soon wishing C.S. Forester had influenced me. Katherine Mansfield too.

'You've only told half the tale,' my inquisitor pointed out. 'You can't walk out on the rest.'

'The rest?'

'Your half.'

'You'd be surprised,' I said.

He left me silent. It became clear to me that the young bugger had done his research and wasn't of a mind to give it up. Still endeavouring to make my day useful, I navigated among notes on dreams new and old. Some dreams are recurrent. One is especially haunting. In this one I have published a book – perhaps of verse, perhaps of stories or essays – which I have no memory of writing. For some reason this phantasmal book is never a novel, which might seem more likely for an author with his name on a dozen. Moreover, I have never published a book of verse, nor of essays; and have only two short stories to my credit in the last three decades. Odd.

The dream book, or such of it as I am permitted to see, has a powerful reality. The difficulty is that I lose my one copy. It melts away or is pilfered by persons unknown before I can begin reading seriously. In search of the book I begin a quest which ranges over much of New Zealand and then even further. I meet people who recall seeing the book and even quote fluently from it. Finally, however, they are no help. Though they have seen it here and there, they have no copy either. The dream is so plausible that it sometimes survives awakening; I rise from bed and hunt frantically among my bookshelves for the missing title. When I fail to find it, I have a daylong sense of loss; the dream can take a week to disperse. I continue eyeing my shelves with suspicion, as if the book might be hiding there. Memory refuses me even its name.

I must take it that my subconscious is doing more than having a playful field day; that it is telling me something of an enlightening nature. As a parable the dream – refined frequently in the thirty years since it first afflicted me – never lacks narrative interest. My first experience of the dream seems to have been sometime soon after my first book appeared – or about where this manuscript begins. Any earlier and it would make no sense. Each book I have published since it began may be seen as another attempt to make good my loss. Come to think, this one too.

Another repetitive dream is more sporadic and less single-minded in character. An editor, who bears some resemblance to a peppery

Bulgarian who once employed me in Paris, commissions me to investigate life's meaning. This is literally a story to die for. I start by interviewing a distinguished scientist. 'Why,' I ask, 'is it all such a riddle?'

He is tremendously excited.

'I'm glad you asked that question,' he replies.

'Meaning what?'

'Meaning I should be able to give you a firm answer twenty thousand years from now.'

I try a distinguished philosopher. 'You have to define your terms,' he says, or something to that effect.

I look at him blankly. 'Terms?'

'Life,' he points out, 'is under no obligation to have meaning.'

At that point I give up. I inform my editor that he had best commission a writer of more imaginative character.

The third dream is less frustrating, if equally mystifying. I am living in a house which owes little to the waking world; I have lived there, it seems, for many years. I am aware, all the same, that there are doors in the house through which I have never passed. Finally, on impulse, I push one open. With mounting exhilaration I find myself in a large, airy and lavishly furnished room filling with rose-coloured light. I am given to understand that this is where I now live. I have since been told that this is a commonplace dream, familiar to many and recorded by Jung. For the life of me – and Jung's too for that matter – I can't find it commonplace. Something or someone appears to be drawing my attention to the contents of my subconscious. For there is no doubt about it. This is where I continue to live. I have neglected to note that the room is rich in unwritten books, too many of them mine.

Here I am, then, perhaps later the same day. My visitor has gone, wisps of pipe smoke in his wake and his tape recorder now hopelessly tangled. Allow me to be first to acknowledge that my new-found associate Francis Richards, if he exists, is no fool after all. For I seem to be at my desk again; I appear to be writing. Though what? An absurd question. I have always relied on the next chapter to tell me. This one has just slid into place.

Four

The 1950s were expiring astern as sunset cooled; the inaugural hour of a virgin decade was almost upon us. Our ship, the cumbersome SS *Oronsay*, a vessel long dedicated to populating the South Pacific with optimistic migrants, was closing with the sandy capes of northern New Zealand. Diminutive islets outcropped to starboard: surf flew up formidable cliffs to port. A lighthouse began to blink on the promontory called Cape Reinga. Legend asserted that it was here the Maori spirit disappeared into subterranean dark following death of the flesh. It was my first encounter with the melancholy silhouettes of New Zealand's northernmost limb. I allowed myself excitement at last. Had other New Zealand writers, their fugitive years ending, felt the same mix of fear and euphoria as they made their stealthy way home?

Gillian, my wife, was considering the coast too.

'So how does it look?' she asked.

'Out of ten?'

'Out of ten.'

'Nine,' I reported.

'Why not ten?'

'Too much like hard work.'

We had been weeks waiting. There was little left to be said. It was my twenty-eighth year. My first book had just been published. Our first child was soon to be born. And that was my equally pregnant land bulking ahead. What did I ask of it? Innocence perhaps? The silences of a land not altogether blighted by man? The silences of a people trying to discover what they were about in South Sea? Such silences might tell me that I was a long way from London. They didn't tell me where I was, or who. Not yet.

We sailed among the islands of the Hauraki Gulf on a sunlit summer morning. Off Devonport's North Head we were met by the customary pilot boat. Scrambling aboard was a journalist in need of an interview. A file of newspaper clippings rustled in his hand: reviews of *The New Zealanders*. 'It seems your first book is having some success in London,' he said with a faint air of grievance.

Perhaps he was a disgruntled author. Anyway it was plain that he felt some mistake had been made; that, if these reviews weren't bogus, I shouldn't be back in the country. Received wisdom said that New Zealand writers who sailed away seldom sailed back. Katherine Mansfield, the country's longest living star in the literary firmament, established the convention by disappearing in the direction of literary London and never returning. Latter-day contenders for her crown, sometimes to be seen as downcast itinerants in London or Paris, continued to reinforce the custom. As for the suspicious journalist, I could see his next question coming.

Did I consider myself, he asked, the successor to Katherine Mansfield? (In 1959 any New Zealander who had written a respectable sentence was alleged to be the new Mansfield, regardless of gender.) I thought not, I said. I considered myself merely the successor of my parents, grandparents and great-grandparents. Did that make sense?

It would have to. He made none of me.

On the Auckland waterfront the *Oronsay* finished discharging human freight. My parents were on the wharf to help us find our land legs. We stayed at first in an outer reach of suburban Auckland. Summer's lethargy was thick on the land, difficult to accommodate after the liveliness of London. Only the beaches were busy, and yachts on the harbour. Otherwise the place was as mute as the moon. That evening there was a family party to welcome us home. My favourite uncles were there – gentle Joe Kearon and burly Dick Shadbolt. They and my father soon cornered me. This trio of 1930s left-wingers didn't much wish to know about literary success, or London reviews, which was a relief. They took my calling for granted. Had I been a drainlayer, they wouldn't have been critical of my drains either.

No, they wanted to know about the Soviet Union. This was difficult. They wanted good news, nothing less. I pointed out evasively that it was now more than two years since I was afoot in the Soviet Union; that I said most of what I had to say in letters written home at the time. Perhaps they were reluctant to believe what pen and ink said. Perhaps they needed to hear me say it. It was something of an inquisition. I shifted uneasily in my seat, knowing I was bound to say the wrong thing; that there was no escape. So I pushed on. The Soviet Union? Worse than my worst expectation, I told them. A monstrosity. A perversion. Desperate to make myself understood, I added that New Zealand was more authentically socialist than the Soviet Union ever had been. At this point voices were raised. Among other things it was suggested that I had been bewitched by Trotskyites, underhand enemies of the people. Beliefs of a lifetime were imperilled. I pulled back. There was too much distress. The evening then meandered peacefully to its end. I supposed I had left them something to ponder on. Not that this gave me pleasure. It was not my business to rob people of peace of mind.

Yet I had. I did. Truth at any price? I once thought so.

My parents hurried us off to their new house in the old gold-mining town of Waihi. Gillian, five months pregnant, found Auckland's humidity trying. After telephoning old friends, people I once thought allies, I didn't find the city congenial either.

'You're making enemies,' one warned.

I had a slightly sick feeling. 'Me?' I asked. 'How?'

'Publishing,' he explained.

'Am I supposed not to publish?' I said.

He fidgeted. Finally he said, 'Perhaps not so soon.'

I was baffled. Was I supposed not to earn a living?

Another, a writer for whom I had always had respect, and from whom I had taken example, had an uneasy sound in his voice. It was not one I had heard before. 'You must come over before you head down country,' he said.

I decided that he didn't mean it. I was aware that his mature stories deserved publication ahead of my apprentice work. But since when had justice flourished in the literary world?

Nevertheless I began to feel guilty about jumping the queue. Further scuttlebutt informed me that I had recently said something heretical in a radio interview which had given offence to the novelist Frank Sargeson, though no one could recall what impiety I had uttered. I wasn't disposed to investigate. The complaint was bound to be petty. A wispily bearded pixie of a man in a Parisian beret, Sargeson was then, and for years after, known as the grand old man of New Zealand letters. Vain and petulant, alert to slights, and possessed of a schoolboy's smutty snigger, he liked young men sitting attentively at his feet, desirably those who didn't talk out of turn. His political views were often bizarre. He argued that historians might eventually decide that Hitler had served a historical purpose and might one day be seen as a good thing. His interest in his quiescent juniors proved the kiss of death for more than a few. I number near a dozen victims; there may have been more. This isn't to argue that a serial killer was on the loose among lettered New Zealanders in the middle of the 20th century, though a case might have been made for the existence of an efficient assassin as one young writer after another sank from sight. The exceptions, significantly, were often women; most notably Janet Frame. Almost alone among her contemporaries this shy woman survived the 20th century with some grace. Even Katherine Mansfield, long in her Fontainebleu grave, wasn't spared Sargesonian sniping. As casualties mounted it seemed Sargeson might soon be the one New Zealand writer worth posterity's gaze. Was that his hope? Obsessively literary, he was never not aware of posterity. Typical Sargeson acolytes tended to produce just one tidy and tiny book before disappearing. (For anyone brave enough the ingredients of an interesting crime novel are still there.) I now think myself lucky to have given offence to Sargeson so early; I could have fallen by the wayside too. At the time it merely seemed that I had made a bad beginning back in New Zealand. Coolness wasn't to diminish, though the summer was warm.

We left Auckland, skirting the pastoral Waikato, crossing the canals of the Hauraki plains, and travelling through the dramatic and steep-walled Karangahake Gorge, the road chipped from perpendicular cliff-face, the once befouled Ohinemuri River racing through boulders below. It wasn't many years since the gorge seethed with men delving sweatily for gold. There were thudding quartz crushers, and horse-drawn coaches carrying away bullion under armed guard. The dream of quick wealth from alluvial gold, the dream that sustained nomad diggers from California, Victoria, then New Zealand's Otago and Westland, finally perished here; here colour was ensnared underground in quartz rock. Backbreaking labour was necessary to win it, and capital. The day of the romantic fossicker, the grizzled prospector pan in hand, was done. The entrepreneurs took over: companies with shareholders to satisfy.

Now there were just a few cottages, an abandoned schoolhouse on a hill. Self-sown Californian pines had begun darkening hillside and riverside, smothering native growth. The vista now had something austerely of Siberian valleys. Beyond the gorge was the remnant of Waikino village. A pub, post office, a few houses among fern – and, on the far bank of the river, the ruins of the powerful Golden Crown battery, once drumming night and day, reducing quartz to powder and purging the gold with a stiff dose of cyanide.

Waikino is vivid in my first memories of the world. My father worked in the nearby Golden Dawn mine. We lived in a half-derelict cottage above the river and beside a railway track, linked by foot-bridge to Waikino village. The footbridge was frightening, with the river seething below. Small wonder I remember it. My mother informed me that I was less than two years old when we lived in that cottage. Two years? Could that be right?

If so I had come full circle. If I was to make sense of New Zealand, where better to begin than where my recall reached? Memory offered more nourishment than literary envy and erudite feuds.

The cottage was still there, just. The roof was bright with rust; windows were broken. It was also abandoned. I looked no further. I was never again going to see the place through the eyes of a terrified two-year-old on a shaky bridge.

Further on, we found the town of Waihi beyond an avenue of tall phoenix palms. The ridges and tortuous summits of the Coromandel rose to their rear. We lived in Waihi too, when my father was working in the Martha mine, using gelignite to blast apart reefs of quartz.

Waihi was more to my liking. Unlike Auckland suburbia, it made sense; there was a feeling of a potent past in the streets of one-time miner's cottages, in the mansions inhabited by mine managers, in the basilica-like ruin of the pumphouse which once served the Martha mine, the richest and longest-lived in the then British Empire. Walking beside my father I learned of the infamous Waihi strike of 1913. Prisons were emptied of reliable thugs. These unlovely individuals were issued with batons and sometimes firearms and sent out to subdue striking miners. They did this with success. Brutality triumphed. Strike-leader Frederick George Evans was clubbed to death. Others were run out of town as their homes blazed. Some survived the strife to become scarred foundation members of the infant Labour Party.

Waihi remains a landmark in New Zealand labour history. It is possible to see it as the country's one colonial revolt – unless one counts the felling of the British flagstaff, and the lowering of the Union Jack, by the axe-happy Maori rebel Hone Heke in 1845. (See my novel *The House of Strife*.) When New Zealand becomes a republic, something long overdue, the Waihi strike may be revered as a revolt against distant British mine-owners by nationalist-minded miners. They failed to see why British capitalists should pocket New Zealand's wealth. Colonial politicians, craving Britain's good opinion, knew what the strike was about. It wasn't about pounds, shillings and pence; or even about hazardous working conditions. It was about who owned New Zealand. They denounced the strikers as traitors to the British Empire. Rebels they may have been; traitors never.

After an absence of twenty-five years my parents had just moved back to Waihi. Housing was cheap there, since the Martha mine closed, and my father's retirement was near. They meant to settle here when my father had wired up his last telegraph pole. (Well, perhaps. They had never settled anywhere.) It was possible to see their move back to goldless Waihi as sentimental. They came here in the depression, a young married couple with their first child. Perhaps they found happiness here, for two or three years, before sackings made them transient again.

Anyway they were back. And here Gillian and I were, at least for a few weeks, waiting on the future to show itself. We enjoyed Waihi, with its magnificent ocean beach just minutes away. Drinking in the Rob Roy with my father, I discovered the strike still alive in the rambling pubs of the town; the names of 1913's scabs were still recalled with disgust.

I met up with an old friend in Waihi, the artist Eric Lee-Johnson. I first met him on the Hokianga, in the north, six years earlier. He looked to be there forever, wedded to that sandy, subtropical region in both life and art. I wrote and directed a documentary film about this Hokianga hermit. In the course of this modest enterprise Eric gave me eyes to see beyond the rubble and scrappy lumber left by forester and farmer; to see the essential New Zealand. My early short stories owed much to his paintings.

Eric's second marriage had foundered on the Hokianga. Perhaps the isolation was too great, friends too few, a common New Zealand complaint. Eric had no easy explanation; he shook his head sadly. All that mattered was that his pretty blonde wife Vivienne disappeared over the hills with a local man. With his third wife, Elizabeth, Eric had put the painful past behind him and moved to Waihi. Like my parents, they were attracted by inexpensive housing. Eric was already finding subjects worth his attention in the ransacked hills.

Not for the first time, Eric put me in touch with post-pioneer New Zealand. The New Zealand, that is, which hungered for its history, thirsted for its stories. Eric encouraged me to think that some might be mine to tell.

Five

I was fathered by the frontier, though I was slow to learn it. No one felt the need to tell me, not even my ostensible parents. Nor were my teachers any more informative. In that respect, in common with most of my contemporaries, I was like some sinfully conceived child whose origins had to be hidden. Some precocious detective work on my part might have disclosed facts gleaming suggestively among the trivia of my existence. Such research, had I been of a mind to engage in it, and of an age to interpret it, might have told me that my English-born great-grandfather Benjamin Shadbolt, among his many robust pioneer roles, was a tamer of horses, a timberman, and sheep farmer too; that my New Zealand-born grandfather Ernest Shadbolt was a bush-burner, timberman and farmer; that even my far less robust father began adult life as a farmer and miner before winning a licence to level New Zealand landscapes with explosives. In other words I had three pioneer generations peering over my shoulder; and that was not to tally my great-great-grandfather, Thomas Perham, a gold-seeker slain by a bushranger's bullet in Australia's outback.

Yet these forebears appeared to have no existence. They certainly had little in the classroom. They were seldom referred to in our textbooks. Even the Maoris, at large in the land for five hundred years, appeared to be interlopers on the landscape. The flora often seemed equally ill at ease. We knew more of England's oaks and Wordsworth's daffodils than of New Zealand kauri and kowhai. We knew more of England's Wars of the Roses than of the Anglo-Maori wars in our neighbourhood, wars in which 1200 poorly armed tribesmen battled 18,000 Britons, often with respectable result. We knew little enough of the rebel Te Kooti, long in exile just one or two

30

miles from the house in which I grew up, the Te Kooti who used the Old Testament to pitiless effect in his campaign against colonists and their Maori allies. None of this belonged to us. The country didn't belong to us, not yet. It was as though New Zealand had risen magically from the ocean: that its towns and cities, mines and mills, roads and railways, were the consequence of some virgin birth. What we did know was England, with Ireland, Wales and Scotland misty runners-up. We belonged to the British Empire. We belonged to Britain. We saluted an alien king or his costumed representatives. Buttressing our education was the belief that there was little of our land worth knowing: no history, no literature, no art, no culture. This was a familiar frontier lament, frequently indulged in by bookish luminaries. Brimming with self pity and bemoaning their isolation from cosmopolitan Europe, they gave the appearance of detesting their rough-cast fellow countrymen and loathing their land. If so, what was the point? It wasn't my intention to join this martyrs' chorus; there were better things to grumble about. Like Yeats in pre-1916 Ireland, many of us imagined we lived where motley was worn. We were wrong. There was nothing motley, nothing inconsequential, about the muscular men who won fresh worlds from moist wilderness; worlds in which their wives and children would one day prosper. Without their labour, without their sacrifice, I might not have been more than a Hertfordshire poacher and amateur burglar.

Summer grew warmer still in Waihi's nest of hills. Another child of the frontier, Barry Mitcalfe, rang from the far north: from Ahipara, a small and largely Maori community at the southern end of Ninety Mile Beach. His voice was warm. Those edgy Auckland voices ceased to matter. When Barry welcomed me back he meant it. When he said he liked *The New Zealanders* he seemed to mean that too. 'I wish to hell I'd written it,' he claimed. I heard all that was good in my country in his joky and generous voice. 'A couple of your stories gave me an erection,' he disclosed. 'No New Zealand writer has done that to me before.'

That was an original literary yardstick, to say the least.

As always, Barry made light of his own work. Teaching in the far north, involving himself with the community there, left him with little time for things literary. Yet not long before he was – with his fluent verse and robust prose – one of the most promising young

New Zealand writers. His head start on his contemporaries may have been due to his lettered background. Barry's mother Gwen was the nearest friend of the ailing New Zealand novelist Robin Hyde. She also figured in one of Hyde's novels. The Mitcalfes gave Hyde sanctuary during one of her several breakdowns. Anyway Barry grew up thinking authorship the most natural of human activities. Perhaps he also grew up knowing it perilous. When he died early in 1985, better known as a rural guru or political activist, the novels he seemed destined to write remained unwritten.

I once asked Barry if he had some childhood memory of Robin Hyde. 'She was just an irritable old woman to me,' he said disappointingly. Actually she couldn't have been more than thirty. Irritability wasn't evident in her work. Wit was. And compassion.

Her novel *Passport to Hell*, in which she slips into the skin of an anarchic soldier in the trenches of France, is surely the most extraordinary written by a New Zealand woman. As an act of transferred identity there is nothing by a male contemporary to match it. There was nothing by a female contemporary to rival it either. If death permitted her out on parole, for a dinner party at Titirangi perhaps, I would ensure she sat between Mansfield and the equally tragic Ron Morrieson at the head of the table. Like them, and too many others, she never lived to hear the applause which was her due; there was next to none, anyway, in her brief life.

Years later with my actress wife Bridget Armstrong near to hand I was for the first time well placed to kick start literary history. I encouraged Bridget to arrange, write and act in a one-woman show drawing on Hyde's life and work. For the thousands who saw it, in New Zealand and England, the experience was magical. It was certainly a lyrical impersonation. Even Hyde herself appeared to be taking an interest. Bridget claimed to hear pots and pans mysteriously banging in our kitchen during the season, and sometimes furniture being shifted after we had gone to bed.

'Why don't you come up?' Barry said. 'Let's go on an expedition together.'

I gave him no time for second thoughts.

I hitchhiked two hundred miles north and made it to the Mitcalfes by dusk. Barbara was warm, Barry ebullient. Our reunion was festive. There was the smell of beer and freshly caught fish frying in the pan. I fell asleep on a Mitcalfe couch. Outside there was the rumble of surf on ninety miles of sand. (Actually the beach is nearer ninety kilometres long, but I wasn't counting.).

Next morning, before breakfast, I walked through dunes and down to the beach. With wild ocean filling my ears I meditated on Allen Curnow's lines: *Surf is a deafness/ All islanders suffer from.* The beach, with a mist of fine spray, curved on and on and disappeared in distance. Maori children galloped horses along the surf. Others collected shellfish. Memory couldn't be faulted. The vista was even more mesmerising than I remembered. Barefoot Barry joined me on my walk. He was as ruddy, plump and exuberant as ever. And more Maori than most Maori.

'You were a long time gone,' he observed.

'Too long,' I agreed.

'At least you didn't become another fake Mansfield.'

'Now you mention it,' I said.

'Good,' he said. 'So where are we going?'

Provisioned up, looking sufficiently serious, we left for Cape Reinga. There were several in our party. Barry's Maori neighbour Busby Te Paa. A tribal elder and composer of waiata (Maori verse) named Pat Kerehoma. Barry's boy Michael. And a couple of Barry's fellow schoolteachers. The single-minded road to New Zealand's far north was rough, deeply fissured, and dusty. More than once we were up to our axles in sand. Then it was all hands to the pumps, or all shoulders to the car's rump.

We stopped at the village of Te Kao – New Zealand's last store, and the last gasoline pump. Here, from a small cottage in a plantation of banana trees, we picked up another Maori elder, Joe Conrad, the wise old man of the north. Yes, he had Polish blood. And yes, he had heard of a Polish writer with a name much as his. They may be related; who knew? Joe was to be our guide to Reinga. We travelled on. To right and left, as the land narrowed, were glimpses of great dunes. Then hills grew, and valleys, and scrubby semi-deserts of gumland where diggers – Maori, Dalmatian, and Anglo-Saxon – once toiled to bring the lucrative fossil residue of once mighty forest to the surface. There were few relics of the once rowdy communities of diggers. The hills had long been stripped of gum.

We halted often. Joe Conrad had a story for every stop. He

pointed out the sites of old fortresses and recounted tales of battle and bravery. Here, for example, the first firearm in the far north was discharged. A local chief purchased it from a passing English skipper. He used it in defence of a tribal fortress. When he had demonstrated its value by levelling a foeman, he lent it to the opposition. It seemed only fair to do so. No one was going to say that the battle was decided by a tawdry bullet. This may have been chivalrous. It was also fatal. The first round from the rival tribe caught him amidships. There were no further stories of adversaries presented with firearms. Chivalry would have to find a new home.

Joe pointed out the rugged heights which summoned the spirit to the world of Hine-nui-te-po, the goddess of darkness and death. Such markers were necessary, especially in seasons of war, when the sandy boulevard filled with spectral traffic. In such seasons the spirits could be heard as a giant fluttering overhead. Confusion could be great. On the hill called Haumu, guardian spirits knotted the grass to point newcomers in the right direction. On the height called Maringi-noa the phantoms of the dead looked their last on New Zealand and shed tears for things mortal. Finally, after crossing the creek called Waioterata (the Maori equivalent of the waters of Lethe), beyond which no traveller returns, they leapt from the limbs of an aged pohutukawa tree growing mysteriously, sans soil, from rock at the tip of Cape Reinga. There curtains of kelp parted to reveal the murky hereafter.

Joe told us that a missionary, trying to rid the land of pagan susperstition, once attempted to fell the sacred tree. His axe-marks could still be seen. The missionary came, of course, to a deservedly bad end. (This tale turns out to be short of true. In fact, like most villains, the insensitive cleric flourished as the bay tree.)

In the late afternoon we reached the lighthouse, the legendary tree far below and the Tasman Sea blending with the Pacific's wild currents. Here New Zealand ended. Here the world began. It was barely three weeks since I looked on that rippling reach of ocean as an exile returned. On that first day of 1960 I saw New Zealand as a strange land. I had already I painted myself into that picture, become part of the panorama. It was as if I had climbed into a mirror to look out on the world. I felt an unfamiliar rejoicing. Was some passing spirit at work in me? If so, a benign one; in this aweing place I find myself aloft on gentle wings.

Was New Zealand to be discovered by diving into Maori lore? Was that how New Zealanders might, in the poet Allen Curnow's memorable phrase, master 'the trick of standing upright here'? The problem was that the lore left in the landscape by those of Europe's colour was discounted. It suggested that our forefathers were crude cretins and villains. We had a story too; New Zealand's virtues were not exclusively Maori. Yet the likes of Busby Te Paa, Pat Kerehoma and Joe Conrad made me unmistakably at home here. In their company I was no lost child of the frontier.

The lighthouse brought us back to the European world. It was no less warm than the Maori. The head lighthouse keeper, Bill Kemp and his wife Kitty threw open their schoolhouse, and let us camp there. It was a boisterous evening. At three am, still passably sober, I made the nightly report on climatic conditions to the Meteorological Service in Wellington. I also said hello from Bill. The duty officer at the far end of the line didn't seem surprised by a new voice from Cape Reinga. I informed him that the wind was about thirty knots, and the sky clear. At this rate I might soon be throwing the switch to illuminate the lighthouse. A night later I did.

With Joe Conrad we trailed across terrain full of whispers. Then Barry and I clambered down to the sea, and the sacred tree. Joe, elderly and less agile, didn't keep us company; he urged caution, however, in the vicinity of the tree. He didn't mean just physically. Anyway Barry and I remained at a decent distance. The wind muttered faintly overhead. The kelp rose and fell. Imagination had much to work on.

As if to confirm it, Barry that evening passed me some of his recent translations of Maori verse – waiata and karakia (sacred songs). I read them in a feeble light of a naked bulb. The lighthouse generator drummed next door. The voices of our party were subdued; even laughter was muted. Barry's poems were readable and resonant, as richly allusive as anything by T.S. Eliot.

The heron has flown
The canoe is gone
The river is no haven,
The root is drawn from the earth,
But in Otahu, the place of birth,

You cannot die, there is no death,
You dart like the shag beneath
The dark waters of the stream,
Dive like a gannet to a death
In the deep where small fish gleam.

'What do you think?' Barry asked.
'I hope my grandchildren read them,' I said.

Back in Waihi there was a message from Jim and Jacquie Baxter. They had found us a dwelling for the year – in semi-rural Upper Hutt, about twenty miles from Wellington. It belonged to a back-to-the-soil academic now proselytising in Canada. The place was a little eccentric, Jim and Jacquie said, but we should like it. Eccentric? What did that mean?

Another message. Brian Brake, the brilliant young photographer with whom I once worked on documentary films, was also back in the country. In three or four years he had become one of the world's most sought-after image-makers. His photographs of Communist China – the work of one of the first Western photographers made welcome there – had been published in a dozen countries; he was already winning international awards. His portrait of Mao Tse Tung, walking reflectively in the Forbidden City, was already familiar world-wide. Brian had just finished photographing the Indian monsoon. He now wished to chance his arm on his native land. He had an assignment for *National Geographic*. Was I interested in travelling with him and writing the text? I took fewer than five seconds to confirm my interest.

Almost buried under baggage, behind the wheel of a shiny Jaguar, Brian turned up in Waihi. We travelled south to Christchurch to meet the current editor of *Geographic*, then on a visit to New Zealand. He was a gently spoken man. He asked if I was familiar with *Geographic*. Why, yes, I claimed. My doctor had it in his waiting room; my dentist too. This was a mistake; the editor winced. It was not how he preferred *Geographic* seen. It was never meant to distract from the sound of a dentist's drill. Nevertheless he offered me US$2000 plus $500 expenses for a text. I was impressed. I reminded myself that I was in good company. Joseph Conrad also wrote for *Geographic*.

So. We had a house. I had work. I also had a modest grant from the New Zealand State Literary Fund to subsidise work on the novel I thought I was writing.

It seemed too easy. It was.

Six

With our child two or three months away, Gillian and I flew to Wellington. Jim and Jacquie Baxter met us at Wellington's new airport. Much had happened in the three years since we last saw the Baxters – to us, to them. Jim had unexpectedly embraced Catholicism. Less surprisingly I had surrendered the last shreds of my Marxism. I had survived the Soviet Union and much of the rest of Eastern Europe. Jim had been to Asia, to Japan and India, an experience already colouring his verse. As always Jim was a leap ahead of his detractors. Just when they thought they had his number, he was elsewhere. He was now earnestly involved with Alcoholics Anonymous. I had no argument with this, or with anything which kept Jim in business. The problem was that Jim was incapable of doing anything by halves. He regaled me with tales of minor miracles in his vicinity: of praying to the Virgin for fiscal assistance, and finding a five pound note underfoot. I nodded judiciously when he told me this. I didn't know what I was supposed to think. He also disconcerted sober, run of the mill Catholics by falling unprompted to his knees in prayer. His sincerity couldn't be doubted. To an outsider his devotion could be touching. Jim's difficulty wasn't in the realm of faith; it was in the domain of everyday excess. Someone had compassionately found him a home in education, editing and writing texts for scholastic publications. This allowed him long periods of useful freedom. His office had a side door opening on a busy Wellington street. It meant he could come and go unobserved, more or less as mood took him. His mood often took him. His superiors didn't take Jim to task on the length of his absences. No one could say poets were undervalued in New Zealand. Though his typewriter was often heard, his fellow workers suspected that poetry was being produced by the state-subsidised yard. In his new verse he picturedhimself as a beleaguered bureaucrat strangling in the tentacles of the omnipresent state. Jim needed his masks. This masquerade, however, was more than usually implausible. The omnipresent state was serving him generously, and with considerable patience.

Wellington – sunlit, serene and summery – flashed past the car windows. The Baxters had a car. This was new. So was the experience of Jim's driving. He frequently and unnervingly took his eyes off the road to ensure that I wasn't missing the point of his current monologue. When I attempted to say something appropriate to the reunion, it surfaced as a gasp of fright. Jim failed to acknowledge my condition. He merely smiled benevolently as imperilled motorists sounded their horns.

We left the harbour behind and travelled along the Hutt river. The state housing estates of Lower Hutt passed, then Upper Hutt too. The traffic thinned. This was a relief. The vista was more rustic by the minute. There were glimpses of grazing sheep and fattening cattle. Willows overhung the road. Cicadas entrenched in roadside trees grew loud above the sound of the car.

We arrived at a cluster of houses called Te Marua. As promised, our dwelling was picturesque. A rippling stream divided it, with decorative ducks sailing through a watery corridor. The living room and bedroom area was A-frame in form and set among silver birches. A hazardous footbridge spanned the stream, above the gliding ducks, linking it to a kitchen and guest room. It was an exceptionally airy place. And the ducks were friendly. Life there would be an adventure, not least in storm.

By early February, Brian Brake and I had begun travelling for the waiting rooms of the western world. Certainly for *National Geographic*'s six million subscribers. Brian was working to an exhausting timetable. First we sped north, to Russell in the Bay of Islands, a new experience for me. Nowhere is there a site more endowed with New Zealand's first collisions with history. Circling the globe, Captain Cook was bewitched by the place. Whalers by the score anchored here between bouts with ocean giants. The hell-hole of the Pacific, some said. Populated by 'the very refuse of society', added an appalled Charles Darwin. The Russell beach was lined with grog-shops. The missionaries camped no more than a mile across the bay. Here God and the Devil glowered at each other for three ill-tempered decades. Here the gentle French voyager Marion du Fresne, in love with the notion of the noble savage, was slain by the tribesmen he sought to befriend. Here the missionary Thomas Kendall took a Maori wife and traded in muskets and fell dramatically from grace. Though there were eventually converts in plenty, it cannot be said God was victorious. There was war too, when the reckless young Maori Hone Heke four times felled the British flagstaff above the bay. Here – encountering Maori fortresses for the first time – British regiments were left in bloody disarray. These tales, as vivid as any in colonial literature, as wild as those of America's west, remained feebly chronicled where on record at all. For some reason New Zealand writers had scrupulously avoided telling them. The mystery would dog me for decades. It might have been charitable to put it down to national amnesia, to New Zealanders' indifference to their history. Or was it fear of that history?

Meanwhile Brian and I had a practical problem. He needed a photograph of big-game fishermen pursuing their sport. The waters off the Bay of Islands are home to some of the biggest sharks and swordfish in creation. Zane Grey, the writer of pulp fiction (*Riders of the Purple Sage* and others), made the place a marine playground when he began hauling in monsters here in the 1920s. Brian and I, travelling in the best-equipped launch in the Bay, and with the most distinguished guide, had less luck. For three days we bounced about on bruising sea, waiting for an oceanic brute to strike. There wasn't a wisp of agitated water.

'I have to get one,' Brian said in despair.

That night we were drinking in the bar of the Duke of Marlborough, the Bay's one surviving grog-shop, when we learned that a large swordfish was being brought in and weighed.

Panic followed. It was now dark outside. How win a photograph? A pupil of Cartier Bresson, Brian was an available light photographer; as a matter of aesthetic principle he didn't use artificial illumination. (He had even photographed performers in the Peking opera by candlelight.) Aesthetic principle, however, was unhelpful in present circumstances. Brian wrestled with his conscience and finally decided that he must use a flash gun for the first time in his professional life. The difficulty was that he didn't know how. We raced to his hotel room and found an instruction book. I read relevant passages aloud while he untangled cables and joined batteries and bulb to a camera. We had no time for a trial run. Still in confusion, we hurried down to the jetty. I managed to trip on a cable. The wonder was that there wasn't more damage done. The swordfish weighed in at close to a world record. Still shiny with seawater, it was a magnificent creature. That couldn't be said for its grinning killer. He was a skinny, bow-legged, squinty-eyed little man in floral shorts and a silly hat. Perhaps a small-town bank manager out for a day's fun. Anyway he was not an impressive example of homo sapiens. In his present pose, beside his catch, he shamed our species.

Miraculously, all things considered, Brian persuaded his flash to work. We returned to the Duke of Marlborough, our mood melancholy. It had not been a pleasing day. Brian had violated deeply felt tenets. And I hoped never to see another big-game fisherman.

We dawdled down the North Island on dusty roads. In a back country barn we kept an appointment with a man named Godfrey Bowen, sheep shearer extraordinary. He was teaching a dozen young men the essentials of their trade. Trade? For Bowen it was a religion; he was the high priest of his calling. As a young accountant, working in his father's sawmill, sometimes shearing on contract with his burly brothers, he had been appalled by the cruelty and inefficiency of the business. It did not sit well with King Solomon's Biblical admonition: 'Be thou diligent to know the state of thy flocks and look well to thy herds'. A man of religion, Bowen embraced this personally. Looking well to his herds, he took a brutal and bloody occupation and made it humane; he had also made it a spectator sport which pulled in crowds by the tens of thousands. He had given five royal performances in Britain. In Russia, in the then Soviet Union, Premier Nikita Krushchev made Bowen a 'Hero of Socialist Labour'. The Edmund Hillary of the rural world, Bowen scaled a fleecy Everest. His first time out, he broke all past records by shearing 456 sheep in 540 minutes. Until then three dozen sheep had been thought a decent day's tally. To prove his record no mistake, he repeated it again and again.

The story couldn't but be New Zealand's. If nothing else it served to remind me that my homeland wasn't short of marvels. I was reminded of an equally inventive fellow countryman whose acquaintance I once made. Bill Hamilton was a high country farmer and an inveterate tinkerer with never a day's formal training as a designer and engineer. A lover of his land's wild places, a trout fisherman too, Bill was often frustrated by his inability to get far enough upriver to pull in big trout from alpine pools and streams. A special kind of craft was needed, one which would skim over shallow rivers and lakes. He gave the problem his earnest attention. And he came up with the jet boat where scores of professional designers had failed. There was now not a land in the world without Hamilton jets travelling its waterways, and all because of a New Zealand farmer who wanted fish for supper.

There was no time to linger; our timetable was tight. We drove through Auckland and then seventy miles on to the Ngaruawahia regatta. It is one of the liveliest events in the Maori calendar. Canoes glided on the wide Waikato as they did in pre-European days. Brian moved soft-footed and impish among the crowd. I still marvelled at his capacity to remain unobtrusive with two or three cameras swinging around his neck. He came and went before his subjects knew he had been there. Toward the day's end I sat on the riverbank, in the shade of willows, and listened to an old Maori recount legends of the river. At one point he grasped my shoulder solemnly. 'I can tell you one, two and three. But I can never tell you four. That is mine. Four is what makes me Maori.'

He didn't have to explain.

We roved down the South Island's slender and mountain-girt western coast – or simply the Coast, as most New Zealanders call it. Community after community was celebrating the anniversary of the discovery of alluvial gold in the Coast's dark forest and billowing streams in the 1860s. It wasn't quite the full century (that would have to wait until 1965 or thereabouts) but no matter. Coasters never spurn an excuse for celebration. We stayed in a hotel at Ross, just south of Hokitika. At the height of the gold rush here, with frantic skippers losing ship after ship on the river bar, Hokitika had – aside from gaming houses, brothels and billiard parlours – a twelve hundred seat opera house. Ross had no such architectural opulence, but as a goldfield it was as rich. It was home to the huge nugget known as the Honourable Roddy which, at 99 ounces, was the largest found in New Zealand. The spectacular find was presented patriotically to Buckingham Palace and melted down for a monarch's tea service. Or so goes Coast lore. The tale of the Honourable Roddy would be repeated again and again; the wealth of the region now resided in distant vaults. Riches had left no residue here, other than in goldfield legend. Ross was now a village of rusty rooftops and mildewed dwellings, two hotels, a store, a timber mill, and a fire-bell. A few old men, sons and grandsons of the original gold-seekers, still panned gritty alpine streams. For the purposes of celebration, many had grown beards and fitted themselves out in the garb of their forefathers. Brian and I seemed to be the only citizens of the 20th century resident in the town.

While waiting on celebration to begin in earnest I left Brian and his busy camera and took the road down to the glaciers. The territory was new to me and the more marvellous for that. The glaciers – the Fox and Franz Josef – shimmered between half-tropic vegetation. Valleys filled with the sound of cracking ice. Mountain torrents milky with powdered rock roared seaward. The retreat of the glaciers has been steady, with no more than small fluctuations, for centuries now. Yet they remained impressive. As aweing was the sight of the world in the making, the rubble left by their retreat. Vegetation, here scanty, there thick, was slowly colonising the floor of the valley. This was how much of the planet must have looked as the last ice age ended and glacial sheets shrank; we were in a laboratory of creation. Man was a puny witness of proceedings. I tried to imagine what footsore Polynesians thought as they first happened on the scene. They knew nothing of ice. Nor had they a word for snow; they called it huka, or foam. They might have seen the gleaming glaciers as a highway to the gods. Who would not?

The weekend arrived. So did a couple of thousand Coasters. The pubs did epic business. The City Hotel, where we bedded, had its busiest day since its boisterous opening in 1865. I wandered away for sobriety's sake. The wondrously dissonant Kakotahi miner's band, decorative in red shirts and white moleskins, was demonstrating that the Coast was far from indifferent to its past. It has been said that this musically imaginative troupe has long brought melody to a harsh land. It has to be said that melody was not much in evidence that day. Conductors have always been suspect. Bandsmen are required only to play the same tune at the same time and sometimes they are known to.

Meanwhile movie cameras rolled. Wrinkled old men regaled me with anecdotes of the Coast. One taught me to pan for gold's colour. There was always drink at hand. I retired to my room in confusion and fatigue. Mine? The bed appeared to be occupied. Whoever it was, the prone figure wasn't me. After some indecision I shook the intruder's shoulder.

'You have the wrong room,' I suggested cautiously

He looked up blearily. 'No,' he told me. 'This is the right one.'

'But these are my belongings,' I pointed out.

He acknowledged this. And explained, 'Mrs Taylor [the publican's wife] put me to bed here. She said you're a decent joker and wouldn't mind.'

Who was I to quibble? This was the Coast. I had established a reputation as a decent joker.

The bar was busy until six next morning. As one pianist collapsed another took over. Others slept where they fell; the bar was carpeted with snoring celebrants. We stepped gingerly among them, seeking breakfast. A recumbent figure rose to grapple with the piano again. Someone else stirred and reached for a liquid breakfast. Red-eyed from lack of sleep, Brian and I deduced that it was time to move on. We had been warned that the rest of the weekend might be rowdier.

We took a dizzying road up into the South Island's alpine divide, pausing at the hamlet of Arthur's Pass. Brian had grown up here, son of the village storekeeper. Such an environment, with snowy summits bulking above alpine forest, was conducive to fitness. It also fed the imagination. Brian had a Box Brownie in his hand at the age of ten. His first photographs, however, were less of mighty peaks than delicate alpine flora. As a photographer, Brian was always painterly. His interest however, was now in fauna of human form. We lunched there, with people crowding to shake the hand of the newly famous local boy. Brian was quiet as we drove away. I thought I could identify his silence. I had known it too, and a little of it lingered. It was the wistful silence of an undecided expatriate.

Seven

We reached Mount Possession station, in the South Island high country. The weather was cool and exhilarating. Weathered sheepmen, tasting the nip in the air, judged autumn's first snowfall near. That meant some twenty-five thousand sheep would soon have to be mustered from tussocky heights to graze on low-lying winter pasture. Our host was Sam Chaffey, a man as formidable as the 100,000 acres he managed. There was a dinner party before the muster began. Neighbours drove in from equally remote stations. Their talk was of weather, of early mustering, and of the way the high country was steadily slipping into corporate hands, many of them foreign. Sam, for example, ran Mount Possession station for a British company. Few at the dinner still farmed the land of their fathers. We consumed high country mutton and drank canned Beaujolais.

There was another surprise. At the meal's end Sam climbed authoritatively to his feet. 'Who's for outside?' he asked. The males rose and silently departed, leaving their womenfolk to exchange recipes. Outside, on the front lawn, the men stood in a circle and urinated as one. With so many efficient bladders working, it was something of a torrent. Discreet inquiry produced the information that this procedure was a dinner party custom in the Canterbury high country. No one knew when it began. No matter. New Zealand, more than most countries, needed native rituals. But must it involve pissing on the land? The Maoris, whose territory this once was, might have relieved themselves more delicately. At least I liked to think so.

The autumn muster began with a dozen musterers and two freeloaders.

We weaved up into the hills with a tractor and trailer bumping behind with our provisions. Hiking along a high ridge we came in sight of Samuel Butler's Mesopotamia station, far below. The landscape still looked as lonely as he pictured it in *Erewhon*. Only one thing troubled me. How the hell did he haul a piano so high?

Frost spiked the grass outside our overnight hut. Winter was never far away in these mountains. We rose at chilly six and climbed into our woollens. Breakfast was mutton chops fresh from the frypan. Lunch, up on the heights, would be cold mutton.

There were three beats for the muster. The rugged top beat, following the snowline from peak to peak, was a route to make weekend mountaineers look flighty. The middle beat was more moderate, but still no boulevard. The lower beat was meant to scoop up sheep grazing mountain flanks. I correctly divined that the lower beat would suit me admirably. Brian, who knew where the best pictures were, took the top beat with veteran musterers; he was fit enough to foot it with the hardiest in this terrain. So he should be, with an Arthur's Pass boyhood.

A gentle, bearded, and weatherbeaten man named Gerry was my sole companion on the low beat. Gerry was the classic itinerant of the New Zealand back country. He was also the archetypal man alone of the New Zealand novel, though he wore this distinction lightly. Aside from his enterprising dogs, he travelled light – to shear here, muster there, working his way from station to station, wherever needed. Unless called out by blizzard, to rake sheep from snowdrifts, he saw out winter comfortably in town. He didn't treat the land lightly. He loved it and wasn't shy about showing it. Several times that day I caught him gazing out on vistas of cloud, rock and snow-tipped heights. I also saw him fixing an alpine flower in his hat. Familiarity with the high country appeared to engender reverence.

'You don't carry a camera?' he asked.

'No,' I explained. 'My pictures are in my head.'

He smiled shyly. 'Mine too,' he said.

The climbs were cruel. Thorny matagauri bushes – the species imaginatively renamed wild Irishman – scraped our legs. We pushed noisily across shingle slides, the residue of glacier and avalanche. If this was the low beat, the top beat must be murder. Again and again Gerry sent his dogs uphill to fetch in stragglers. That didn't preclude him from following the dogs up, to make sure the ground cleared; this could mean a steep climb of one or two thousand feet.

Late in the day Gerry's alert eye picked up three sheep on a far mountain flank. At that stage in proceedings the truant threesome could easily have been forgotten. (I was losing count of the thousands of feet Gerry must have climbed.) But no. Painstaking Gerry went after these stragglers too. He wasn't performing for me, or to demonstrate his reliability to his boss. Self-respect was the issue here.

'You'll be all right by yourself?' he asked me.

'Of course,' I insisted, and hoped it true.

'Just follow the creek,' he said. 'You'll come to our hut.'

The next hours ranked among the loneliest of my life. Trying to find a easy route home, I was blocked by giant boulders and saturated by snow-fed streams. Shivering, I heard no human sound. I didn't even hear a sheep's far bleat. Or, for that matter, a phrase of birdsong. I toiled uphill and slithered downhill. The wonder is that Samuel Butler survived this territory sane. My respect for that Victorian worthy was increasing fast.

Yet there was life in this landscape after all. After two or three hours of hardship, with dusk not too distant, there was an eerie cackling above me. Two colourfully winged creatures circled and settled nearby. They gazed at me with as much surprise as I goggled at them. I had met New Zealand's unique mountain parrot, the antic kea. Among sheepmen they had a mixed press. Some respected them as fellow creatures of the mountains. Others loathed them as killers of lambs.

After they established that I served no useful purpose they floated off. I stumbled the last hundred yards home to our hut. I was in time to see three sheep dispatched, for the dogs and dinner. Dinner, of course, would be mutton chops.

'So what do you think of the high country?' one musterer asked.

'It takes the breath away,' I said truthfully.

I barely had time for a mouthful of mutton. Then sleep found me.

Slowly, over three or four days, several mobs became one: there were soon more than twenty thousand sheep on the march, though no one was counting. The temperature was kinder. By noon, as we trudged, sweat shone on our faces. Our route took us past a large lake set in terrain of copper-coloured tussock. Lakeside poplars dripped autumnal colour on the waters. Brian saw a magnificent picture in the making. We sped ahead of mob and musterers to place ourselves in an advantageous position for Brian's cameras. The mob, however, had a mind of its own. Refusing to oblige with a picturesque pose, it was pushing uphill, veering away from the lake. Brian saw his composition falling part.

I came up with a wild proposal. I would work my way surreptitiously down to the lakeside, behind a long ridge, and attempt to entice stragglers over the ridge. The entire mob might then follow.

'How will you entice them?' Brian said.

'I'll bleat,' I disclosed.

'Bleat?'

'Bleat,' I confirmed.

Brian concluded that he was travelling with a lunatic. Not that I was optimistic either.

Soon I was working along the ridge on hands and knees. It was distinctly undignified, but who was to see? Then came my pièce de résistance. I bleated and bleated again. There was a long and rather stunned silence. Then a lone sheep's head lifted above the ridge. With mounting confidence in my powers of mimicry, I bleated again. This produced two or three more inquisitive sheep. They gazed at me with interest as they rose along the ridge. Three more bleats and I felt I was winning. There were now a score of sheep trying to make sense of me, some moving tentatively towards the lake. After a few fits and starts the rest of the mob began to follow. I rose to my feet and signalled Brian to the effect that he now had most of thirty thousand sheep at his disposal.

Minutes later he had a lyrical picture. It didn't, of course, show a sweaty and self-sacrificing writer crawling through tussock and thorn bush, leading the mob. Nor did Brian record my abrasions and bruised knees. Small wonder that writers are a moody breed.

I remembered, too late, why I quit film-making for writing. With a cameraman I had spent three days trying to film a river at sunset. First time around the sunset was too feeble to film. The second time there was camera trouble. On the third we had drizzle. Rain dripped miserably from my nose and mosquitoes grazed on my legs. And I thought: Dear God, it wouldn't take me more than a minute to write the damn sunset, without even leaving my desk.

With assistance from suggestible readers, my sunsets have since been superior too.

Eight

We left Canterbury behind and pushed down the South Island with the great glacier-smoothed schist plateau of Central Otago rearing to our right. Little gold-towns – Naseby, Clyde and Arrowtown – persisted in this stark terrain. While Brian fattened his file I walked the territory on my own account. It was still easy to visualise thousands of diggers stumbling footsore into the flinty interior, often perishing in rockfall, flood and blizzard.

In Queenstown, above the loveliest lake in the land, we treated ourselves to comfortable hotel beds and an expensive Beaujolais. Beyond dining room windows sunset took its leave of the peaks of Otago. Enough was suddenly a surfeit. I had New Zealand coming out my ears.

Next morning we drove through glowing countryside to the mining village of Arrowtown. We paused only to pick mushrooms under yellowing maples. In the village itself there were deep drifts of fallen leaves. Some had been swept into heaps by the inhabitants of the tiny miners' cottages. There was an arresting picture here, though Brian was puzzled how best to win it. To demonstrate my power of invention again, I ventured out with a box of matches and set two or three of these heaps alight. An obliging local joined me with a rake and made himself part of the picture. The smoke drifted among the trees and Victorian cottages as the old man raked leaves into even larger pyres. Giddy with delight, Brian had to concede that writers might have their uses.

Congratulating ourselves on our morning toil, we treated ourselves to beer in an old Arrowtown pub. A copy of the *Otago Daily Times* spread on the bar told us that a royal marriage was in the making. Princess Margaret, sister of the Queen, was to marry a commoner, a photographer named Anthony Armstrong Jones. Brian approved; it elevated his profession. Besides he knew Armstrong Jones and thought well of him as a fellow photographer.

We took our hoard of mushrooms to the A-frame house of a Swiss friend of Brian's and there lunched lavishly. Back at the hotel a cable awaited Brian. It requested his presence in Westminster Abbey as the official photographer for the royal wedding. Brian decided he couldn't say no. He did a swift calculation of New Zealand days now at his disposal. Our *Geographic* joyride was near its end.

With the dust of Otago billowing behind, we journeyed on to Dunedin. There, while Brian viewed that sturdy Victorian city through a lens, we stayed with Charles Brasch, poet, essayist, editor of the literary magazine *Landfall*, and benefactor of the arts. It was only the second time we had met. The first time he alarmed me by lamenting, apropos of the arts in New Zealand, 'There are so few of us.' He seemed to see New Zealand writers and painters as members of a furtive sect. I didn't find this healthy or helpful. (He wasn't alone in literary paranoia. Frank Sargeson, for example, persuaded himself that his kindly neighbours wanted to burn his books and plant him on the pyre.) The descendant of an affluent goldfield merchant, Charles was a gentle, sensitive and wealthy man who meant well and was a generous host. For the most part, however, I found him difficult company. He couldn't bring himself to enjoy the company of his fellow New Zealanders, from whom he remained remote for most of his life. I failed to imagine what he made of the colourless vernacular fiction then in favour with New Zealand writers and which, for want of better, he frequently published. That didn't mean I – or purveyors of prose less shopsoiled – qualified for Charles' approval. He deplored the New Zealand accent, for example, which I distinctly had. He saw uncouth philistines where I merely saw ruggedly egalitarian fellow countrymen. The walls of his elegant family home on Maori Hill were crammed with paintings. I marvelled at an exquisite Frances Hodgkins watercolour above my bed. More to the point Charles' collection gave me my first glimpse of Colin McCahon's South Island paintings. Until then McCahon had been no more than a name to me, someone spoken of disparagingly by North Island painters. ('Graffiti from a celestial lavatory,' said the uncharitable poet A.R.D. Fairburn, who should have known better.) I was overwhelmed by the majesty of McCahon's work. No one could now complain that we were missing out on a Michelangelo or Matisse. There was greatness afoot in my land. McCahon was no member of a furtive sect. 'I saw,' he was to say in a moving credo, 'something logical, orderly and beautiful belonging to the land and not yet to its people. Not yet understood or communicated, not even yet really invented.' But Colin could invent it, and would.

Charles terminated my trance by pressing the latest issue of *Landfall* upon me. There was a distinctly acceptable review of *The New Zealanders* there, two or three pages long. 'I trust this makes up for the disagreeable ones,' he said.

It did. Charles and I might have had our differences, but there was no lack of benevolent intention on his part. Perhaps he was trying to help me forget and forgive the more outrageous attacks on my person, not to speak of my prose. Perhaps. Charles was too soft-spoken for me to be sure. Also he had fallen in love with Brian, which could only confuse matters.

After dinner with Charles we walked down town to say hello to Maurice Duggan, Dunedin's current Robert Burns fellow in literature. Maurice had a rather draughty dwelling near the university clock tower. With security and a salary for the first time in his writing life, he was awash with stories and novellas composed in marvellously measured prose. No New Zealand storyteller could turn a phrase better. Though I had known Maurice for six or seven years, and admired his stories greatly, I had never found him easy company; he always seemed alert for a slight, jibe or put-down from his peers. So it proved again. Nervously, I talked of the journey Brian and I had just done, and of our adventures along the way. I suggested that the expatriate, world-wandering New Zealander, as I had been for some years, tended to think of his country in terms of one or two remembered and revered localities. The surprise on return was finding the land so wildly diverse.

There was nothing profound in this observation; it seemed obvious to me. To my dismay, though, Maurice bridled defensively, taking harmless comment as criticism. He appeared to think I was saying that *his* work should be more diverse. 'One is given one's piece of rock and one carves it as one will,' he said abruptly, or something to that effect. And indeed he had been elegantly chiselling domestic rock, Katherine Mansfield fashion, since he began writing. There was nothing wrong with that, with sticking to one's patch and making the most of it, and I hurried to say so. It was too late. The damage was done. Maurice imagined I was needling him. Such rampant sensitivity made me wonder if I had been unwise to put London behind me. Hardly a month home, I was already wondering whether I could last the distance. Were New Zealand writers naturally testy, or did I bring it on my own head? Conversational collapse was tempered by the arrival of the poet Fleur Adcock. Dunedin had been her base since her marriage to fellow poet Alistair Campbell ended. Both had been friends of Gillian's and mine when we lived in Wellington in the 1950s. Fleur wore her familiar feline expression. She said little, smoked and drank quietly. Her eyes moved beadily from person to person. She seemed to have everyone in the room summed up sexually and socially. Before long I deduced that Fleur and Maurice were suffering through an unhappy affair. The pace at which drinks were downed tended to confirm it.

It was time to move again. Brian and I had discovered enough of New Zealand to satisfy *Geographic*. We had also discovered more than enough to please ourselves; we were already planning a book which would tell New Zealand's tale with word and image. Back in Wellington our ways parted. I joined Gillian among the willows and ducks of Te Marua. Medical opinion said her time was near. Brian flew off to keep his rendezvous with royalty. The past months were as memorable as any in our lives.

Nine

I began to forget the loss of fragile literary friendships. There were gains. At a PEN meeting I met tall, amiable Ian Cross. He also had caused local heartburn by publishing prematurely – in his case a taut and vivid novel named *The God Boy*. I had read his dazzling London reviews; there were reviews of similar generosity in New York. He had since published another tale of anguished adolescence called *The Backward Sex*. There was a third on the way. Like Sylvia Ashton Warner – whose *Spinster* was currently a best-seller in the United States – Ian seemed to have sprung out of nowhere. He hadn't published in local literary magazines. He may not even have known of their existence. In short, he hadn't been licensed. Until *The God Boy* he had been a busy journalist, chief reporter of Wellington's morning daily *The Dominion*. Beyond that was a chapter of adventure in Latin America, which included gun-running to Latin rebels. Outside his fiction he was conventional in character and dress, often to be seen as a vociferous rugby fan on Saturday afternoons. As an everyday bloke, in short. This possibly infuriated his detractors all the more. His talent for appearing ordinary, while producing far from ordinary fiction, made him a mystery to friends. He and the equally unsuspected Sylvia Ashton-Warner had remodelled the face of New Zealand literature. Their success, when I was living in London, had certainly emboldened me to push on and publish *The New Zealanders*. I confided this to Ian. It turned out that he was also nursing wounds. Maurice Duggan, incomprehensibly outraged by the Cross novels, perhaps because he – a one-time Catholic boy himself – felt he should have written them, had bitterly accused Ian of riding to success on the backs of other New Zealand authors, whatever that meant. Ian was bewildered. So

53

was I. There was one good thing to emerge from this unattractive episode. I was no longer alone. I didn't buy a ticket back to London.

There were matters more earth-moving, if not of the raunchy Hemingway sort. In the middle of 1960 I became the father of a male child. (He would be named Sean, which had something to do with my admiration for Irish playwrights.) Gillian's pregnancy was tense to the end. With the baby three weeks overdue, she was taken into Lower Hutt hospital for observation. Then, while I was preparing a modest evening meal, the telephone rang. It was our doctor. The baby's heartbeat was faint. The child was possibly in peril. Gillian was being wheeled urgently into the operating theatre for a Caesarian. I called up a taxi, explained my problem, and was driven to Lower Hutt at illegal speeds, with a traffic officer soon sounding his siren in dogged pursuit. A compassionate man, a husband and father himself, he didn't hand out a ticket. Instead he sped off ahead of us, his siren sounding, clearing the route to the hospital.

I met our doctor in the hospital foyer. In my anxiety I misheard what he said. After vanishing into the bowels of the building he returned to say, seemingly, 'You've got a mare.' Though I thought that a ribald statement of the position, I took it that he meant Gillian had given birth to a girl. For the next fifteen minutes I remained under the impression that I was the father of a fresh-minted female. Gillian was sleeping off anaesthetic. There was no sign of the baby.

'So where's my daughter?' I asked.

'Daughter?' the doctor said in bewilderment.

'You said I had a mare,' I pointed out.

'I said an heir,' he informed me.

'An heir?'

'An heir,' he said with unshakable authority.

My confusion couldn't have been larger. In imagination I had already been walking a beach with a daughter, showing her the sea, tiny fish and strange shells.

'If it's a girl you want,' the doctor said, 'it's easy to have another shot at it.'

So I imagined walking a beach with a son, showing him the sea, tiny fish and strange shells.

Efficient nurses eventually permitted me sight of my child. As I leaned over his cot, a tiny bubble formed in the corner of his mouth.

Then an eloquent finger moved. There was a faint whimper. He was distinctly alive. I sighed with relief. An heir indeed. A prince too.

I was driven home, still elated. There was no need for speed. I had most of a lifetime left to consider the mystery of these hours. I was surprisingly empty of ambition. Fatherhood suggested that it wouldn't matter if I never wrote another line.

Waking toward morning, after too little sleep, I dressed warmly and wandered outside to contemplate the sky. Stars became faint. The eastern horizon grew pale. The lumpy Rimutaka ranges lifted into the light. What I lacked, it seemed, was ritual, some proven form of celebration. I didn't know where to begin. I breakfasted and took another taxi to the hospital. Gillian was still groggy. Our son had survived his first night on our planet. A nurse placed him in my arms.

I hadn't had time to ring anyone with the news. So I boarded a train into the city and hiked to Jim Baxter's office. Who better to be first with the news? He had already anticipated the event in a memorable poem:

Cicadas drumming
For the march of your exhausted manic friends
Bugle as well for your first child's coming
He (or it might be she) will step down
From the womb's fondling night to a world where three
white ducks sail toward their placid ends.

He soberly heard out my narrative of the night. Silent, he took my arm, shepherded me from his office and steered me in the direction of Wellington's Catholic cathedral. There he left me in a pew and went forward to light a candle for Gillian and our child; and to whisper a brief prayer to the Virgin on the side.

Ritual was what I wanted. Ritual was what I had. I was on my knees too.

Jim helped me to my feet and led me off to coffee. Elation couldn't last. On past experience I should have known ambush likely. A magazine open on Jim's desk recalled me to the petty side of my profession. In its pages a critic best called Smith had lately ripped into *The New Zealanders* in surgical fashion. He argued that I was a book-burning fascist. At least this was original. Critic Jones, a colleague of Smith's, had merely denounced me as a loose-living beatnik. The distinctive thing about the two reviews was their theological character. Both appeared to be judging me guilty of heresy. Neither Smith nor Jones could find a kind word for anything in the book. Not a word. Not a line. Not a page. This was remarkable in itself. So clean a sweep invited suspicion. It might have been a coincidence that both reviewers were associates of Sargeson. It was also possible that the two pieces didn't have their beginnings in Sargeson's Auckland cottage. Critic Jones even seemed to be saying that I should ship back to unenlightened London. That was a sly one. A loose-living beatnik? I couldn't read Jack Kerouac. And I found Ginsberg's *Howl* no more than a moan. As for New Zealand hybrid hipsters, I thought them illiterate. Not that it mattered; not that any of this would in a month.

The New Zealanders might have been less than a masterpiece, but there was little in it to justify literary hysteria. Even Charles Brasch – no near ally – was moved to send a letter of sympathy. 'A brew of malice and envy,' he judged. To say that I was poleaxed is to put it mildly. Both Smith and Jones were, as might be expected, embittered and unpublished writers. As for Sargeson, he had, on the strength of three or four influential books, considerable mana as the old man of New Zealand letters. He surely had nothing to fear from my little book.

Jim Baxter, loyal and loveable Jim – the person who did more than most to set me on a my present path – was also quick with consolation. Of doctrinaire and humourless Jones, a onetime friend of his, Jim said, 'If only he stopped knocking fellow writers, and wrote about his adventures in the urinals of London, he might amount to something.' Jim didn't envisage this as likely. Smith, an academic, was famed for falling asleep in his own lectures.

Brian Brake wrote from London, after the royal wedding. From his privileged vantage point in Westminster Abbey, Brian saw the Queen as furious with everyone involved; she couldn't wait to get the ceremony over and done. She turned her back on her sister, and her sister's commoner husband, and careered out of the abbey at indecent speed. I thought monarchs only behaved like that in movies. Then again, that is what the monarchy mostly is. A bad movie. It is difficult not to see the Queen as the whip-cracking ringmaster of a silly circus.

Now for a narrative of more uplifting nature. In sixty minutes or less, New Zealand took two gold medals in this year's Olympics in Rome. Peter Snell won the 800 metres and Murray Halberg the 5000 metres. It was Murray Halberg's triumph which moved me. We went to the same school, a year apart. He was a gentle, sandy haired and modestly sport-loving boy. He was a fast rugby winger, a cricketer talented with both bat and ball, and a strong middle-distance runner. Though I had cheered him on in Auckland school championships, I remembered him best as an adversary on the rugby field, especially in my one attempt to bring him down in a tackle. Fat chance. He was forty yards up the field before I shakily picked myself off the ground.

A year later someone did level him in a lasting tackle. He was rushed to hospital. His left shoulder and arm were damaged, veins and arteries were ruptured, blood clots were forming. His parents were fetched and informed he was dying. Though it was not yet apparent to those coming and going tearfully from his bedside, Murray had already determined not to die. And survive he did with a paralysed left arm and little hope of ever engaging in first class sport. Rugby was forever out of the question. Cricket too. At length he found himself wandering wistfully back to athletics, strengthening his damaged frame with long walks and determined jogs. He began cross-country running. At the end of his first full season, returned to middle distances, he was running close to New Zealand record times – and this when he still had to get fellow athletes to help him dress and undress and cut up his meat when he sat to a meal. Within a year, while training as a teacher, he was running near four minute miles. This won him an invitation to compete against the best milers in the United States, at the Benjamin Franklin mile at Philadelphia. Sportswriters couldn't believe what they saw when Murray stepped off his plane and stripped for a training run. According to one journalist, he looked, 'more like a refugee from a Korean prisoner of war camp than an athlete.'

Murray had the best answer to that jibe. He coasted past his high-powered US rivals to win without effort. Asked his opinion of their performance, he replied, 'I don't know. I never saw them.'

That run put him in contention for the 1500 metres at the Melbourne Olympics of 1956. By this time there was no doubting his physical stamina. His long, hard runs had kept him in peak form. His mental stamina was another thing. In the roaring Melbourne stadium, with the Olympic flame flaring above, his nerves undid him. He couldn't believe that he belonged there at all. He was tired of hearing that he didn't look like an athlete with his skinny physique and crippled arm. He was beginning to believe it himself. What was he doing up against the fastest 1500 metre runners in the world? He finished a mediocre eleventh in a field of twelve. Tired, edgy, and near nervous breakdown, he couldn't face friends back home in Auckland. Instead he borrowed a sleeping bag and roamed lonely through New Zealand's heartland. He hiked along rough roads, followed remote tracks, slept under the stars, and woke to sunrises beyond white peaks. He even found himself writing a poem in celebration of his native land. Next time he planned to serve New Zealand better. Next time – at the Rome Olympics in 1960 – he wasn't going to be an also-ran. Next time he was going to take on the world in the 5000 metres, not the 1500 metres of sour Melbourne memory; he had decided that the longer distance served him best. Murray also had a secret weapon which would be useful in the final fight to the line. From the time he began running Murray had nourished himself on Greek legend, on the tales of the heroes who became as gods in the shade of Mount Olympus. Might he become one with them in a stadium crowned by the Olympic flame? Soon he could think of little else. The 23-year-old was tuning his will to win as finely as his wiry body. The race of his life had begun. It would last four years. Friends saw a new and ruthless quality in the once easy-going runner. With his coach, Arthur Lydiard, Murray was already planning the Rome race. The success of the plan depended on Murray's stamina. As the field shook into shape for the final battle, Murray would strike; he would shock and scatter the field with a cruel sprint to the front. His enormous stamina might carry him the rest of the way.

The plan was tested at the British Commonwealth Games in 1958. It worked. He waltzed through the best runners in the Commonwealth for the easiest of wins. Murray then went alone to Rome, not to run, but to meditate. He wanted to look out on the stadium where the Olympic flame would burn in 1960. He meant to be ready this time; he meant to oblige the gods of Greece with the run of his life. Yet with first sight of Rome's large and empty *Stadio*

Olympico he panicked again. It wasn't the panic he knew in Melbourne. It was something more mysterious. As he confessed to me later, he felt that someone was nudging his shoulder and saying: 'Too soon. Too soon for you here. Go. Go quickly.'

Who was it? Murray never did find out. It was certainly no one visible. After only a few seconds he fled the stadium. He flew on to Athens and found the crumbled track and marble terraces where the first modern games were held in 1896. He jogged around the track, no longer doubting himself. When the call came, he would sweat the blood of the old heroes.

That call came. He took his heat of the 5000 metres without strain, slipping unobtrusively into second place to qualify for the final. No one gave much attention to the scrawny New Zealander with the wobbly arm action; he was far from favourite. Eyes were on the strongly built Australians and Germans. Murray by contrast seemed to have no muscles at all – except, as his coach said, those which carried him over the ground.

Waiting in a tunnel under the stadium he heard the crowd thundering, then long-lasting applause. What? Who? A delirious New Zealander came running with news. Murray's friend and team mate Peter Snell had just taken the 800 metres for New Zealand. As an omen Snell's triumph couldn't be bettered. If Snell could win, so could he. The 5000 metre contestants now took the stage. Murray didn't look at his rivals. Instead he looked up to the Olympic flame and made a silent vow to his longtime friends of legend. 'Just once,' he begged them. 'Just one title. Just one bite at the apple. That's all, I promise.' Then the starter's pistol cracked. From the first the pace was fast, perhaps fast enough for Murray's strategy to work. He trailed the field comfortably. Again no one noticed him. But no fellow athlete was never to forget him. After eight laps he began overtaking his opponents one by one. Then the insignificant black-clad New Zealander brought 60,000 spectators to their feet. He had begun to sprint with stunning strength. Journalists were laconic: 'The guy's gone mad,' one judged. And: 'Doesn't he know how many laps are left?'

Murray knew exactly how many laps were left. Three. Three laps to build a lead and hold it against all comers. Three laps to push his slight body further than it had gone before. With two laps left he held a twenty yard lead on a German champion. But he was weakening fast – his head rolling in distress, his teeth bared. And his German opponent was chopping away at his lead. It was no longer a commonplace Olympic final; it was the stuff of legend, with two men sweating the blood of heroes. Murray could see the last lap looming, the ribbon strung across the track. His body clamoured for release and rest. Beyond that tape, he told himself, he need no longer fret about his mortal body. Beyond that tape he would be one with the gods and heroes of Greece. The German fell away, diminished by the pace. Murray had the finish line to himself. He fell into the tape and rolled to the ground. Other half-dead athletes sprawled around. They were suffering too, but none more than the gaunt winner. For he was surviving his greatest shock since that rugby tackle, ten years before, had left him shattered and near death. He had never felt less a hero, less an apprentice god; he had never felt more mortal. He was, after all, just an ordinary and terribly tired human being with most of his life still to live. Officials and friends gathered anxiously about the prone and seemingly lifeless figure. Then, with relief, they saw the faintest of smiles.

Just once. Just one title. Just one bite at the apple. That's all. I promise.

Put that life in a fiction, in a novel or story? Forget it. I now save Murray's story for disbelieving dinner parties. The printed word doesn't do it justice. Besides, there's nothing to beat an old-fashioned yarn. Telling it keeps my hand in, as they say.

The year lengthened. Our son grew. New people began calling on us at Te Marua. One was Marilyn Duckworth, Fleur Adcock's sister. A lean, elegant novelist, as cool in prose as her sister in verse, Marilyn had just published her first book and had two more on the way. Though I wasn't altogether in sympathy with her work, what mattered was that she needed company. We made her welcome. Others didn't. The otherwise saintly Charles Brasch, perhaps prompted by a distaste for attractive young women, said it unfortunate that so immature a writer as Marilyn had been published in London. It gave the English the wrong idea about New Zealand literature, Charles said. What wrong idea? It was never clear. He seemed to be saying that, if he had his way, Marilyn's work should be heaved on to a bonfire. This was the way Stalin's literary commissars carried on.

Marilyn, small wonder, was extremely shy and growing even less talkative. What preserved her from life-size paralysis was that she and her sister Fleur were a Bronte-like pair, encapsuled and competitive in their own imaginative world. For much of their shared childhood they needed no others.

Another caller was an essayist of distinction named Dennis McEldowney. He was brought to our house by a neighbour, a writer of thrillers. (Let it never be said that the scruffy foothills of the Rimutaka ranges were innocent of literature.) Dennis's life was the male half of a moving love story.

Dennis had been born with the complex and congenital heart condition known as Fallot's tetralogy which once meant early death for most victims as it cut off oxygen to the muscles, and left the patient's skin with a bluish tinge. Those suffering the condition were commonly known as blue babies. Dennis was one such. In his infancy doctors diagnosed a routine if potentially fatal heart defect and gave him a fair chance of surviving until the age of eight. His eighth birthday came and went. No one thought to tell Dennis that his demise was overdue. So he went on living, if in a feeble way. The world, however, slowly closed down on him, day by day, until he became altogether invalid. Breathlessness made him immobile, and immobility in turn atrophied his muscles. From the age of twelve, and for years to come, all he knew of the world was his bedroom. He sometimes felt that the rest of the world was an elaborate hoax. Yet his existence wasn't all unhappy. Continuous unhappiness, he wryly recorded, required a strength of mind he did not possess. He read widely and well, wrote for magazines and published short stories. By the age of twenty, however, his life had become even more circumscribed. An hour listening to the radio could leave him exhausted.

By his twenty-fifth year modern heart surgery had begun giving hope to those with congenital heart defects. Doctors took a second look at Dennis and diagnosed him as a miraculously surviving blue baby (or blue adult) after all. He was flown from his native Christchurch to Auckland for an operation to alleviate his condition. 'Left it a bit late, haven't you?' said the nurse who undressed him. In 1950 he became the oldest New Zealand blue baby to go on the operating table.

For a time, as he slept under anaesthetic, the operation was touch and go. In the end it was pronounced a success. While recuperating he was introduced to a slight, blonde girl named Zoe Greenhough, a little older than himself, with a similar medical history. Encouraged by their triumph with Dennis, which was making newspaper headlines, heart surgeons decided they could risk operating on her too. Soon afterwards Zoe displaced Dennis as the country's oldest blue baby. The young couple, with much in common, kept in touch. That was as far as their relationship could go. Dennis couldn't support himself, let alone a wife. Also Dennis was far from out of the woods, unlike Zoe. She had been able to take an office job and lead a far more strenuous life than he could. A half mile remained the limit of his walking range. Mentally there were problems too. Outside his bedroom, for the first time in a decade, he went into panic with sight of the sky. On the plus side, however, he was now able to write at more length and taste the sweets of literary success. In the late 1950s he published his first book, a short and sensitive account of his invalid years and his emergence into the world again. A reviewer in London's *New Statesman* compared his gently evocative prose with Proust's. In New Zealand it was judged book of the year. 'My way in the world has only begun,' he reported prophetically.

For by 1960 there were even larger advances in heart surgery. He was once more on an operating table. Overnight his walking range became two or three miles. He could stroll city streets without a minder. He could even catch a bus by himself once he had learned the trick of paying for the ticket. Finally, at the age of forty-one, he took his first job. Though his academic qualifications were next to nil, he was soon to become editor of the Auckland University Press. Under his care, the press was to become the most vital academic press in the country.

There were other, more important matters. There was Zoe. From the time they first met in hospital Dennis had hoped for marriage. Now, seventeen years later, it was possible. Their marriage made headlines much as their operations once had. After their years in confinement, they remained excitable youngsters rather than a quiet middle-aged couple. A rose in a neighbourhood garden, a bird singing in a tree, could bring their day to a standstill.

In 1960, the year of my first meeting with Dennis, he was between the two operations which eventually gave him freedom. For two hours he was lively in conversation. Then he grew quiet. There was a bluish tinge to his lips. We saw him to his neighbour's vehicle. After his excursion into the outer world, Dennis would be in bed for at least a week. That had never deterred him. I had a glimpse of the love of life behind his survival. And his love of Zoe.

Those two hours with Dennis, thirty years ago, were to prove durable. Dennis made other friendships flimsy.

Ten

I had a mystery visit from a Soviet diplomat by name of Lutsky. What did he want? He wasn't disposed to make it clear. His wife and my wife talked about child-rearing in Russia and New Zealand. Mrs Lutsky clucked over Sean. Perhaps something I said early in the encounter suggested that I was unlikely to be a useful contact for Mr Lutsky. So there we were. I would never know what the meeting was about. I later learned that Comrade Lutsky was the KGB man in the Soviet legation. He left behind some Soviet magazines and a puzzled New Zealander. No doubt he was followed to Te Marua by some dedicated employee of the New Zealand Security Intelligence Service; Soviet diplomats were always followed. In this case they had a poser. The weekend cottage next to our dwelling was owned by the civil servant most concerned with New Zealand's foreign affairs. He had been under a cloud as a left-leaning liberal. That cloud would be even murkier, with Mr Lutsky visiting Te Marua in his KGB limousine. It would surely be seen as suspicious; there would be another query or two on my SIS file. (Which existed; I was once within arm's reach of it.)

There was a visitor even more mysterious than Mr Lutsky. He was an Italian by name of Renato Amato. Tired of the malicious nicknames bestowed on him by mocking workmates, he had recently renamed himself Michael. In his late twenties, he had been a travelling salesman for most of his four years in New Zealand. He had lately married a pretty blonde Scots girl named Sheena, fathered a son, found less nomadic employment, and become a student at Victoria University; he had also become president of that university's literary society.

Ostensibly his visit was to ask me to contribute a story to that society's annual literary journal. He also wanted me to give a talk. I found a half-finished story I promised to complete. And we set a date for the talk. Actually, however, his visit had more to do with the arcane corridors of authorship. Having read *The New Zealanders* he needed to look me over. Under the mistaken impression that I was in possession of the requisite magic, he wished my advice on publishing a book of *his* stories. He had written several, it seemed; and was now at work on an autobiographical novel set in Italy in the Second World War. In Italian? No. In English. Abandoning his native tongue for another language, I suggested, was rather risky. Even the likes of Nabokov and Conrad had been unable to do it overnight. My visitor didn't seem to hear me. He didn't want to hear.

My reservations melted after he left, and as I looked through the stories he placed in my reluctant hands. Though at times they had the slightly stiff tone of competent translation, they made powerful reading. Italy was sometimes the setting of his stories. The rest were generated by his New Zealand experience. This wasn't the work of a dilettante student out to impress a girlfriend. One or two of the stories read like Pavese or Moravia. I suspected that he had been here before. I rang him to say that the stories impressed me. But were they really his first? Really? There was a silence. Finally he admitted they were not. He had published two or three in Italy. Not in anything important. In newspapers mostly. He also kept literary company in postwar Rome. The playwright Tennessee Williams had tried to seduce him. He had been on talking terms with the novelist Gore Vidal. He had for a time been involved romantically with a cousin of Cesar Pavese's. So what was he doing in New Zealand? And why should he need my advice? At that time I was poorly placed to ladle out literary wisdom. My novel, begun in London, sweated over across the Indian ocean, had gone aground on New Zealand. It was too Faulknerian to be true. And it wasn't. True, that is.

In the course of our first meeting, Michael Amato (the name I remember him by) ventured to say, 'Do you ever think you might be a one-book writer?'

'Every morning,' I told him. 'After midnight too.'

He touched a raw spot. Few New Zealand storytellers progressed far beyond their first books. That was true even of John Mulgan with his brief if monumental *Man Alone*. New Zealand was a land of literary kamikazes. Those who did publish were often suffering from tuberculosis, alcoholism and worse. Suicide was not unknown. (In other words, portents were poor.) Robin Hyde, after walking her way through ravaged China, had been beaten and raped by Japanese soldiers before she killed herself in the first month of the war. John Mulgan, after surviving strife in Greece and Africa, had killed himself in war's last month. No one seemed to notice the symmetry.

I put my novel aside. There was a literary competition attached to Wellington's annual festival. Entries were to be anonymous and the prize worthwhile. In need of the money I wrote a story to fill an otherwise lacklustre Sunday. It was largely about a suburban man attempting to relive the life of his tree-felling pioneer ancestors on a stubborn patch of land. The story was drawn from my own family. Faulkner wasn't hiding out there in the scrub. It worked. A tickle at the back of my neck told me I had found my theme.

As promised, I gave my talk to the literary society. I didn't learn much more about Michael Amato. He asked some shrewd and informed questions afterward. These made it even more clear that he had been around.

The student meeting ended, I was waylaid as I worked my way to the door. A young Samoan student shuffled shyly up to me with a sheaf of manuscript. He was soft-spoken, gentle, probably easily hurt. I dreaded having to pass an opinion on his work. His name was Albert Wendt; I learned that he was twenty years old and had been writing for a year or two already.

Then the expected question. Would I read his work? I attempted to say no. I wasn't up to it.

I took the stories home. I needed only to read the first paragraph on the first page to see that I was in the presence of a bona fide writer. The rest of the page suggested that he might even be an important one. The land of Robert Louis Stevenson still lacked an indigenous author. And Stevenson was no influence on Albert. He wrote as a duck to water. Even his shakiest prose was filled with the colours of Polynesia – not Stevenson's colours, nor Michener's. This wasn't *South Pacific*. There was no Bloody Mary here.

A royalty cheque for three hundred pounds arrived in from London. It looked likely to be the last the three impressions of *The New Zealanders* would earn me; there was no present prospect of a fourth. And we had already spent my New York advance. Nevertheless we raced out recklessly to buy a second-hand car suffering only slightly from rust. With Sean talkative in the back seat, we pushed it hundreds of miles, from one end of summer to the other.

Eleven

*T*he season had begun dismally, with an election. The three-year Labour government went down to deserved and humiliating defeat. Prime Minister Walter Nash, the old man of New Zealand politics, couldn't make his mind up about anything; he couldn't even appoint a high commissioner in London. And he couldn't delegate. The wretched thing about the party's term was that it turned on many of its longtime supporters in matters large and small – conspicuously on those who argued that Maoris should not be excluded from sporting teams visiting South Africa's apartheid-polluted land. It was a contemptible government, though I voted for it. The alternative was worse.

The last weeks of 1960 trickled away. I needed someone to tell me that my novel was a disaster. Since no one obliged, I finally confessed it to myself. I was glad to see the rear of the year. My desk there reeked with sweats of writerly frustration. The lone joy of the year was son Sean – now seven months old. In a burst of early summer sunshine we drove up the coast to the oceanside village of Paekakariki, to visit the poet Denis Glover and his wife Kura. On the way we christened Sean with seawater from a wild ocean beach. The ceremony may have been makeshift, but with spray on our faces and foaming sea at our feet it didn't lack majesty. We bore him away to Denis and Kura.

Kura clucked maternally and Denis pronounced Sean a most manly child. As always I was glad of Denis's sardonic company; he was as terse as his distinguished and delicately wrought lyrics. There was no New Zealand literary figure I respected more, even when the bottle had the better of him. (Which was frequent.) For one thing Denis – a onetime navy man who survived Arctic convoys to

Murmansk in the war, and steered troop-filled landing craft ashore in Normandy on D-Day – knew that literature didn't have to be high-minded. It was also meant to entertain. This boxer turned poet took a malicious pleasure in upsetting preening contemporaries. The punches he threw seldom went wide.

'Has Sargeson been getting at you?' he asked.

I mumbled inaudibly.

'Writers are their own worst enemies,' he reported.

'Sometimes,' I agreed.

'If I had my way,' he went on, 'writing should be a capital offence. Writers could have the choice of rope, axe or firing squad. But no possibility of reprieve.'

This was rather sensational.

'Why?' I asked.

'So only those who really need to write would risk it,' he explained.

Summer warmed and another year loomed. We began packing to leave Te Marua and I cleared the decks, burning my manuscript along with the rest of the year's rubbish.

Through Christmas we stayed at my parents' most recent dwelling, this one beside surf-fringed Waihi Beach. My long-legged teenage sister Julia was there, and my uncle Joe Kearon. On New Year's Day, 1961, a year to the day since our return, Gillian and I drove north, through Auckland, Northland, and on to Cape Reinga. Bill and Kitty Kemp welcomed us to the lighthouse. The vista below was still rich in untranslated messages. Now the paint was dry; I was mired in the picture. A year ago I was on the outside looking in. I was now on the inside looking out. The questions remained the same. What to make of those messages? What to make of this land? What to make of myself?

Holidaying done and another year begun, Gillian and I braced for life back in Wellington. One thing detained us before we left the north. The novelist Sylvia Ashton-Warner lived twenty minutes from my parents. Rumour said she was sensitive and reclusive and didn't care for visitors. After much hesitation, ready for a stiff reception, I telephoned her. She wasn't cool. She was delighted. She insisted that we come to dinner that night. I warned Gillian that the evening might be difficult. Gossip said that Sylvia was embittered by New Zealand reaction to her second novel, *Incense to Idols*, though *Time* magazine thought it a masterpiece. While I admired *Spinster*, her first, I thought *Incense to Idols* a picturesque catastrophe, romanticism gone mad. I should have to fall back on the pretence that I had yet to read the book.

Sylvia and her school headmaster husband Keith Henderson lived in, of all places, a village called Bethlehem. (Judea was just down the road.) We found their bright-lit schoolhouse in the dusk. There were trees around, and school buildings. I parked and shut off the engine. There was a piano being played energetically within the house. Keith appeared on the verandah and descended a flight of steps to welcome us. Sylvia was slower appearing. The unseen pianist continued attacking Chopin with passion. Presumably Sylvia was waiting on her moment. Keith made small talk until we heard a terminal crash of chords. The music continued to reverberate as she floated regally across the verandah and down the steps, a filmy gown billowing behind her, a brimming champagne glass held high. What were we supposed to make of this apparition? At the least it left us in little doubt that we were in the presence of the most distinctive writer in New Zealand history. No one could have foreseen her international success with *Spinster*, the tale of a heartsick schoolteacher in a New Zealand country school. Meanwhile we seemed to be in a movie. Or perhaps in a novel called *Incense to Idols*.

'I have been looking forward to this,' she announced.

'Oh?' I said with disbelief.

'Ever since I published *Spinster*, I have been waiting for another New Zealand writer to call,' she explained. 'Summers come and summers go. But no one ever comes. No one. Ever. Until today. You shall always be my very special friend.'

'I'm honoured,' I said, not altogether untruthfully.

They led us into the house. The interior was modest. There was no sign, not yet, of the royalties roaring in from New York and London. Or of the income deriving from the Hollywood movie of *Spinster* (with Shirley MacLaine starring). Perhaps they didn't know what to do with the money. Anyway it remained a rural New Zealand schoolteacher's dwelling. Another bottle of champagne was broken out. Dinner was roast lamb and potatoes afloat in mint sauce. I had a feeling Keith prepared it. Sylvia appeared to have less menial matters on her mind. Gossip proved accurate. She was still smarting from the critical barrage lately levelled at her work. She was not going to forgive New Zealand easily. Like Sargeson, she thrived on imagined enmity. She needed to be seen leading the charge against philistines. Otherwise her persona would fall apart. In that respect she had more in common with other New Zealand writers than she was likely to admit. Her future contracts were to include a clause saying that her books were only to be available in Europe and the United States; not on any account in her own country. This was unique, and I said so. What of the thousands of New Zealanders who would now have no chance to read her?

She was indifferent: 'If they *really* liked my work *that* much, then they can get friends in England and the United States to buy copies,' she said. She had more to think about anyway. What to do with her royalties, for example. Perhaps she should travel; she had already had a trial run with a visit to Australia. (To buy a pair of gloves, she explained to inquisitive journalists.) She and Keith had spent their adult lives teaching in remote New Zealand communities. They had seen little of cities. 'I should like to go to Japan,' she disclosed. 'What do you think?'

I suggested that Japan might be overwhelming.

'Good,' she said. 'I wish to be whelmed.'

She had another novel on the way. 'When I finish this one,' she predicted, 'I shall be an old woman.' Meanwhile news of the Hollywood movie of *Spinster* was ageing her fast.

It was time to leave. Keith, with a torch, led us to our car. 'We are fellow spirits,' Sylvia whispered.

This was extravagant, especially on the strength of one evening. I was polite enough not to differ. Gillian and I drove off into the night. Not for the first time I found myself thinking that New Zealanders, one way and another, were a puzzling people. Perhaps it had something to do with the introverted and highly-strung nature of islanders. (They are people who see far too much of each other.) A Sri Lankan diplomat once assured me that the inhabitants of his diminutive land were much the same. Meanwhile, though Sylvia might like to think otherwise, her homeland had been her making.

Wellington was warm with summer on our return. We had an inner-city flat, in Glenmore Street, clinging to the edge of Wellington's menacing earthquake fault-line. We looked out on the heaving greenery of the city's botanical gardens. I was less and less happy about living in Wellington. There had to be point in my existence there; I couldn't find it. I waited for something to happen; my novel was no longer going to.

Among trivial mail there was a letter from Mike Bessie, my New York editor. *The New Zealanders* had been published in the United States. The reviews on publication day were pleasing. The *New York Times* and the *New York Herald-Tribune* treated it warmly, and at length. Yet even that didn't lift my spirits. I couldn't see myself writing again. This, though I didn't know it yet, was a romantic indulgence on the part of most novelists. Angela Carter's proposition that writers write to be loved might be true. It was certainly true that they needed to be stroked now and then.

Gillian was working for the populist and notoriously salacious weekly *Truth*. She wrote a couple of columns and the book page. The latter did something to improve the journal's character. The original plan was that Gillian would leave Sean in a day-care centre while she worked. I immediately determined that my son was not going to be dumped in this dire establishment, filled with anguished, runny-nosed infants. Never, I said. I announced suicidally that I would look after Sean myself, at home. I would write while he slept. This wasn't practical. For one thing my son seldom slept. After a week of minding Sean, of changing nappies, preparing his food, walking him in the gardens and averaging no more than three lines a day, I sensed lunacy looming. Hadn't Cyril Connolly said that the greatest enemy of the young writer was the perambulator in the hallway? Meanwhile Marilyn Duckworth, who lived a mile away, and had heard of my problem, generously raced to help. She already managed to write with two small children on hand; she said a third wouldn't be a problem. She would, she said, enjoy having Sean around. Did she believe this? I did my best to. I began taking Sean up to Marilyn's before I began work in the morning and collecting him early in the afternoon.

This routine worked; it also had awkward consequences. Marilyn and I didn't know each other well. Within weeks we knew each other too well. When I arrived to collect Sean, there was always a welcoming coffee and an hour of trade talk. More proved hazardous. For reasons so far unexplained she was restless in her marriage. (She was hardly out of her teens when she married.) I was deeply depressed in mine – though, if asked, I should have denied it vehemently. My discontent didn't derive from marriage in itself. It was with where marriage had marooned me. I wanted New Zealand's warm and wild north, the sweep of Ninety Mile Beach, the serpentine estuaries of the Hokianga, the mangrove-girt tides. In other words the New Zealand that haunted me as an expatriate; the country I invented and revised in story after story, in a dim London basement. Gillian, on the other hand, needed people, her Wellington friends, the instant thrills of journalism. The gap between us was not to be bridged. Economics decided the issue: at the moment Gillian was earning and, despite impressive communiques from New York, I was not. As for Marilyn's house, I wasn't unaware of a sexual ripple in the atmosphere. I tried to pretend that it didn't exist. Perhaps Marilyn did too. On second thought perhaps she didn't.

There was a phone call late one morning. Marilyn told me she had a problem. No, it wasn't Sean. He was asleep. Nor was it with her daughters. They were off with their grandmother. Yet it was a problem, she insisted, of life or death. Could I come quickly? Of course, I said. I stopped trying to polish a rough paragraph and headed up into the hills to Marilyn's house. Alarm bells should have been ringing. They weren't.

When I arrived there was no blood on the floor; nor was flame roaring through the roof. There was no intruder, so far as I could see, and no rapist. The house was serene and sunlit. Life and death? Marilyn might have been flushed, but she was not in conspicuous disarray. She was coolly dressed in jeans and T-shirt. Her problem, it turned out, was merely of a confessional nature; she couldn't keep silent any longer. What she said was rather sensational. 'I think I'm dying,' she whispered in my ear. Minutes later, weak in the knees, we sank to the floor. This seemed to have a desperate inevitability. It did. It should have been squalid. It wasn't.

What followed was mostly news to me. Fiction, including my own, might have forewarned me. I was both sick with remorse and light-headed with relief. The latter had something to do with respite from my fettered condition in Wellington. Guilt, however, won out. I found it all rather shocking, more so because it didn't stop there. Marilyn continued to baby-sit Sean. And we continued to talk affectionately on the telephone. Virtue still had no place in the scheme of things.

A short story – the first written since return to New Zealand – won me a hundred pounds in prize money. The story, as explained earlier, derived from the robust eccentric behaviour of a relative encapsulated in suburbia who broke free and headed into the wilderness to emulate his forest-clearing forebears. Though I failed to notice at first, the story was also about me. It signalled that I might have more stories to tell, narratives which might not be mistaken for those of anyone else. Having heard their message, I found several more queuing to be told. I had another book.

Twelve

*I*an Cross rang, unusually breathless. 'Patrick White is in town,' he told me.

'Patrick White? Here? In Wellington?' I was slow taking it in. Did gods descend from Olympus?

'I've just met him in Parsons' coffee bar,' Ian explained. 'He's here for a few days, staying with a cousin.'

His cousin, Peggy Garland, was known to me; next day I received an invitation to a soirée for the great man. By chance Charles Brasch was also in Wellington. I took him along with me. I had been urging Charles to read Patrick White for some years, ever since I encountered *The Tree of Man* and then *The Aunt's Story* and *Voss*. Charles tended to sniff when Australian writers were mentioned. He had a pained look when I persisted in praising any. It was possible that I had overdone this in respect of White.

Australia's future Nobel laureate proved to be a tall, stiff man somewhat military in bearing. (So stiff that he sometimes seemed to tipping dangerously backward.) He was also awkwardly gentle. Smiles didn't come easily. He plainly found social occasions difficult, especially among strangers in an unfamiliar country. I discovered myself mute when we were introduced. I was even more inarticulate when he announced that he had been reading *The New Zealanders* all afternoon. 'I haven't been able to put it down,' he added. 'My word, you are a spellbinder.' I hope I record this right: he certainly used the word spellbinder. He took my arm and steered me to a chair. 'Now,' he said. 'I must know more about you. How did you come to write that book?'

More surprisingly, he added, 'By the way, I think Victor Gollancz the wrong London publisher for you. He has a reputation for picking up and discarding young writers. My publisher, Eyre and Spottiswoode, is far more stable. I shall write to them, and suggest they take you on.'

I managed, after a time, to muster questions about *him* and *his* work. He wasn't averse to answering them. In distilled form, and in something less than fifteen minutes, I got most his life story. Out of nowhere, talking of his beginnings, he said, 'My bitch of a mother carried me off to London in her womb so I would be born English.'

I found myself without a word to say. Was it his custom to denounce his mother intemperately to total strangers? Later I learned that this bitter tale of his beginnings wasn't true anyway. Rancour didn't begin and end with his mother; it seethed again when he spoke of Australian reviewers. Australian writers. Australians in general. He seldom allowed facts to trip him. For example, he talked of his monumental novel *The Tree of Man* being savagely reviewed by *Time* magazine. As it happens it was that review, in the middle 1950s, which persuaded me to rush off to the nearest bookshop and buy the book. I wasn't the only one. With excitable readers racing to the shops, who needed commonplace plaudits? But he went on. It seemed he knew of the *Time* reviewer, an Australian by origin, and had him on a hit list. 'I'll get him one day,' he announced. Get him? I was even more alarmed. Was this the literary life in the raw? Perhaps distinguished writers should be read and not met. Then there was the matter of the one New Zealand review he had read of his work.

'By someone with your Christian name,' he remembered.

'Duggan,' I suggested hastily.

'That's right. Maurice Duggan. He tore me to shreds too, in a magazine called *Landfall*. 'Do you publish there too?'

'Not reviews,' I replied quickly.

'Don't,' he advised.

He didn't have to warn me a second time. In any case I was familiar with the New Zealand review which incensed him. Maurice Duggan had been slightly mystified by the dense and traditional texture of *The Tree of Man*. On the whole, though, his review had been mild-mannered; and far from injurious. Like many a cautious critic, he simply hedged his bets. I felt I should make some protest. Instead I mischievously introduced Patrick to Charles Brasch, editor of the magazine which published the offensive review. They appeared to get on. Lordly Australian met up with lofty New Zealander; they recognised each other immediately. Having monopolised the eminent guest too long, I was led off to make myself known to others at the soirée. From the side of my vision I watched Charles and Patrick in increasingly intimate conversation. I felt I had done my duty by Australian-New Zealand relations – which have always been next to non-existent.

When departures began Patrick followed me to my car. 'Please keep in touch,' he asked, and gave me his address. 'Let me know if I can do any more for you. And if you're ever in Sydney please dine with me.'

'I will,' I promised.

Ian Cross, when I later told him of this encounter, sardonically suggested that Patrick may have mistaken me, on the strength of one or two stories with sympathetic homosexual characters, as of his sexual persuasion too. As ever, I had no opinion on the subject.

I drove Charles back to his lodging. 'White is a most pleasant man,' he observed.

'You'll have to read him now,' I suggested.

'I mean to,' he said.

It was all right after all. Patrick White was no Australian literary lout.

Life was leaving much to be desired. The weather had cooled. Marilyn and I had begun agreeing to terminate our affair. The proposition was whole-hearted on my part, less fervent on hers. I picked her up sometimes at a coffee house called the Mon Marie. Sometimes we just sat in a car parked at Oriental Bay and looked at the lights of Wellington across the water. There was no future in this. Sometimes I just drove her home. We found more and more ingenious ways of making each other miserable. I was also appalled by the fluency of the untruths I was learning to tell.

On sunny afternoons I walked Sean in the Botanical Gardens. He had a marvellous chuckle. He loved the frog fountain. Bless frogs and princesses wherever they are. Innocence. Must we lose it? Apparently. And as most women are born knowing, you've got to kiss a lot of old frogs to find a handsome prince.

Thirteen

A couple of itinerants, Barry Crump and his girlfriend Jean Watson, both writers, took a room above ours in the Glenmore Street establishment; they shared our kitchen. Barry had been shooting rabbits in the North Island back country for most of the past year. He thought it time to chance his arm as an author again, at least as long as winter lasted. And why not? His first book, *A Good Keen Man*, was said to have sold a stunning fifty thousand copies in hardback. This tended to put rabbit shooting in the shade. Poet Kevin Ireland was in large part responsible for this publishing phenomenon. He first met Crump as a young deer-culler with literary ambition and in need of tuition. Kevin smoothed down rough edges and gave his surprising protégé weekly tuition in constructing a narrative. As editor of a literary magazine he also published his stories. To my eternal discredit, I played a part in this. I had written out Crump's first literary contract, the most enriching a New Zealand author had ever had. In less spendthrift hands the money might have ensured him a lifelong income. In a second large mistake, I turned down his proposal that I act as his literary agent. I might have had a lifetime income too.

Barry and Jean had aweing appetites. They consumed at least a dozen eggs and a pound of bacon every morning; our kitchen reeked of their breakfast fry-ups. Jean, who had an original view of the world, and whose delicate little tale of her days on the road with Crump, *Standing in the Rain*, would be far more impressive than anything Crump ever published, wondered aloud whether Barry would win the Nobel Prize for literature in the coming year. Managing a straight face, as tactful as I could be, I explained that authors who walked off with the Nobel Prize generally had a prior

78

reputation in Sweden, which Barry hadn't. And *A Good Keen Man* was after all his first book. Not wanting to disappoint her, I pointed out that Barry, as the first writer to win a large New Zealand readership in years, had already had a fair share of good fortune. His yarn spinning, I hastened to add, was not to be despised. Without a compost of legend and lore, New Zealand literature was going to remain anaemic. Possibly I believed this. If so, I soon wished I didn't.

Dizzied by the city, waist-deep in royalties, and beset by dubious and druggy hangers-on, Barry soon revealed himself as something of a pen-pushing Frankenstein raving out of control. His flair for heavy drinking and beating up women far exceeded his talent for telling sometimes plagiarised tales of the back country. The horror didn't end there. He would be responsible for the death of four or five schoolboys unwisely left in his care for a costly adventure holiday with the famous author. By the time of his own death, in 1996, Crump's weathered features had even won a place on a New Zealand postage stamp. By that time he was even garlanded with an MBE. Tears were shed, some of them genuine. I remembered the females in his life, women with bruised faces and swollen eyes hidden behind heavy make-up and dark glasses; and one I took to hospital with a fractured arm. On his death he was widely mourned for his comic gift. The joke, however, had long soured. With his devoted Jean discarded, he finished up ingloriously, not with a Nobel Prize but selling Toyota pick-up trucks in television commercials. Jean's *Standing in the Rain*, was rightly seen as superior to anything that Crump ever published. This persuaded me that justice was not unknown in literature's realm.

Maurice Duggan, never at a loss in coining a vivid phrase, had it about right when he called Crump an anecdotal ape. Maurice didn't live to see the ape gazing out of a postage stamp. It was as ugly an episode as any in New Zealand letters.

That leaves me with this footnote. Years later, on a late summer day in March 1975, Crump turned up at my Titirangi house on a motor cycle. Stripped sweaty to the waist, I was scything long grass around my property. Glad of an excuse for a break, I offered Barry a beer.

He held up a hand. 'No,' he said solemnly.

I was meant to be impressed. I fetched myself a beer anyway. He drank water.

'So what's this all about?' I asked.

'I'm dry,' he said. 'I've become a Bahai. No drink. No drugs.'

'A Bahai? You?' I barely killed a smile.

'That's right.'

'This is no joke, Barry?'

'I've never been more serious in my life,' he claimed. 'I've brought some Bahai literature along. You should have a think about it too.'

'Me?'

'You could do worse.'

That may have been true. Crump's gift for self-advertisement, on the other hand, left me suspicious. His conversion to the Bahai faith might make a few headlines and sell a few books. I suspected they sold far fewer these days. New Zealand had begun to outgrow this soiled son of the outback.

Some weeks later, in London, I walked into my favourite Maida Vale pub. There Crump sat over a pint of beer. I couldn't hide my astonishment. It seemed he was in pursuit of a runaway wife currently hiding out in London. In no hurry to make her captive, he invited me to join him in a pint.

'I thought you weren't,' I said.

'Weren't?'

'Drinking,' I said. 'Last time we met you told me you were a dry Bahai. You even tried to recruit me.'

'That was back in Auckland,' he pointed out.

'What's so different?'

'No one knows who I am around here,' he explained. 'Anyway what's a beer between friends?'

I sank my pint with some satisfaction. I had long suspected him to be a charlatan playing up to paying customers. As the years passed he had grown even more shameless. I spent a squalid day sparing his wife further damage. It was my good luck that I was never to see him again.

Optimism gone, Marilyn decided to escape to Auckland to write her next novel. She had a literary grant which should support her and pay for child-minding in Wellington while she was away. We had a long and largely cheerless conversation. She made me promise to attempt to visit her in Auckland. Then I drove her home. Two days later she was gone. A week or two later I pointed the car toward

Auckland. That was imprudent.

My route led me up the west coast of the North Island, around the elegant volcanic cone of Mount Taranaki, and into the King Country, the limestone terrain of my childhood. Otherwise the route had little to commend it. The car climbed over rugged ridges, swooped into valleys. Then misty hills parted. Te Kuiti, my home town if ever I had one, disclosed itself far below. A noisy flock of teenage boys, out for a weekend jaunt, were pushing bicycles uphill. I parked on the roadside and watched them pass. Then I realised I was looking for myself among them. Though I stared intently enough I failed to sight anyone answering to my description. It was the same further downhill. There was a lusty game of rugby in progress on the town's football ground. My onetime club, Waitete, was playing. If tempted, I could easily have hauled on shorts and my club colours, laced up my boots and joined in the fray. But temptation wasn't placed in my way. Much as I wished it, no familiar face rose from the crowd to reproach me for having given the game away, the sheep-shaven hills of Te Kuiti too. I was now a stranger here. If I met up with an old schoolmate, what would I say? What could I say? The townsfolk who remembered me would possibly have seen me as overdue for a bad end; on present showing they might even have been right.

Marilyn and I met in a motel just north of Auckland. A magnificent ocean beach became the setting for our long talks and walks. Rain didn't daunt us. This time we knew our affair finished. For one thing, it had to be. I finally delivered her to a bed and breakfast house in Auckland where she would write her next novel. I drove reluctantly home to my desk.

There little had changed. I looked out on the medley of vegetation bordering Wellington's botanic gardens. Silver birches alternated attractively with evergreen native pohutukawa. Since May I had been watching leaves colour and fall. It was now July; there was just one leaf left. Colouring, withering, surviving wind and rain, it had held on tenaciously for weeks. My eye returned to it again and again as I worked, or tried to. The lone leaf was ludicrously out of step with the seasons. Didn't it know it had a duty to disappear? Apparently not. On the first day of August I was on the point of terminating my vigil. This way was madness. I rearranged my desk and turned my back on the delinquent leaf. When I looked up again, an hour later, the leaf had flown. So had much else. There was a letter from Marilyn. She seemed more at peace too. In Auckland, lonely, she had fallen into the arms of a more receptive writer. Once again I found myself wondering at the time and effort authors put into the making of misery. On the other hand matters might be worse. I had only to contemplate the chaos Crump left behind him.

Gillian was pregnant again. That revised almost everything. A warmish day suggested that winter might be passing and spring near. So might some lucrative work. *Geographic* wanted Brian Brake and I to go to China. Their own journalists and photographers couldn't travel there on American passports. We might, on our New Zealand documents. Besides, we had both been to China; Brian knew the ropes, and I had bounced off them. Brian was knocking on diplomatic doors in London and Geneva. I could do nothing. I waited on word from Brian.

It was a month or more before he decided that he was wasting his time with slippery diplomats. The news was dismaying; I had been counting on the largesse. I had a timely call from Washington. 'Is there something else you'd like to do for us?' the editor of *Geographic* asked.

Off the top of my head I heard myself suggesting Western Samoa. After forty years as a New Zealand protectorate, it was about to win independence. Besides, I had friends there, most conspicuously the young Samoan writer Albert Wendt. A sortie into tropical Polynesia might do much for my spirits.

Before I flew to Samoa, Gillian and I moved again, this time to a house high above the city, in the suburb of Kelburn. Wellington harbour was wildly beautiful below, sometimes glittering, often stormy. We let part of the house to a young couple about to be married – Max and Janet. They were slow making a showing after the ceremony. Finally a distressed Janet arrived minus Max. There had been a turbulent bachelor party for Max the night before. Hoping to sober himself, Max had gone outside. There was a car there he presumed to be the property of a friend. It tempted Max to take an overdue doze. He opened the unlocked vehicle and fell inside. The rightful owner of the car, putting out his cat, viewed this with alarm. He opened the door of the vehicle and tried to drag Max out. Max then threw a punch which left the aggrieved citizen prone on the pavement. Lights flashed on in nearby houses. People began running. The police arrived and arrested Max. His victim was carried away in an ambulance. Max's wedding day dawned in a police cell. Later that morning he made an appearance before a magistrate, not a minister of religion. The unfeeling magistrate was unimpressed by the news that Max's nuptials were near. He sentenced him to a month's prison for assault. The wedding? Very well, then. He gave Max permission to marry in the company of two prison guards. So Max and Janet married, kissed, and Max was raced off to serve his sentence. Festivities proceeded without the bridegroom. It was a cruel world.

Fourteen

I packed for my Samoan assignment and flew off in mid-December. Our second child was now five or six weeks away. At steamy Apia airport Albert Wendt was waiting with family and friends. They rushed me off, past lagoon and coral reef, along pot-holed road fringed by coconut palms. The sun shone warmly. The earthly paradise of a hundred Pacific fictions paraded past. Villages were neat, churches huge, Samoans muscular. Apia was largely a shanty town. There was just one hotel of moment, named for its proprietor Aggie Grey. Though she vigorously denied it, Aggie was said to be the original of the brothel-keeping Bloody Mary in James Michener's *Tales of the South Pacific* and the musical on which it was based. There was a post office and a few government buildings. Otherwise markets, shops, and twenty thousand people. Western Samoa as a whole had only one hundred and fifty thousand. It had been a German colony until overrun by New Zealand at the beginning of the First World War. Some German traces remained, especially in surnames (such as Albert's; he had a German grandfather).

Albert's father, Henry Wendt, was the town plumber; his home and business sat under palms just back from the waterfront and next to Western Samoa's prison. Prisoners were often seen sitting on the walls conversing with passersby and often with the Wendt family. Albert assured me that they were a rough crew, some of them murderers, though they looked harmless to me. Escape would be easy, but where to? A Pacific island offered no escape routes. Meanwhile the extensive Wendt family, with four generations resident, took me crushingly to its bosom. I went to church with them in a borrowed white suit. I sat beside Albert's ancient grandmother and heard her stories of another, older Samoa: the many-coloured land Robert Louis Stevenson knew. She was marvellously knowledgable, in touch with the unseen things of this world. She perfectly predicted her demise. On a Monday morning, soon after my visit, she asked that her grave be dug. She took a critical interest in the project as it progressed. On the following Friday, as scheduled, she retired comfortably to her grave.

Seeking to orient me, Albert took me up steep and slippery Mount Vae'a where Stevenson's bones and the ashes of his American wife Fanny are buried. Teams of grieving Samoan matai – or chieftains – had carried their remains to the summit. It was challenge enough without coffins to carry.

A spluttering bus took us around Upolu, the most populated island of those which compose Samoa. It was a leisurely means of travel. We sometimes waited five minutes for a village maiden to finish brushing her hair before scrambling aboard. We could wait longer for our driver to finish a conversation with a disembarking passenger. Such halts meant that more interest could be taken in me. Europeans were seldom seen on rickety Samoan buses. So what, they asked, was I doing aboard? Albert explained: 'This man is learning about Samoa. He is a tusitala – a teller of tales.'

'Ah,' our awed fellow travellers said, as if it explained everything. 'A *tusitala.*'

Robert Louis Stevenson and me both. But without *Treasure Island* to my name.

Unlike other Polynesians, who retain tribal memories of the migrations which peopled virtually every outcrop of land in the South Pacific, Samoans don't concede that their beginnings were elsewhere. They insist that they have always been on their island home. They don't even concede that they are a Polynesian people, cousin to New Zealand Maori, Tahitians, Tongans, Hawaiians or Cook Islanders. Those islanders can style themselves Polynesians if they wish. Samoans have no intention of so doing. They are Samoan. No archaeologist or anthropologist dare tell them different. Such stubborn pride possibly drove New Zealand administrators to drink. It certainly drove them to turn guns on peacefully demonstrating Samoans in the 1920s. It was New Zealand's blackest feat of arms. Conspicuous among the dead was the paramount chief Tamasese, the leader of the independence movement. His young nephew took up the bloody standard. I spent an evening with this now elderly Tamasese. He was a cultivated and witty man, a reader of the English *Guardian* and the *New York Times*, and a life-lover rather than an ideologist. Nor did he nurse a lasting grievance. New Zealand's lethal involvement in the affairs of his land was tactfully forgotten. Death, however, sat distinctly on his shoulder; he was not a healthy man. In a few days more his race would have been run, his life's work done; Western Samoa would be the Pacific's first Polynesian state. Would his successors be as cultivated and informed?

I felt unease. New Zealand, when it withdrew from Samoa, would not leave universal suffrage behind. Electoral power would continue to reside in the hands of family heads, the five thousand matai, or chiefs. They alone would have the vote. It meant that no women would have a say in affairs of state and for that matter only a minority of men. The one escape from ancient thralldom for the humble and poor would remain migration to New Zealand, if they could win a permit and find the money. It seemed to me that this lunatic arrangement, approved by the United Nations, could only entrench traditional privilege; the propertied of Samoa, and that included the distinguished Tamasese family, would be still more prosperous. It also provided for corruption on a daunting scale. No one in New Zealand seemed to have noticed, though New Zealand was to continue to subsidise Samoa. Politicians were possibly glad to have truculent Samoa off their hands. If that meant a few million a year disappearing into privileged pockets, so be it: peace might be cheap at the price.

Anyway I wished I felt better about it. I joined in the celebration, if rather quietly.

Fifteen

The first day of 1962 was Samoa's. Celebration of independence was long and loud and attuned to dramatic drumbeats. Prime Minister Holyoake and assorted politicians and civil servants comprised the New Zealand presence. Holyoake, never in doubt of his importance to the occasion, made use of proceedings to refresh himself with an especially deep sleep. No one dared tap his shoulder and tell him that Samoa had become the Pacific's first Polynesian state while he slumbered. If Samoans were offended, they were too polite to show it. It wasn't one of history's great moments.

I had my problems too. A New Zealand official arrived at my side with a cable from Gillian. She had gone into Wellington hospital. It looked as if another Caesarian might be necessary. And here I was, stranded, flightless, in mid-Pacific. My panic was ended by an obliging New Zealand diplomat. Hearing of my dilemma, he offered me a flight home courtesy of the Royal New Zealand Air Force. 'The least we can do,' he told me.

I could breathe again. There were advantages to life in a small land. The diplomat was a reader of mine.

Sunlit New Zealand coast lifted from the Pacific. The DC-4 rolled to a halt on the runway of Wellington airport. In the habit now, I all but fell to my knees with Samoan fervour. I was back in time for the birth of my second son. Nurses, as they did a dozen times a day, reported that they had never seen a boy with so lusty a pair of lungs.

'Do you think he'll turn out a writer too?' one asked.

'God help us.' I said.

'God will,' she said unnervingly.

Nevertheless we found a second Celtic name. And a second

playwright. Brendan he would be.

1961 was gone. I have faint memory of much of 1962, though I remain reasonably sure it existed. Most of it concerned money. Money explained my employment in a bakery where I laboured mightily to bring forth the perfect bun. I began at 4 pm on Thursday, finished forty hours later at 8 am on Saturday morning, and have never been able to look a bun in the eye since. Unseemly hours, shortage of sleep and two bouts of pneumonia suggested that I might soon be an apprentice member of Katherine Mansfield's consumptive club. Was the woman *never* going to get off my back? Visiting me on my sickbed, Ian Cross, his latest book in hand, was decently consoling. 'You can't die on us yet,' he protested cheerfully. You'll become *the* writer of the 1960s with the rest of us also-rans.'

'Sorry,' I said through my fever.

Though it was slow coming, and identifiably mine, I heard laughter.

Finally deciding that life must have more to it than this, I rose from my sickbed. Better books than buns. Aware of the perils, and against my better judgement, I began reviewing for the *New Zealand Listener* and, later, the *Sydney Bulletin*. The literary editor of the *Bulletin* wanted a disinterested reviewer – ie, an impartial New Zealander – to ruminate on Australian fiction. Australian literary pages, he informed me, were filled with petty feuds. As a New Zealander I would presumably be free of local malice. Anxious to oblige, I thought better of disclosing that I had an amiable connection with Patrick White, a name then guaranteed to arouse Australian ire and envy in roughly equal measure. Besides, I didn't want to disillusion the editor or upset his kindly view of New Zealanders. 'You could try reviewing New Zealand fiction yourself,' I suggested.

I wasn't especially surprised when he flew off to Hollywood soon after and there began writing racy biographies of long-dead movie stars. They were poorly placed to pursue feuds.

The new literary editor of the *Bulletin* may not have known of my arrangement with his predecessor. Or perhaps he had mischief in mind. Anyway it happened that Frank Sargeson's collected short stories arrived in the mail. Payment of twenty pounds was promised. My first thought was to wrap up the book and return it to sender.

On second thought twenty pounds was twenty pounds, an impressive sum for an impecunious reviewer in the 1960s. More to the point, it was twenty pounds I currently lacked. It would provide my family with groceries for a fortnight. Other freelance writers must have been in that position. Now it was my turn. Was I to retain my rectitude or feed my family? Reader, I wrote the review. I fed my family. As for the review, I would now happily pay myself five hundred pounds not to write it. At the time, I thought it an honest appraisal of Sargeson's work. Honesty, however, is no defence in such matters; it didn't save me from the gallows. In the thirty years since, save as a favour to a needy friend, I have never reviewed a novel. I suspect I no longer know how. If so, God is good.

Let me be fair. There was an occasion when a review proved inspirational. One Friday night Max and Janet, our newly-wed tenants downstairs, had their first large marital clash. Their voices drifted upstairs, becoming more and more audible. Then dishes were thrown. Gillian and I looked at each other weakly and decided against intervening. Finally a door slammed. Searching for peace of mind Max had stomped off into the bitter Wellington night. The house shuddered and settled. I returned to the copy of a Raymond Chandler anthology I was reading for review. In imagination I was walking the sultry streets of Los Angeles with Phillip Marlowe, the prince of private eyes, and revelling in the resourceful touch of a master storyteller. 'When in doubt,' Chandler advised fellow writers, 'have a man come into the room with a gun.'

There was no gun. There was, however, a ringing telephone. Max was on the line. He was in police custody. The news was almost as impressive as someone with an unsociable firearm.

'Don't tell me you've knocked out a neighbour again,' I said.

'Nothing so simple,' he said. 'I've been picked up as a peeping Tom.'

'You?' I laughed.

'I'm serious,' he insisted.

Finally I had to be too.

When Max barged off into the night he followed his feet into the shadowy botanical gardens. There he drifted in circles until his distress diminished. Turning for home, he had a disagreeable encounter with two policemen carrying high-powered torches. These were thrust blindingly in his face. 'This is the bugger,' one announced. 'I know his face.' It was Max's misfortune that this constable had seen him before. He had been an arresting officer the night of Max's noisy prenuptial night out with the boys.

'So what have you got to say for yourself this time?' the constable asked.

Max had a great deal to say for himself, much of it obscene. He was even more distraught when he learned he was to be charged with trespassing on private property and loitering with intent – in short, of being a peeping Tom. Whatever way one looked at it, his situation was becoming more ignominious by the minute.

'Me?' Max said. 'A peeping Tom?'

'A bloody wanker,' the constable said. 'You've been peering in the windows of little old ladies.'

'Who says?'

'The neighbour of a little old lady.'

'I've been home all night. Ask my wife.'

'We have a reliable witness. A respectable businessman. He says he saw you quite plainly, peering into windows. In a red sweater, same as you're wearing now.'

There was only one thing to be said. Max said it.

'Shit,' he said.

Marched off to a holding cell in the Wellington police station, stripped of shoelaces and belt lest he attempt to hang himself, Max managed to get a telephone call to me.

'Get me out of here,' he croaked.

'That mightn't be easy,' I said.

It wasn't. There was a short court appearance next morning with Max miserable and humiliated and struggling to keep his trousers aloft. Then there was a conference with Max's lawyer. This was disheartening. The lawyer was young, nervous and totally inept. I suspected it was his first time in court.

'My advice is that you plead guilty,' he told Max.

'Plead guilty?' Max was stunned. 'For something I didn't do?'

'We can always plead mitigating circumstances. We could say you were drunk and looking for a student party in the vicinity.'

'That's still saying guilty,' Max pointed out.

'True,' the lawyer agreed. 'On the other hand it might mean a lesser charge.'

'You don't understand. I was at home having a fight with my wife.'

'That evidence may not be helpful,' the lawyer went on. 'The fact of the matter is that it is your word against that of their witness. Your word against that of a prominent and respected citizen. You don't have a hope.'

'What do you think?' Max asked me.

'Give me a chance,' I said.

I hadn't been reading Raymond Chandler for nothing. How would Phillip Marlowe have handled things? Solid sleuthing was needed. That afternoon I took Max to the scene of his alleged transgression. I got him to retrace his steps to and from the botanical gardens. The route took us past the dwelling of the citizen who was said to have seen a red-jerseyed Max leering sinisterly through women's windows. One thing was apparent. There was no way in the world in which the witness could have seen Max from his upstairs vantage point. Parapets of adjoining buildings would have narrowed his view; he could have seen nothing but a patch of an indifferently lit suburban street. Max had walked the near side of the street. The peeping Tom, assuming there was one, could well have walked the far side. He would have passed by while the alert citizen was on the phone to the police. It seemed he had been some time raising law enforcers.

It was clear cut, then. I returned to Max's lawyer and reported my findings, along with useful facts and figures. Phillip Marlowe had never done a more thorough day's work.

'Ah,' said the lawyer. 'Interesting.'

'You had Max pleading guilty,' I pointed out.

'No one's perfect,' he said.

This was confirmed at the court hearing. The police put their case plausibly. Their lone witness then took the stand. Asked to identify Max, he shook his head.

'He isn't the man,' he said, turning to the police prosecutor for help. 'His wasn't the face I saw.'

That should have been the end. Max had been picked up and fitted up on the strength of his earlier misdemeanour. Perplexingly, it wasn't the end. Presenting the case for the defence, Max's lawyer began labouring through the information I had gathered. He didn't miss a fact or figure and looked likely to go on forever.

The magistrate coughed discreetly. 'There's no need to persist with this,' he said.

'Sir?' the lawyer asked.

'The defendant hasn't been identified,' the magistrate pointed out. 'There is no case to answer. There hasn't been for some time.'

There was a long and embarrassing silence in the court.

Max looked at me. I looked at Max. The lawyer looked at his feet.

'Let's go,' I said. 'I've got a review to write.'

Later that day, the Chandler review written with new-found authority, I found myself wondering how the episode might have ended had Max been brown and not white, Maori and not European. He would probably have been persuaded to plead guilty; he might have got a year behind bars.

One up to Phillip Marlowe.

Sixteen

Since book reviewing wasn't improving my character, I persuaded the editor of *Geographic* that their coverage of Asia was poor, particularly of the countries comprising Malaysia, which had just won independence from Britain. 'So what should we do about it?' he asked.

'Send me there,' I proposed.

After some reflection, he did. There was, however, a flaw in the arrangement. The flaw was me. Travel and tension had left me with large intestinal woes. It was first judged to be an obscure tropical disease. Finally, and more competently, it was diagnosed as colitis, a disorder which specialised in bringing writers low. Otherwise I was no wiser for making its acquaintance. It was commonplace diarrhoea to me. I suffered through the jungles of Sarawak, staggered through the bogs of Borneo, and bounced sickeningly about the Sulu Sea in a boat filled with a terrifying team of Gurkhas on anti-pirate patrol. At the least it left me less introspective. On my way back to New Zealand, via Brunei, I passed through Australia wild-eyed, having just missed a revolution by minutes. In Sydney Patrick White looked me over judiciously and asked, 'Did you see any head-hunters?'

'Of retiring nature,' I reported.

'And no dried heads.'

'Just a wartime selection.'

'You wish my view?' he asked.

'By all means,' I said.

'We don't need another Joseph Conrad,' he announced.

That put me in my place.

'The best narratives are in our back yard,' Patrick explained. 'We don't have to hunt them in the jungle.'

To prove his point he showed me over the modest patch of Australia he and his life companion Manoly Lascaris had farmed while waiting for the world to discover Patrick's novels; where the couple grew and sold fruit and vegetables and milked cows and, by way of a sideline, stitched together the commonplaces of existence in a novel known as *The Tree of Man*. He didn't need to explain further.

I was back in Wellington early in 1963. In my absence I had been awarded Dunedin's Robert Burns fellowship in letters, which was a promising start for any year. First I needed a rest after the ravages of Asia. I grabbed up Gillian and the children and drove north to the beat of surf on Ninety Mile Beach. Reliable, it worked its magic again. I began singing for my supper, trying to earn my *Geographic* fee.

I had never felt less literary. *The New Zealanders* was a long way behind me. I could no longer imagine why it should ever have interested anyone, least of all Patrick White. In a rented caravan I managed to manufacture a few inches of *Geographic* prose most mornings. Then I took the boys to the beach. We gathered toheroa and tuatua with Maori neighbours and netted flounder with Barry Mitcalfe and other locals. For a time it seemed I might daydream there forever. On a good day – of which there were many – we pulled in something up to a hundred mullet; and delivered them around the village.

The boys were often knee-deep in adventure. Investigating a bucket of toheroa, Brendan found a shell snapping shut on his finger. Yells. Grief. So Sean had to investigate too. Then there were two little boys careering tearfully through the house in the grip of monster molluscs. The toheroa were illicit. The season for gathering them legally was gone. As I dug for them with a Maori neighbour, I asked, 'Who is the ranger around here?'

'I am,' he said dourly.

'You?' I said with disbelief.

'The last fellow got run down by a truck,' he explained.

'Run down?' I said with wonder.

'In broad daylight, in the main street of Kaitaia. No one knows whose truck.'

We dug again, thoughtfully.

It was suddenly time to leave for Dunedin. I had yet to shake off colitis; I imagined that sun, sea and love of children might deliver me from affliction. That proved optimistic.

We arrived in Dunedin after a 600-mile journey almost the length of the land; and took over a derelict university house in Union Street just a short walk from the slum setting of John A. Lee's *Children of the Poor*. A youthful rogue and vagabond and absconder from lawful custody, later as a celebrated and one-armed survivor of the Western Front, Lee had become, by dint of his flamboyant oratory, the country's most conspicuous politician, racking up the largest electoral majorities in New Zealand's history until knifed in the back by envious fellow politicians. But it was as a novelist – with narratives of his delinquent life, his days on the run, and the trenches of France – that Lee was to leave a lasting mark. *Children of the Poor* had long seemed to me the one pre-1940 New Zealand novel certain of survival. My earliest encounter with the book was in a school library. For the first time I understood what hair-raising meant; not a strand of my hair failed to levitate as I read the unforgettable opening lines: *This is the story of how I became a thief, and in time very much of an outlaw, running and skulking from the police, and of the circumstances which made my sister a daughter of the streets.* George Bernard Shaw justly called the book 'a whopper.'

Preparing for Dunedin, I read the novel again and found I was right the first time round. Yet the country's critical consensus said otherwise. Lee didn't exist. He had no place in the nation's literary vocabulary. Nor in the political, for that matter. When I delivered the eulogy at his funeral in 1982 I couldn't help noting that few former Labour colleagues were present. His still wasn't a name to be uttered with abandon.

I once asked him how he would feel if offered a knighthood, as briefly seemed possible.

He mused on that.

'Well,' he said with a sly twinkle, 'I don't think I'd say no. It isn't that I want to be Sir John. The fact is that I've always wanted to go to bed with a lady. Waking next to Lady Lee would suit me fine.'

He never got that knighthood or bedded Lady Lee, though he lived another fifteen years. Old scores didn't die with him.

I mentioned Lee to our pleasant Dunedin grocer, hoping he might direct me to the street where Lee lived. 'We do not,' he said coolly, 'talk of John A. Lee around here.'

Of the writer who exposed new world poverty? Of the politician who did more than most to end it? To my dismay even Charles Brasch, Dunedin's most distinguished literary gentleman, poet, editor and a man who should know better, failed to talk of Lee without a wrinkling of nose.

They spoke more in Dunedin of Robert Burns, an emasculated bard now two centuries sober. He now sat bored out of his mind, suffering barrages of bird shit in the centre of the city; condemned to exist as a statue in the leafy Octagon. I had mixed feelings about Dunedin. Its smug and synthetic Scottishness tended to madden me. But the old Victorian buildings were genuine. I wished its citizens would see themselves as inhabiting one of the new world's most distinctive cities, one which matched pioneer aspiration. Instead they boasted absurdly of their 'Edinburgh of the South'. Who needed a southern Edinburgh with a northern one still stolidly in business?

Two items in the above account should be qualified. Our grocer was a pleasant man otherwise. A large bouquet of flowers came with our first grocery order. I took that to be the kinder side of the city – the ostensibly virtuous community that Lee blew the whistle on in 1933.

And Charles Brasch, whatever his flaws, was said to be the benefactor who put up the money for the Robert Burns fellowship – the first university-based writers' fellowship in New Zealand. Which was paying my bills. It was not for me to grumble.

Seventeen

Arriving in Dunedin, driving along Union Street, we sighted Dennis McEldowney hurrying to welcome us. He was dressed for Dunedin's cool summer – corduroys and sweater. But he was walking. His recent operation to rectify his heart condition had left him agile in the world for the first time since he was six years old. He had come to Dunedin to be near family, to take a job, and begin life at the ripe age of 41 years. A lecturer in the English Department, Bob Robertson, was in the house to give us the key, and to help us settle in. Bob was a fetching fellow, full of lively opinions. He dealt freely with New Zealand writers in his lectures. This was regarded as revolutionary. I had the impression that few of his academic colleagues had read a line of verse by a New Zealand writer, or a paragraph of a New Zealand novel. That, of course, might be their good luck.

Dennis McEldowney called to tell me that people in the English Department were relieved to see I was happily domestic. Had they expected a wild-eyed and boozy bohemian? It turned out that the Burns Fellowship had been under a cloud, perhaps even in peril. Three recent predecessors had left scandal in their wake. Ian Cross, the first fellow, treated it as a straightforward job. Clocked in at nine, finished at five, and wrote a novel. Not just any old novel either; as substantial a chronicle of society as any written here. Then came Maurice Duggan, a married man, his wife left behind in Auckland. Maurice seemed permanently camped in the Captain Cook hotel, glass in hand; he also had a public affair with the poet Fleur Adcock. Adultery, at least of the visible sort, did not go down well in Dunedin. Another predecessor, whose appointment was mysterious, and not especially decorative, smashed furniture at a faculty function and left lecturers and professors fearful of social gatherings for some time after. Another fellow, the elderly poet Ron Mason, must have seemed safe enough. But no. Now fifty-six years old and dizzied by the young women in his vicinity, he made seriously improper advances to a young female student while ostensibly passing judgment on her poems. He was rushed off to a hospital for rest and rehabilitation. The official version was a nervous breakdown. His longtime mistress was flown in from Auckland. After decades of serene companionship they were rushed into matrimony. No one could say Dunedin lacked excitement. A fourth fellow was to be arrested for punching a policeman.

Now in his creative twilight, Ron Mason was still in town. He took me off to a Burns night in the Dunedin Town Hall. There was whisky and haggis and a bobbing sea of bald heads. I suspected that few of those present would have given Scotland's bawdy national poet the time of day were he alive. Ron took the function seriously and imagined I might too. I disappointed him by backing off. I sank even lower in his estimation when I professed admiration of the Russian poet Yevtushenko.

'That young pup,' Ron said.

Ron's political opinions were platitudinous, largely second-hand and mostly derived from the 1930s. If he had been an elderly man next door, a neighbour I yarned with over the back fence, this wouldn't have disconcerted me. Even right-wing opinions wouldn't. But this man wasn't a neighbour leaning casually on the back fence. He was a man who, in his youth, wrote some of the most vivid lines ever written by a New Zealander; a poet Dylan Thomas respected. Why did he disappoint me? I felt the lack was mine but suspected it wasn't. Never once did I hear him say anything out of the ordinary.

Jim Baxter was another young pup. Probably me too.

Bob Robertson was lecturing on my story 'After the Depression' to students of English. He wondered if I could bring myself to sit in. At first I found the prospect terrifying. I finally agreed to attend after he promised not to draw attention to my presence. I slipped into a back seat as the lecture began. I also kept my head down. This was unnecessary. Two or three hundred students were attentively scribbling down everything Bob said. It was not my story he was summarising, but his own. 'A homeless and footsore man, woman and child wandering a dusty road,' he said. 'What does this say to you? What does it remind you of?' Now Bob mentioned it, the beleaguered threesome of my story might be seen as the Holy Family. This was daunting. It may have been due to the fact that I failed English in my short and unrewarding encounter with the academy. And there I was listening to a learned lecture on my work. If I hadn't failed English, I should never have written 'After the Depression'. That gave me something to think on.

Eighteen

On midwinter day, in 1963, my second book of stories, *Summer Fires and Winter Country*, was published in London. Again the reviews were kindly, also in New Zealand when copies of the book arrived from Britain. This gave me less satisfaction than it should. It was three years since most had been written. I had been in Dunedin five months with little new to show for it. That was, apart from several thousand worthy words which I hoped might lead me into a large novel. Was this a consequence of residing in an English Department? Was it the academy on my back? I felt the need to be mischievous; to write something irreverent and unworthy. With next to no premeditation, I put *Strangers and Journeys* aside – or the manuscript which would one day be that novel – and began writing a comic picaresque. I seemed my own man again. Gillian said she heard me whistling as I walked along Union Street to my office.

I flew to Wellington to pick up the Katherine Mansfield award – for the story called 'Homecoming' in *Summer Fires and Winter Country*. Michael Amato met me at Wellington airport with a wide smile and drove me up into the familiar hills of Kelburn. 'You don't have to tell me why you're here,' he said.

'You know?'

'Congratulations.'

The award wasn't yet public. The winner was to be announced by the Governor General at a starchy function. Though Michael had an entry too, he had received no invitation to the function; he was out of luck again. Despite disappointment he remained a generous friend. I wished his stories could find a publisher in book form. It seemed no one in New Zealand, save a few admirers, was interested in a young Italian survivor of his country's civil war. His Italian stories, those which drew on his life as a teenage runaway in a war-cursed land, were comparable with those of Cesare Pavese. His New Zealand stories were unique, resembling nothing else in the country's literature. Possibly that accounted for his difficulty finding a publisher for his stories: they didn't conform to local expectation. They concerned themselves more with human fate than with the country's puritan shortcomings. They were too cosmopolitan; literary New Zealanders cherish their provincialism. (Men alone unite.) In that respect Michael and I saw the outsider in each other. That was enough. We sat up late talking, long after red-eyed Sheena had gone to bed. Suddenly Michael said, 'I know about you, you know.'

I wasn't sure what he meant.

'I know enough to write about you,' he explained.

Was this a threat?

Apparently not. He promised, 'If you don't get round to writing about yourself, I will.'

'I see.'

'On the other hand,' he went on, 'you are equally free to write about me.'

'So it depends on who lives long enough?' I asked.

'You could say that,' he agreed.

The award function was reasonably sedate. The one flutter of anarchy came from the Governor General, Sir Bernard Fergusson, a sometime author himself, a wartime Chindit in the battle for Burma and, despite his monocle and comic opera appearance, a man of the world. In presenting the award he noted wryly that many of the stories referred to by the judges dealt with Maori-European themes, or had Maori characters. (My award-winning story was no exception.) He invited those at the function – a hundred or more – to look around and consider how many Maori were present. The answer was none; there was not one Maori present. He pressed this point home. 'I think New Zealanders should ask themselves why,' he suggested.

There was an uncomfortable shuffling in the audience. Then a long silence. The Queen's emissary wasn't supposed to carry on like this, to say anything pertinent.

There was one astonishing breach of taste. On the platform, with the Fergussons, the judges, and officials and sponsors, was a young woman eye-catchingly costumed and coiffured as the young Katherine Mansfield – much as in the familiar Anne Estelle Rice painting of Mansfield of 1922. Were we meant to be amused? Were we to think this clever? I found it bizarre.

Next day, walking along Lambton Quay before catching my plane home to Dunedin, I encountered a woman author involved in organising the function. Pleasantries were passed. Then I chanced a cautious complaint about the ersatz Mansfield presiding over the ceremony. I expressed the hope that it wouldn't be done again; that she wouldn't become a feature of the event.

My acquaintance looked at me strangely. 'What woman?' she said.

'The woman dressed as Mansfield. On the right hand side of the platform. She even had a Mansfield fringe.'

'There was,' I was informed firmly, 'no one dressed as Mansfield on the platform. Not on the right hand side, nor on the left.'

'I saw her,' I insisted.

'*You* might have. I didn't. And I'm sure no one else did.'

I was shaken. I record this for the sake of veracity. Might she make a spectral appearance every time an award is made in her name? After all she was, wasn't she, a pupil of Gurdjieff; perhaps she learned a posthumous trick or two from that mystic.

There is a sequel. Years later, in conversation with John Garrett, Professor of English at Canterbury University, and judge of the Mansfield award that night, I told him of the incident. I expected a polite laugh.

But John had news for me. He had seen her too.

Nineteen

In the first week of 1964 we farewelled Dunedin friends and pointed our car north. The largest consequence of our Dunedin stay, the first draft of *Among the Cinders*, was buried in our baggage. I had the hope that it might make 1963 worthwhile. There was also the all but forsaken half draft of the novel titled *Strangers and Journeys* to be considered. I tried not to consider it and mostly didn't as we drove across the Canterbury Plains, the snow-streaked Southern Alps shimmering to our left. After a night with relatives in Christchurch we took the winding road to Banks Peninsula. Then we rolled downhill into Shadbolt territory, the inlets of Akaroa harbour luminous on all sides. This was where my father's family began in New Zealand. Not for the first time I regretted that I knew little of their story beyond unreliable lore. Might it profit me to track their story down? I didn't see myself, not then, as possessing the stamina for a fat family saga. Such as I did know had coloured one or two short stories and, in my Dunedin year, something of *Among the Cinders* too. Making free with my ancestors had done me no discernible damage, though one or two relatives thereafter refused to speak to me, or even to acknowledge my existence. When they were obliged to admit that I might exist, their favourite canard was that Gillian wrote my stories, and that these were then shamelessly published under my name.

Meanwhile the Shadbolt pub, one of New Zealand's rowdier 19th century watering holes, still survived on the seafront of Duvauchelle Bay. Nearby was the little Shadbolt church and finally and shakily the Shadbolt homestead, now a barn with an unpromising lean. This was where patriarch Benjamin Shadbolt presided with his wife Elizabeth and his sixteen children. We found their overgrown graves on a hilltop high above the hamlet of Duvauchelle. According to his headstone, Benjamin was 'esteemed by all who knew him'. For what? According to obituarists, he was famous for his generosity. This affluent village squire never refused a bed and a job to some dusty down and out. The mystery was where his money came from. One family story said he was a remittance man, a ne'er do well paid to remain out of sight of respectable relatives. That seemed more than likely. There was much to suggest something suspect in his past.

There was. Years later, at a family funeral in 1989, not too late, I would learn that this burly and benevolent pillar of propriety had originally been an inhabitant of Britain's penal colonies, a transported convict shuffling in chains. I might have guessed that I was the descendant of some scarred Magwitch. Through childhood and adolescence *Great Expectations* had been my favourite Dickens novel; I read it again and again, identifying powerfully with Pip and weeping for Magwitch. So was it mere coincidence that I have several times been involved with long-term prisoners? I have even had a hand in freeing one or two. That may mean nothing. If so, everything is meaningless and the world a puny place.

As our smoky car climbed out of Banks Peninsula, I looked back on ancestral acres; on land farmed by my father, grandfather and great-grandfather. Having had my first sip of a piquant family past, I looked ahead. The future was in need of thought too.

The car-ferry carried us away from the South Island. We stayed with Michael and Sheena Amato in Wellington, a few doors away from where we lived unhappily in 1962. They were glad to see us; the Amato marriage had lately been turbulent. Michael's jealousy was explosive. There had just been a scene at a party: shouts and sobs, beer thrown, fists used to effect. Nevertheless Michael was writing well. The Amatos wanted us to stay in Wellington, to buy a house neighbouring theirs. Presumably they hoped that their marriage might be more serene with the Shadbolts nearby. Chain-smoking Michael kept me up till 2 am (with a bottle of whisky) in a last-ditch attempt to persuade me of Wellington's virtues. I should miss him, Sheena too. She was moist-eyed when we continued north.

Dusty with travel, we reached Auckland's edge and passed a night or two with my Uncle Joe among the orchards and vineyards of Henderson Valley. His spartan cottage was unchanged. Joe's potent

Dalmatian sherry tasted much the same. There was the usual piquant mix of reading matter on his bedside table: the Bible, *Rubayat of Omar Khayam*, *Paradise Lost*, the collected works of Shakespeare, Winwood Read's *The Martyrdom of Man*, and the latest issue of the Communist Party weekly *The People's Voice*. With enough money saved to cover the gap until his old age pension arrived, he had resigned from a road gang: he pronounced himself retired. He seemed to be acknowledging that there could now be no more to his life: no wife, no children, and friends few since his working life ended. Just this austere dwelling, worn linoleum on the floor, curtainless windows, outdoor dunny, and soon the undertaker. My grief undiminished, I attempted to behave as the affectionate son he should have had. Did he notice? I appeared to concern him rather more than he did me. With a wife and two sons to support, I had no job, no prospects, no roof overhead. Just a car and enough blankets to bed down warm at night. After the gypsy journey north we were looking even more frayed.

'And how is this stomach trouble of yours?' Joe asked, meaning colitis.

'It's still with me,' I confessed.

'So you're still swallowing pills?'

'Still,' I had to admit.

'Throw the bloody things away,' he urged. 'Dose yourself with this at the end of your working day.' He presented me with a half gallon flagon of rather rich sherry.

A week or two later, perhaps even less, I tipped my remaining pills and potions down into our long drop, never to be seen again. Nor was colitis.

We left the car with Joe and voyaged off into the Hauraki Gulf. Brendan's second birthday was celebrated at my parents' house on Waiheke Island. Chubby Brendan was already a bubbling winner of hearts. Sean was the lean and thoughtful one. Both were more lovable by the month.

Meanwhile I read the classified columns of the *New Zealand Herald* with mounting dismay. Auckland rents were murderously high. It became plain that it was better to buy than rent. We would use the royalties from *Gift of the Sea,* a pictorial book done with Brian Brake, due any day now. The cheque should serve as a deposit on a house. We might muster a mortgage from someone. (Though if I were a bank manager I would see a poor risk.) I left Gillian and the boys on the island and returned to the mainland to reconnoitre the terrain. Auckland it had to be. If I failed to survive as a professional novelist – and no New Zealander then had – then perhaps I might find a niche on a newspaper. I drove out through West Auckland, the part of the city I knew best, looking for somewhere to plant the family. I was taken by green Titirangi: the houses sequestered among the trees, the bird-filled bushland and sunny harbour views. This was the New Zealand I dreamed about in smoggy London winters. I rang Gillian. 'I've found the location,' I reported. 'All we do now is find the house.'

She arrived next day, with the boys, on the Waiheke ferry. At Titirangi we met up with the suburb's sole land agent. He took us down a road winding past the fern-fringed beaches and rocky inlets of the Manukau harbour's tidal coastline. Then he halted outside a modest dwelling half-hidden in fern. Though the rooms were small, there were large views. The place didn't feel cramped. There was a basement I could use as a workplace. The price was £3500. Sean and I set out on a reconnaissance, following a bush track to the water. Sean scooted adventurously ahead. When I caught up with him he was paddling along a little crescent beach overhung by red-blooming pohutukawa. 'Look at all this, Dad,' he piped. 'Look.'

Bold Brendan, not to be outdone, plunged into the tide too.

The place was as good as ours from that moment. I fetched Joe to inspect the house. He found flaws, but mostly approved. It was the boys' endorsement which decided the issue. I also envisaged a productive life here, a place where I might stand or fall as a novelist. I located a helpful man, a reader of my stories, willing to arrange a mortgage. 'I think you're a reasonable risk,' he said.

I didn't enlighten him.

We retreated to Ninety Mile Beach until the Titirangi house was legally ours. That would be another month or two. Meanwhile we had sun, surf and silvery fish flashing beyond the breakers. Though the idyll wasn't intended to last, it had its temptations. Did we really need to be near Auckland? I found a leaky caravan in which I could work, trimming *Among the Cinders* to tolerable size while waves thumped nearby. In the afternoon I fished for the family larder and dug tuatua from the sands. We seldom lacked seafood. After an outing, we often arrived home to find a bag of crayfish and paua on our front step, gifts from Maori neighbours. When the boys looked likely to become bored, I took them on adventure hikes through the sandhills and gathered sea-whittled objects from the shore.

Visitors arrived, sometimes to stay. The most conspicuous occupant of our lumpy kitchen couch, fresh from the trenches of literary London, was the English novelist Colin MacInnes, the lean and lively interpreter of mid-century England, far from his beloved Soho. He was also long way from the bon vivant I recalled from my London years. There was now a melancholy in the man, as if the 1950s had cruelly dumped him and the 1960s were now conspiring to kick him while he was down. In those days he was often cruelly called Colin McWithit. With it he had been. But what was this grizzled ideologist of the turbulent sixties doing in one of New Zealand's loneliest corners? Ostensibly he was writing a book on New Zealand and Australia for *Time-Life* books. He was also, it appeared, looking for friends and allies in outposts of the English speaking world. I was plainly a possibility. Having read my stories in *Summer Fires and Winter Country,* he seemed to think I could offer him some clue to New Zealand's character. I protested that I was a novelist, not a seer or sociologist. He refused to hear. He wasn't to be disillusioned. Like many before him, he saw paradise rearing around in New Zealand's far north. He found the region's distinctive blend of European and Polynesian arousing, especially the attractive Dalmatian-Maori shading of young men. I had to hasten him out of pubs when his advances promised to pass beyond idle admiration. I took him home to watch rising tide and migrant bird and down a few more bottles as the westering sun coloured the Tasman.

'The long wash of Australasian seas,' I heard him murmur, almost to himself.

'What's that?' I asked.

'Tennyson,' Colin said.

Colin never lacked a good quote.

When not collecting material for *Time-Life,* he worked on a novel. He woke at six, or an even unholier hour; I heard a furtive clinking as he lifted his first bottle of beer from the refrigerator and began writing. By breakfast he would have sunk two or three bottles and written a chapter. Some writers lived dangerously, none more than Colin.

In the last weeks of his life, in 1976, he would write asking me to find him a haven in or near Ninety Mile Beach, somewhere a long way from the slings and arrows of literary London. The metropolis no longer needed him. His celebrated London trilogy was already forgotten. He was crusty and bitter and, in the week I last saw him, beginning to feud with cancer. Before I could find him an antipodean sanctuary I was reading his obituaries. His departure was in keeping with his character; he enjoyed having the last word. His last request was that friends dump him in the North Sea when his expiry date came round. His friends, though inexperienced in such matters, did their best to oblige. Colin, however, was a long time sinking; his friends weren't aware that corpses need to be attached to weights. Nor were they successful in pushing him down with oars. Again and again he bobbed up from the waters, apparently with something yet to say. Finally a knowledgeable fisherman was called in to give expert advice.

Impressed by Colin's capacity to continue writing in makeshift surroundings, I finished the manuscript of *Among the Cinders* with a flourish and mailed it to London from our tiny village post office. The local postmistress was impressed, handling the package as if it contained explosive. 'A novel?' she said.

'A novel,' I confirmed.

'I've never had one of those before,' she marvelled.

'Nor have I,' I said.

Twenty

Our northern idyll was soon at an end. This was confirmed by a telephone call from Wellington, from Sheena Amato. Michael had just died. How, why? Sheena wasn't coherent. But the cause of his death, at the age of thirty-five, appeared to have been a cerebral haemorrhage. 'What am I to do with his work?' Sheena asked despairingly.

'Keep it safe,' was all I could think to say.

Still shaky, I took a long walk, five sandy miles up the beach and five back again. There had to be a mistake. There wasn't. Death made no mistakes. Nor did it ever play fair.

I woke to the fact that I was walking the long and luminous highway which the Maori believed led to the underworld realm of the dead. I imagined Michael floating invisible beside me, looking out the route home to Italy. I like to think I shared the first miles of his journey.

Sometimes life is too cinematic to be credible. As I turned the key in the door of the Titirangi house a lady arrived from the local post office with telegraphic tidings. It was a message of congratulation from my London agent. She informed me that she would have no problem finding a publisher for *Among the Cinders*. My apprenticeship papers suggested that I was no longer a composer of wistful trifles. I was now articled to the rough and ready realm of the novelist.

Back in the city I risked a literary function. That was a mistake. It was an unattractive gathering. After the open spaces and faces of Ninety Mile Beach, literary folk in number had a dispiriting effect. They were at pains to impress me that I didn't impress them. Their problem was that I had just published in New York. I might as well have offered my services as a dartboard and handed out the darts. In hangover next day, I swore off further communication with preening poets and prosing academics. I appeared to have done the right thing in resigning from the republic of letters. (Have I mentioned this? Consider it said.) There was more stimulation in the company of painters. There was certainly more generosity. Colin McCahon's visionary work, which invited me in, told me I was in an heroic land.

Something had gone wrong in New Zealand. Perhaps it was a surfeit of isolation. Our introspective fiction was sour and doomladen. 'Too gloomy to teach,' an Italian professor told me, after attempting to teach it. She waved a hand to the vista of sea and sky, tree and bird, beyond my living room window. 'Why is it,' she asked, 'that New Zealand writers, living in splendour, are all so miserable? They have no joy. No play. It is not how I see your country. Do you feel obliged to be sad? Why so black? Much New Zealand writing is so black that I cannot teach it in my courses. My students sometimes refuse to read it. Why is this, please? Why? Are New Zealanders all so unhappy?'

I wasn't prepared to take responsibility for the country's condition. Nor was I willing to write off my compatriots. New Zealand writers weren't *all* joyless: our poets certainly weren't altogether averse to celebration. One English critic, reviewing a sprightly anthology of New Zealand verse, said he wondered why Katherine Mansfield ever felt she had to leave. So, forty years on, did I.

I am in trouble with this manuscript. I daresay, like most autobiographers or memoirists, I am guilty of striking a romantic pose, though I try to rein myself in. It can't be helped. A writer is a romantic by definition. Even the anti-romantics. *Especially* the supposed anti-romantics. You have to take romanticism seriously to be anti.

Colin McCahon and I, in the flush of new friendship, agreed on the need to affirm, to celebrate from the brink of negation. He also taught me how to grow watercress where all was waterless.

After reading a learned and largely indigestible essay with my lunch I began wondering why Samuel Beckett should be taken seriously and the likes of John Cheever ignored? Beckett seldom troubled himself to find a distance from his obsessions. He and his admirers appeared to think that obsessions were sufficient: they mistook the will for the deed. (With the partial exception of *Waiting for Godot*, perhaps. Sooner or later Beckett had to be lucky.) Cheever, whatever his other qualities, or lack of them, wasn't just a glossy *New Yorker* writer. He had far more to tell us about our 20th century condition than Beckett. He gave his classical themes contemporary flesh; he gave suburban man a role in a prodigious drama. Perhaps my examples aren't good. Nevertheless I rest my case. I was at dinner with V.S. Naipaul shortly afterwards. I was gladdened to learn that he thought Beckett a pretentious trickster too.

I often play with this thought: that if I were to stick a pin in a random page in any New Zealand telephone directory, and come up with a name, I might – if the subject were willing, and if there were a few artefacts and documents to hand – come up with New Zealand's whole story. More than that – given good luck, and an ample supply of shoe leather – I might even, following that one name in the telephone directory back into the past, come up with the story of the entire human race. Individuals we may be, but we carry the story of our species in our heads and hearts. Insignificant as we may seem, as individuals, we trail huge histories, vivid dramas.

Nor are we to be despised.

In 1965 and thereabouts Titirangi had a reputation as a hangout for those involved in the arts and crafts. It was true that there was a reputable vineyard on hand. Otherwise its reputation was more fancy than fact. Perhaps orthodox Aucklanders felt that only art-loving lunatics would be mad enough to return to the dripping forest their 19th century forerunners toppled. (These days they would probably be called eco-freaks.) It was true that there were several craftsmen, mostly potters, working among the tall trees; smoke from their kilns announced them in business. Over the years there have been up to three or four respectable painters, Colin McCahon one of them for a time. Photographers, on the other hand, have flourished. Not the least of them was Brian Brake. He made his base here for ten years before dying in 1988. Of writers there were few. I was the first (and remain the only) novelist. If there have been poets, and there surely must have been, their names are unknown to me. Essayists seem to fare best here. Perhaps the misty climate encourages meditation. For many years a retired professor – a classicist and

Baptist – was the chronicler of our community. He wrote in elaborate and heavily adjectival prose. How he managed to reconcile classicism and Baptism remains a riddle. I sometimes saw him in our tiny post office. He nodded silently. I nodded silently. And we passed on. Did he see me as stealing his thunder? I hope not. I had enough problems in that connection.

One who didn't feel me a threat, and welcomed me with arms wide, was the essayist and art historian Eric McCormick. It would be inexact to call Eric a near neighbour; he lived with his devoted sister Myra two miles toward Auckland. But he seldom seemed far. Eric gave much or most of his life to studies of the emigré New Zealand painter Frances Hodgkins. (Who, I pause to point out, was a contemporary and painterly counterpart of Katherine Mansfield.) Myra, a trained nurse, in her turn gave most of her life to her brother Eric. Incest is not a word to be bandied about, and possibly not helpful, but something like it seemed to cement their relationship for many decades. Not until late in life did Myra learn that Eric, the brother on whom she lavished such love and care, was a homosexual. Then it was only because Eric himself boldly confessed his sexual nature in an essay on his literary beginnings. Myra pretended not to have read the essay. I am sure she did. For from that point – the appearance of the article – Myra's life was all downhill. She was at last obliged to acknowledge that she had invested her emotional capital in a liaison which didn't require it, in a man with need of unlawful love elsewhere. It was a cruel discovery. She turned her face to the wall. Eric's life was soon downhill too. After close to ninety years together, from the cradle to the grave, merely months separated them in death.

There was one other writer of note nearby – nearby meaning a road wandering through a couple of miles of bush country. This was the popular historian Dick Scott. Dick was no novelist, though, with his anecdotal gift, he should have been. It was due to Dick that I discovered Titirangi; he had extolled its pioneer virtues while we were researching on adjoining desks in Wellington's Alexander Turnbull Library. Dick had then been resident in Titirangi two years. Great for children, he reported. Not bad for authors either.

It remains true most of forty years on. I didn't need telling twice. Always a wild yarn-spinner, a novelist *manque*, Dick made the place sound magical. So it has proved.

Twenty-one

There are other things to be said. Dick and I had a past in common. For a time we even had the New Zealand Communist Party in common. In those mid-century years of cold war and witch-hunt such associations weren't wise; they were also monitored by the catastrophically clumsy security intelligence service. Dick had been the editor of trade union journals and the Communist *People's Voice*. In the latter he published several of my early poems and stories under cover of pseudonyms. While editing the Stalinist *People's Voice* Dick also organised a literary competition to demonstrate that there was culture among the comrades. There was also the hope that some hitherto unknown and unlettered son of the working class might make an appearance. It failed to happen. Though the competition was judged by a reliably Party-lining academic, I took first, second and fourth prizes. What made the affair embarrassing was that I had by that time cut my connection with the Party; and that no one had thought to inform the distinguished judge that I was ideologically unsound. The aspirant commissars had to go along with his finding. Nor did any red-blooded proletarian writer climb out of the woodwork. Any so inclined might have been deterred by the news from Hungary, where workers and writers alike were then being shot down.

Dick's subversive wit suggested that he wasn't long for the Party either. He wasn't. The comrades were dizzy with relief.

Dick and I – neighbours now – turned our backs on contemporary matters in favour of what we knew best. We turned, that was, to New Zealand's past. For Dick this meant uncovering the land's least glorious episodes, often to the chagrin of professional historians possessively guarding material they thought theirs by right. Such as

113

Te Whiti, the pacifist Maori prophet, came to life in Dick's pages; he had seldom been seen as more than as a vaguely eccentric Maori tribesman until Dick wrenched him from obscurity and demonstrated that New Zealand had a Gandhi too. My intentions were more modest. I didn't have to dig out documents as Dick did. My material was familiar. My parents had bequeathed me enough material to work and rework for the rest of my life. I fed most of it into the fattening manuscript of *Strangers and Journeys*.

Sometimes our digging into the past was literal. On the site of New Zealand's first commercial vineyard we found the country's first wine press. And enough bottles, intact or shattered, to conclude that business had been busy. In the mountains of the Urewera country Dick's foot kicked against something solid. Clearing the ground around, he excavated a musket which had survived the Anglo-Maori wars.

Perhaps inevitably, it was to those wars, largely neglected until then, that I was eventually to turn – in the trilogy which began with *Season of the Jew*, continued with *Monday's Warriors*, and finished with *The House of Strife*. Without a maverick historian like Dick Scott and a gentle scholar such as Eric McCormick setting me an example, I might never have gone the distance.

In my first years in Titirangi I fished frequently with Tony Atwool, an elderly neighbour in Arapito Road. Tony was always an antidote to literary stress. Currently in his seventies, he had been a Royal Air Force aviator in the First World War. A biplane cockpit gave him a God's eye view of the carnage. No doubt there was danger in it too. He wasn't inclined to discuss the danger. Fifty years on, in the middle 1960s, he was engaging death on a different front. He had been diagnosed as having a serious heart condition. Leaving the doctor's surgery he drove to the nearest cemetery and spent the rest of the day wandering among headstones. He now made that excursion once weekly. 'It helps me get used to the idea,' he explained. 'The best people I know are dead.'

Arapito Road was then a leaf-fringed lane of faulty hearts and furtive hermits. If a pensioner backed his car into a ditch, I was invariably summoned to help heave it back on the road. Such duties fell to me as one of the few males in the vicinity with a dependable heart.

The hermits? A couple of hundred yards upstream from our property lived a human reminder of Titirangi's pioneer beginnings: a bona fide recluse, a survivor of the time when rafts of giant kauri logs crashed down our estuary, to be snared and sold as marine timber. The logs had gone, apart from those deeply mired in mud. The loggers left just one of their number behind. Why? Was there a broken heart in his story? Was there some fear of the city creeping over the horizon? Or was he a remittance man or a commonplace criminal? He must have had reason to remain when his fellows decided to look for a living elsewhere. He resided in a one-room shack among wiry mangroves and fledgling pines. To supplement his pension he collected kauri gum from mangrove roots and presumably had a buyer somewhere. He also picked oysters and netted flounder. His lacks included electricity, radio and telephone and piped water. In the morning he hoisted a flag to let locals know that he was still in the land of the living. This couldn't be said of all in our neighbourhood. Few were far from their last breath.

Closer to home, in a damp house beyond dense foliage, there was a shrivelled man named Darky Broughton. He shared the house with an army of smelly opossums. Though few recalled his name, he was once the best harness racing driver in the land. Whipping sleek horses around racetracks, he brought great prosperity to the owners and trainers who employed him. His wife Lex, whom he treated badly, eventually ran away with a tattooed seaman. It was the scandal of the neighbourhood, still talked about decades later. It was thirty years before shy Lex showed her face in Arapito Road again. She took over the house, chased out the opossums, but shopped furtively in suburbs where her face wasn't known. This wasn't necessary. By that time, of course, Darky was dead and his racetrack feats forgotten.

Tony Atwool's wife was to be counted with the hermits. I never saw her. Even long-standing neighbours seldom did. My informants insisted that she was mad. A madwoman out of a Bronte fiction, in fact. She and Tony lived an extremely sequestered life, in a sunless cottage cloaked with greenery. She left her bed infrequently. Loyal and long-suffering Tony cooked, shopped and cleaned. She read religious tracts. Her voice could often be heard drifting shrilly through the trees. She appeared to be berating Tony for his deficiencies as a spouse; I never quite heard. His one means of escape was the launch moored at the foot of their property. He could flee insanity by taking me fishing. It wasn't fish he wanted. It was company. When Tony called, I went.

On one memorable Monday we motored out into the Manukau harbour and anchored at the edge of a usually rewarding channel. Fat snapper began taking our bait. A score soon flapped on the floor of the launch. Hauling them in, one fish after another, was soon too much like hard work. For Tony this was evidence that homo sapiens was a perverse species. There were groans when fish were few and moans when they were many. The bonanza didn't allow Tony time to talk or me to light my pipe. He was always gently curious about my vocation. But not that day. He wanted to discuss death. How did I see it?

'Death?'

'As a literary man,' he said. 'You think there is a life beyond?'

This was a tall order. I gave him Socrates's thoughts on the subject before he drank the hemlock. Socrates informed grieving friends there were two ways of looking on death favourably. If there was life beyond death, then there was a chance of meeting old and dear friends again. If, on the other hand, there was no life after death, then there was at least the opportunity for a long and refreshing sleep. And who, he asked, does not enjoy a long sleep?

The likes of that literary function were forgotten.

Twenty-two

The war in Vietnam literally sickened me. My gut was in upheaval again, this time not with colitis. By May of 1965 it seemed more than likely that New Zealand would be contributing troops to the squalid conflict. The novel I was supposedly writing seemed far too lightweight. I was appalled to find myself involved with deputations, public meetings, petitions, protests, and letters to the editor. Much of this left me with mixed feelings. Former comrades of the left were again trumpeting their wretched Stalinist rubbish. I thought I'd heard the last of them. On another front, in the correspondence columns of *The Auckland Star*, I debated involvement in Vietnam with the president of the bellicose Auckland Returned Services Association. My daily mail was extraordinary, often with letters of support from old soldiers who survived the trenches of the First World War. I had a surreptitious phone call from Geoffrey Webster, the *Star*'s senior journalist. 'Keep it up,' he pleaded. 'People aren't reading our editorials. They're reading you.'

Actually the *Star* was taking a liberal, anti-war stance. But for how much longer?

Barry Mitcalfe, with next to no political past, and pushed by his Wellington students, had become de facto leader of the protest movement. He rang to ask if I could organise an Auckland committee which would present a broad front against the war.

'Me?'

'You,' he insisted.

I backed out after a couple of preliminary meetings. There were others better equipped. Gillian was pregnant again. It was no minor pregnancy. There were twins on the way.

May 27, 1965, turned out to be as sorry a day as any in New

117

Zealand history. Barry Mitcalfe woke me with an impossibly early phone call. 'The decision's going to be made today,' he told me. 'Ring everyone you know and tell them to ring everyone *they* know. Bombard Parliament with telegrams.'

Barry was weeping as he talked. Telegrams began flying. No use. The decision was made. Though a rift in the Cabinet was rumoured – and Prime Minister Holyoake seemed short of enthusiastic – New Zealand was to send troops to Vietnam.

The mail brought me a long letter from Holyoake. We had exchanged letters before, in connection with more innocuous matters. Even so, I was flattered that I was thought worth a lengthy communication from the Prime Minister. Was guilt unhappily pushing his pen? Though he was a representative of New Zealand's right, Holyoake came from a famously nonconformist family; a distant uncle, celebrated in John Osborne's play *A Subject of Scandal and Concern*, had been the last man tried for blasphemy in England. In his letter this later Holyoake explained the need for New Zealand to stand alongside the United States in Vietnam. Yet it was apparent – if just from the length of his letter – that he wasn't the most lighthearted of men.

I failed to connect with life as I had known it before that day in May. Nor could I write. *This Summer's Dolphin*, the first casualty, sank suddenly from sight. That left me with the manuscript titled *Strangers and Journeys*.

On midwinter day, driving impulsively toward the King Country, I set out to find it again. I needed to breathe the benign atmosphere of childhood; I wanted the landscapes of my early life. Farms and towns flicked past as I drove further into familiar territory. I came up for air in my onetime home town of Te Kuiti. It had never been much of a town and still wasn't. It consisted largely of one long street running parallel with the railway – the railway which, fifty years earlier, fathered a trading post and populated the place with hopeful pioneers. I didn't look out a place to stay; I made the most of what was left of daylight. I parked the car and begin walking. It was years since I last saw the town; longer since I last found it underfoot. Little had changed. The names on shopfronts were the same. Memories ambushed me at every turn. Here was where my brother and I manufactured catapults with the intention of holding off devilish

Japanese invaders; and tested their accuracy on lovers poorly cam-
ouflaged with riverside greenery. There was where I stole a kiss from
Sally McDonald, the town beauty, on the way home from school. She
told me I was silly, which was astute, and mysteriously went on to
marry the neighbourhood bully. I followed the river, once a Maori
canoe route, as it threaded through the town. I glimpsed no one I
knew as I ambled through my past. Did I want a familiar face? The
spell might be broken. I loitered for a time beside the pasture where
our cows grazed, looked up at the house where we once lived. At
length I turned away. Next day I drove out into the country. Frost
coated the land. Water dripped from icy overhead wires. Limestone
bastions patched with forest bulked around. Had my excursion been
worth it? It had.

Strangers and Journeys thawed too. I began to believe that I might
finish it. No one else was going to. No one else was even going to
begin it. I decided to see it not as an elegant exercise, but as my
contribution to the human record. That was as much as any author
might hope for. As I saw the novel, it was a tale of this land, the men
who made it, and the children of this land and those men. As I saw
them, the fathers, Ned Livingstone (the pioneer) and Bill Freeman
(the revolutionary) were men meant to live on an heroic scale. But
neither their time nor their place permitted them a stage. Nor for that
matter their sons garbed in paternal hand-me-downs. I saw what the
novel must be about.

On everything I have written, and have yet to write, I should like
the epigraph: 'Do not understand me too easily.' Who made that
plea? Gide? And possibly every writer.

After three days exploring town and country, I cruised east,
towards steamy Rotorua. I had a note from onetime schoolmate and
fellow novelist Maurice Gee saying he was presently in residence
there with his longstanding companion, an attractive Maori nurse
named Sarah, and their six-year-old son. I hadn't seen Maurice in
years. He would, he said, welcome a visit. I called him from the Te
Kuiti telephone exchange to warn him I was about to arrive. The
duty operator at the post office was a pleasant Maori woman. She
thought she recognised me from somewhere. School? Possibly, I
agreed. A newspaper photograph? That was possible too. Then her
face filled with a smile. 'You're the writer,' she decided. She had been

reading *Among the Cinders*; her husband had given her the book for a birthday present. She and her husband recognised Te Kuiti. They identified people too. Even, she thought, her auntie.

'Don't tell anyone,' I said conspiratorially.

'I promise,' she said with an even larger smile.

Buoyed by the discovery that I was not unknown in these parts, I drove on.

On the way to Rotorua, along roads steeped in history, and lapped by shiny tides of grass, I stopped at Te Awamutu – and not merely for a guide book I had lately been commissioned to compile. There was something I needed to see on my own account. That is, the unique memorials inside and outside St John's Anglican church. Both paid tribute to the heroism of the Maori who took up arms against the British Empire in the 1860s. *Love Your Enemies* exhorted the text within the church, placed there by the officers and men of Queen Victoria's 65th infantry regiment. I suspected there was nothing in the history of human conflict to match this salute to slain foemen. On my way to Rotorua I crossed the battle-site of Orakau, where the Maori of the Waikato region made their last and all but suicidal stand against the British army in 1863. I left the car and paid my silent respects.

Maurice wasn't happy. He couldn't be. With his de facto marriage looking likely to end soon, he was hanging on desperately to his six-year-old son. His partner, Sarah, was embarked on another relationship, with an elderly doctor, while Maurice persisted under the same roof. It was not a situation many men could suffer. But Maurice had always been as much heroic as stoic.

That night the doctor invited us to view his art collection – almost entirely composed of oils on black velvet, paintings of provocatively posed Tahitian women. As pornography, it was run of the mill. As art, poor *Playboy* plagiarism. The painter, a Frenchman by name of Leteeg, was celebrated in one of James Michener's South Pacific tomes. The less his nude studies left to the imagination, the larger their price on the international market. My eyes flickered toward Maurice. He sat impassively in a corner of the room. I had the feeling that he wished to hide his head in his hands. The paintings suggested the nature of the relationship between the doctor and Sarah. There might be a novel in this for Maurice. It was not one I should care to write. Fortunately I was rescued by a female friend of Sarah's. Of mixed blood, French and Maori, Wendy belonged to one of the region's most distinguished families. She saw me in social difficulty and invited me to share her family hot pool. This promised material for a rather livelier narrative. (It would. Years later the night became a carefree episode in *The Lovelock Version* – one which might even have pleased that Italian professor.) While we soaked under a sky dense with stars, in an atmosphere scented with sulphur, Wendy told me the story of her life. This proved unnecessary. It turned out that I had already written it. It was a short story named 'Homecoming,' which she, just to compound coincidence, happened to have read recently. Synchronicity no longer unnerved me, not as it once had.

Next day I left Rotorua behind and dawdled to Waihi. There I stayed with Eric and Elizabeth Lee-Johnson. Eric's watercolours of the North Island interior – of decrepit farmhouses, patchy forest, shattered stumps, rock-strewn riversides, misty hills – remained as enthralling as ever. They did far more for me than the landscapes themselves. His paintings were windows which let light into what I was about in *Strangers and Journeys*. Eric was no stranger in the land; his journey was epic.

With Waihi behind, I pushed up the rocky Coromandel Peninsula. Auckland wasn't far off. Soon I had my first brush with the world I had been busy escaping. I stopped beside the rugged coast, a hot cup of thermos tea in hand, and read a less than favourable review of *Among the Cinders* in the latest *New Zealand Listener*. The reviewer was persuasive; she seemed to know what she was talking about. My life, my work, was worthless. My problem was that it might be true.

Not for long. A few weeks later the twins were born. A girl and a boy, Tui and Daniel. Tui was named for the birds feeding on the kowhai now in golden flood around the Titirangi house. In naming her I wished my tiny daughter sweet with the nectar of the land. My little new son was named in the hope that he dared to be a Daniel. In the words of the negro song: *Didn't my Lord deliver Daniel, deliver Daniel, deliver Daniel? Didn't my Lord deliver Daniel? Then why not every man?*

My current problem was delivering myself from penury. Money, in the form of a commission for a television play, tempted me twice to Wellington. I was to write a segment of a four-part drama which, if made, would be the first full-length New Zealand television play. History-making, in short. I soon had reason to fear the worst. My slice of the drama was to deal with a young girl in autumn. It was to interlock with tales of a young man in spring, an old woman in winter, an old man in summer. This format wasn't original, but I worked on it anyway, adapting an old story of mine for my instalment. The writers of the other three came up with scripts impossible to film or no script at all. My story was judged the only one thought worth producing.

I protested. My story was never meant to stand alone. It didn't make sense alone. The writer's cry of grief was ignored. The machine ground on. The producer was hand-wringing and ineffectual. The cameraman was confused; so was everyone else. The director was an Italian who couldn't read English, especially of an idiomatic nature. For example, when a character was accused (by another character in my script) of having cold feet, the director instructed the actor to look down at his feet and shiver. Dear God in heaven. It couldn't be true.

Nothing good could come of this. Nothing did. My first and last entanglement with television drama ended there.

On the way back to Auckland I found a less wasteful activity than writing for television. Reading a good book, for example. For most of the journey home I was I buried in an extraordinary New Zealand novel titled *The Scarecrow*. A madcap chronicle of small-town New Zealand, it was written by an obscure resident of South Taranaki named Ronald Hugh Morrieson, I wondered why I had never heard of the fellow, why so few had – aside from a perceptive Australian publisher. Long before I reached Auckland I was convinced that I had met with a comic master. His mentors, if any, may have been Dickens or Mark Twain. Not that it mattered. There was never a New Zealand writer more his own man. On my next trip to Wellington I took along his second novel, *Came a Hot Friday*. It confirmed that his first was no accident.

I had a daunting chore in Wellington. That was, to put together a volume of Michael Amato's stories and gather material for a memoir covering his bitterly short life and anguished times. Though we had been corresponding, I hadn't seen his wife Sheena since his death 18 months before. Her welcome was warm. There were also tears. Michael's desk was ready for me, his chair, all his manuscripts. All I had to do was make sense of his life. All? I was suddenly overwhelmed by the impertinence of the project. What did I know? What *could* I know? I sat at his desk, trying it for size. It wasn't altogether uncomfortable.

On my second night Sheena handed me a discoloured document. The language in the document was Italian. There were a couple of fading signatures. Sheena watched my face.

'Is it what I think it is?' I asked

'It is,' she said. 'It turned up yesterday.'

She translated. The document confirmed that one Renato Amato was a fascist of the *Brigate Nere,* Mussolini's infamous black brigade, best known for its atrocities against civilians and prisoners.

I should sooner not have seen it, of course. I also preferred to imagine him coerced, as he possibly was. His often autobiographical stories suggested that he had been an unwilling conscript. They also indicated that he had finished the war in a left-wing partisan unit; that he managed to fight on both sides in the war. Such speculation made the document more palatable. I was shaken all the same, even if nothing was news to me.

With morning sun filling through a Wellington window, at a kitchen table covered in manuscripts, Sheena and I worked back and forward over that life, sometimes in harmony, often in discord. In spite of my best intentions it soon began to seem that a novel, rather than a memoir, was in the making. I asked Sheena how she felt about that prospect. We agreed that the memoir must come first. After publication of his work, I was welcome to his life. The last lines Michael wrote, days before his collapse, continued to haunt me: 'It is a beautiful day, but it is again as it has always been. I am so short of time.'

So he was.

In her distress Sheena consulted a spiritualist medium to see if Michael had more to tell her. She couldn't imagine him not having a last word. If he attempted it, his communication was inaudible. I gave up much of my summer writing the memoir, trying to wrestle him back to the world. Ian Cross at least was impressed.

'It reads like a novel,' he said with approval, and wondered why I groaned.

Twenty-three

A desperate DC-3, possibly the first ever flown, and destined not to fly much longer, circled the island of Rarotonga, the one sizable lump of land in the Cook Islands. Vegetation looked miraculous after hundreds of empty miles. I gazed down on an oceanic oasis of coconut palms, banana plantations, orange groves and more indiscriminate growth. At sea level it was lagoon fringed with coral and ramshackle dwellings. Suddenly our aircraft bumped along a primitive landing strip. There was a terminal building of sorts, a makeshift control tower, and perhaps a hundred people ready to pounce. Ours was the first plane in a fortnight. They said that Tahiti was like this once too. Perhaps. Anyway I was there to witness the last of old Polynesia as it expired. Expire it would when the first jet plane boomed overhead, when the first tourist hotel opened. The entrepeneurs were already investigating the possibilities of the place. As a hint of things to come, hired Rarotongan hands rushed across the landing strip to wreath us with sweet-smelling flowers.

The world's most diminutive state, the Cook Islands constituted fewer than 20,000 people scattered over a dozen atolls and volcanic outcrops. There were now rather more than that number of islanders resident in New Zealand. There would be even more were there more berths on boats, more seats on planes. Even so, the population dwindled yearly. There was something comic opera about 20,000 people having an elected Premier, Cabinet Ministers, heads of departments, and a busy bureaucracy. How could so wispy a place survive such freight?

'Fence the place off,' said one sardonic journalist of my acquaintance. 'Make it a human zoo.'

I decided not to make up my mind on what I found. Or what I

might not.

The Rarotonga Hotel, where I lodged, was South Sea sleazy. The only visitors' accommodation in town, it would have served Somerset Maugham well as a setting for his Samoan story 'Rain'. It was a decrepit barrack-like building, or boarding house, with dining room attached. It housed Europeans – mostly civil servants, lawyers and schoolteachers seconded from New Zealand to help the lilliputian state function. A number of these expatriates seemed in large disrepair, not to say despair. Was it booze, sex, or both? There was something unhappily seedy about several. Their conversation was sexually obsessive. There were feminine murmurs from their rooms at night and often more full-throated sounds. I bedded in Room 13, which wasn't promising. Worse, the last occupant of Room 13 hung himself a month before my arrival. There was no suicide note, so no one knew why. (A romance with a fickle Rarotongan girl was suspected.) I was glad I had a satisfying night's sleep before discovering this. Though there were creaks in the ceiling I continued sleeping well.

The hotel was run by an expatriate couple as down at heel as their establishment: Norm and Beryl. They had once managed pubs in New Zealand and Australia. Norm was stocky and bloated, usually in poor temper with lethargic kitchenmaids. Beryl was skinny and pale and visibly unhappy with her lot. The Rarotongan sun seemed never to have shone on either. They had the complexion of dedicated drinkers.

Norm invited me to their quarters and was at pains to put me right about the Cook Islands. 'There's more going on here than most people know,' he warned me.

'In what way?' I asked.

He looked over his shoulder and said no more. I presumed he was talking chicanery.

'Hang around,' Norm suggested finally. 'You'll see.'

Also permanently resident in the Rarotonga Hotel was an elderly, skinny white-haired and roguish gentleman, a dehydrated seventy, named Julian Dashwood. The one European politician in the Cook Islands' cabinet, he had just published a book about his youthful exploits in the South Sea. Like many Europeans who fetched up here, to beachcomb and bed local women, there was something dingy about the man. As for his political credentials, it wouldn't have surprised me if he had embezzlement in his background. But there he was. A Cabinet Minister. The Right Honourable Julian Dashwood, no less. He gave me a good-natured smile when I passed him in diminutive Avarua, Rarotonga's lone township. He was possibly summing me up. Was I really writing for *Geographic*? Or was I conducting a less literary investigation of the Cooks? I didn't think it necessary to reassure him.

The Prime Minister, Albert Henry, whom I soon encountered, was a genial Maori who had spent much of his adult life in New Zealand exile, flying the flag of Cook Island independence. Charismatic Henry, with his left-wing connections, was never popular with the New Zealand authorities. They backed a safely right-wing local crook as the islands' first Prime Minister; Henry's political party – the CIP or Cook Islands Party – swamped the crook electorally. But I didn't see Albert as a fount of virtue on that score.

There were intriguing human encounters beyond every coconut grove on the road around the island. One was with Rarotonga's resident author, a onetime beachcomber named Ronald Syme. He was a pukka Englishman in dress – white shorts, long stockings, boater hat – and clipped speech. His books were undistinguished examples of the earthly paradise genre as pioneered by the likes of the French novelist Pierre Loti and the English poet Rupert Brooke. They were also clumsily fanciful, with little regard even for botanical facts. Syme was up to the neck in the petty politics of the islands; buzzing importantly in and out of Albert Henry's office he appeared to be, or tried to be, Albert Henry's chief adviser. Did Henry listen to him long?

I did. Or for long enough. In this unlikely South Pacific setting, iced drink in hand, looking out on the surf bursting over the reef, I became aware that I was listening to an unreformed and raving Stalinist. If the KGB had a man in place in the peaceful islands of Polynesia, there to gather intelligence, signal Soviet submarines, win friends, or just report on prospects for a proletarian revolution in Rarotonga, it had to be my dapper companion. All I did, to set him off, was make a few sympathetic sounds concerning colonial blunders in the Pacific. My suspicion was confirmed by the arrival on Rarotonga of a Serbian employee of the United Nations. Ante was

a worldly, humorous, and most entertaining man. I suggested to
Syme that he might enjoy Ante's company. Might I bring him out to
meet Syme? After all, visitors from the larger world were few in
Rarotonga.

Syme gave me a strange look.

'I think not,' he said sharply.

That was that. I had forgotten that for diehard Stalinists Yugosla-
via's Marshal Tito was still, in 1966, persona non grata, the devil
incarnate. Anyway I said no more.

More amiable company was Walter Hambeuchen, an American
journalist and aspirant author. He wrote and printed the only thing
passing for a newspaper on the island. Such news as it carried was
pilfered from short-wave radio. The rest was harmless gossip. The
lean and literally haunted son of a Wall Street stockbroker, Walter
had been combing the beaches of Tahiti and Rarotonga for a decade.
He imagined he would win a novel from this enterprise. Instead a
novel was writing him in established South Sea mode. He married a
stunningly beautiful Tahitian soon after his arrival in the Pacific – yet
another version of Fayaway, Herman Melville's dusky heroine in
Typee. Fayaway, under one name or another, seems to inhabit every
South Pacific novel written since Melville's. In fiction they died
tragically and lingeringly, and Walter's real-life wife conformed to
the convention. In the years since her death he had been sitting out
under starlit Pacific skies, listening to the surf on the reef, night after
night, waiting on her reappearance. He was convinced that she, or
her moonlit ghost, would return. Meanwhile, in daylight, he typed
up trivia for the *Cook Islands News*. His father wanted him to return
to New York and take up a partnership in the family firm. This didn't
appeal to Walter. But then little in this life did. He showed me
photographs of his wife. She was indeed beautiful. Walter drank
sparingly, as if unable to trust himself with alcohol. His eyes were
permanently bloodshot. The romance of South Sea was slowly
destroying him. He was eventually to perish in a motorcycle crash
while on his nightly search for his lost mate. Was the crash deliber-
ate? Neighbouring villagers believed so. Some even claimed that they
had seen Walter and his wahine walking at dusk beside the lagoon.
Walter's was the other half of the South Sea tale.

I cooled my heels in Rarotonga until my photographer arrived. I hoped his aircraft found the place. Acquainting myself with the island wasn't onerous. It was barely more than a volcanic lump laced with coral. It took forty minutes or fewer to circle. Hospitable locals reared from the shrubbery whenever I halted. They seemed to have all the time in the world to gossip. Well, the fact was that *they* had all the time in the world. I didn't. I had a story to write: or at least some wallpaper prose to plaster between *Geographic*'s photographs.

Since I was a lonely stranger in town, one or two families virtually adopted me. There were beach barbecues. There was song. There was dance. The many-scented shore, especially at dusk, with embers of sunset cooling to the west, proved to be all that travel-writers promised of Polynesia. I seemed likely to become one of their number. Surprisingly and dismayingly, I sensed how easy it would be to give the world away. My world, that was. Philosophy, science, political discourse, literature, history – all forms of inquiry into the human condition. Everything for the past 2500 years. Everything since the Athens of Pericles, the Agora of Socrates. The unexamined life, Socrates to the contrary, had something to be said for it. Literary life began to look tawdry; my novels and stories paltry. I read, or attempted to read, a novel by a distinguished English literary gentleman. Though it was full of fine thoughts, I could make no sense of it. For one thing it appeared to be in a foreign language. It *was* in a foreign language. So far as I comprehended matters, literature was now about literature, art about art, philosophy about philosophy, and sex about sex.

In mounting alarm I discussed my condition with an intelligent and articulate schoolteacher friend named Turepu. He had travelled, lived elsewhere, and seen as much as he wanted of the world; he was cheerfully home again, growing citrus on his family land and, with evening, cradling a guitar in his lap. He might have made more of himself had he wished. It wasn't his wish.

'It's hard to be earnest, to study, to think about life, when all around are people who only want to laugh, dance, sing and be happy.' So saying, Turepu strummed his guitar.

This was dangerous stuff. This was what frangipani did, and moonlight through the ironwood trees. Though it was nothing I could safely report to *Geographic*'s six million subscribers, this was what the balmy Cook Islands could do to the reasonably level-headed writer in only a week.

With splendid timing my photographer flew in to remind me of my mission here. His name was Bill Fortune. He was new on *Geographic* and this was his first assignment outside the United States. I didn't find this promising. He was also bumptious and aggressive, a pretty uncouth Midwesterner. Even less propitious. We were about to spend a considerable amount of time together, four weeks at least, voyaging through the Cooks. Bill bore a message to me from a *Geographic* editor: 'Try,' this editor urged, 'to fill your story with as much personal adventure as you can muster.' Personal adventure? I was at a loss to think how this might be managed. Bill Fortune, however, rushed in where authors fear to tread.

While we waited on our vessel, I introduced him to Rarotonga by way of motor-scooter. An inexperienced and incautious traveller, Bill found the sexual electricity of the place dizzying, not least when photographing Rarotonga's champion dance troupe, all fluent brown limbs, twitching thighs and floral garlands in the provocative dance called the tamure. He was a long way from the Midwest. His eyes glazed. Soon they were slits. Within a day or two he had a female companion, a talented dancer and singer from one of Rarotonga's most respectable Maori families. I foresaw trouble, perhaps a vengeful and virtuous male relative cracking open Bill's skull. Would I get him out of the place intact? Would I survive, for that matter? Personal adventure might be the death of me.

Trouble arrived rather casually, from a different direction. Norm, the manager of the hotel, asked a favour of Bill. He had a document which he wished photographed. Might Bill arrange two or three good quality negatives? Innocent Bill saw no reason not to oblige. While he was fetching camera and film, I began reading the document.

'I found it in Julian Dashwood's waste basket,' Norm explained.

I wasn't taken with the sound of that. A hotel manager who rummaged in the waste baskets of his guests?

My reservations dispersed. The document was a recipe for a political explosion, well worth pilfering from anyone's waste basket. It was a letter from the aforesaid Julian Dashwood, the token European in the Cook Islands cabinet, to a dealer in stamps and coins in Australia. It concerned forthcoming stamp and coin issues from the Cook Islands and detailed arrangements by which Dashwood and a certain A.H. (ie, Albert Henry the Prime Minister) might fatten their pockets in the course of the deal. There was nothing in the least subtle about this enterprise. It was all there in black and white, so shameless that I couldn't believe that I read it right; I read it through again and found I was right the first time. Julian Dashwood and Albert Henry were a slimy pair of swindlers. Less than a year after independence, the Cook Islands administration was crawling with corruption.

'What do you think?' Norm asked.

'Fascinating,' I said. 'What are you going to do with it?'

'Use it to keep my job,' he explained. 'They're trying to sack me.'

'Someone should know about this,' I said. 'New Zealand sinks millions into this place.'

Norm shrugged. 'You could write something,' he suggested.

Possibly that had been Norm's hope from the first, why he had approached Bill for photographs. He wanted a favour from me, not from Bill.

'Not until I've finished my *Geographic* chore,' I said. The last thing I needed, at this moment, was a deportation order.

Norm was disappointed in me. I was too. I told myself that the rights and wrongs of Rarotonga were not my present concern. Besides, our vessel was ready for the voyage to the northern Cooks.

Twenty-four

The vessel was the 200-ton *Akatere*, a now sea-weary boat built for the Baltic rather than the temperamental Pacific. God knew what this rust-bucket was doing in Rarotonga, indeed how it made it there at all. The skipper was a short, burly and barefoot Fijian named Archie Pickering. His mission was to carry goods and passengers to the remote atolls of the northern Cooks; and to bring back copra. Bill and I shared a stern cabin, the only respectable passenger accommodation on the vessel. The mattresses smelled powerfully of human sweat; the galley reeked of diesel fumes. The voyage promised to be a test of stomachs. Other passengers bunked sensibly under the stars.

Our departure from Rarotonga was unexpectedly moving. First there were wisps of sorrow. These fast became frantic cries. I had never heard grief to match it. There were people, often elderly, sometimes juvenile, returning to their native islands; the young adults left behind were looking to lead a less constricted life on Rarotonga and, perhaps eventually, New Zealand. The likelihood was that they would never see their elders again, nor their home islands. Thus the sorrow. Their wailing took me back in time. This was how it must have been when venturesome canoe-loads of voyagers set out to find new land, often to perish in the Pacific. Those left behind would never know if the voyages had been successful. Enough must have been. All ninety-three square miles of land and sand were settled before Western voyagers appeared on the horizon. The most surprising feat in maritime history began to seem even more extraordinary as we pushed, day after long day, across the Pacific. There was not a sniff of land to right or left. Bill was less impressed as he surveyed endless ocean. Where, he asked, were the women?

Contemporary Polynesians were less impressive than their for-bears on the great waters of the world. There was a low moaning from deck passengers when we met even a mild swell; most aboard seemed terminally seasick. Prayers became fervent. So how had they done it? How had these delicate souls sailed the Pacific from end to end, from New Zealand in the south, to Hawaii in the north?

The familiar world was soon still further behind. Some days out from Rarotonga I woke to a colourful dawn, coconut palms leaning over a shimmering shore. *Akatere* was drifting, its engines idling. This first rendezvous was with a rather ravishing atoll called Manihiki. It had to be one of the world's most exquisite. Like all or most atolls it rose, at its highest, no more than a dozen fragile feet above the ocean, virtually all sand and coral, with little soil. The marvel was that its thirty-nine islets, comprising two square miles, managed to support six hundred people.

Setting foot ashore involved shooting the reef in classic Polynesian style; Manihiki's lagoon had no entrance. We lowered ourselves by way of rope ladder into a slender longboat. Oarsmen pointed their craft in the direction of land while surf began to beat up on each side. Our steersman eyed the tumbling walls of water and hazardous coral, waiting on his moment. '*Oeu!*' he finally cried. 'Pull!' For a time we seemed to be travelling through a tunnel of foam. Then swinging oars heaved us over coral on to solid shore. Islanders were steadying the longboat and lifting us to reliable ground. Manihiki's first visitors in two months had arrived.

'Jesus,' Bill said. 'Do we have to do that again to get out of here?'

'I can't see any other way out,' I said.

'The hell with it,' he decided. 'I'm staying.'

Land was a large improvement on the open Pacific. Recovering our equilibrium, and our wits, we breakfasted on cool coconut milk. Later we wandered in the direction of Manihiki's central lagoon. Manihiki's barrel-chested shell-divers, the most robust in the Pacific, were anxious to impress us with their submarine skills. Fetching up mother of pearl from the floor of the lagoon – equipped with no more than goggles – meant descents of between 80 and 120 feet; sometimes the divers were absent for three or four minutes. Snorkel-ling on the lagoon surface, I watched them glide with uncanny leisure among clouds of bright fish a dozen fathoms down. They plucked the shell as they might blooms from rainbow forest. Then came the long ascent. None seemed distressed. They dived down for more.

They also showed us how to fish the Manihiki way. It was original, weird and wonderfully beautiful. Two or three fathoms down, around the outer reef, there was a herring-like fish prized by the islanders. These creatures had to be tempted closer to the surface. Divers filled their mouths with shredded coconut meat and dived down until they were among the fish. Then, as they ascended, they began spitting out the coconut. The fish fed furiously, following the divers to within a fathom of the surface. Then came the pièce de résistance. The men ceased to be divers and became underwater anglers. They whipped out tiny rods and lines laced with more coconut. Then they began casting underwater. It became a breathtaking ballet: the arms and legs of the men working, the silver fish flashing as they took the bait. Fish by the score were slung into our boat.

We lunched on the catch, and on barbecued crab. Bill was still wondering gloomily how he could get off the island, his cameras in one piece, without risking the reef again. A helicopter seemed the only alternative; Manihiki was more than a thousand miles from the nearest. Perhaps an SOS to *Geographic* headquarters in Washington? Bill reluctantly conceded that as unrealistic too. Meanwhile *Akatere* was unloading foodstuffs into longboats and taking aboard some thirty ton of Manihiki copra. There was other, human cargo. Some twenty young people were quitting the atoll for new lives in New Zealand. It was easy to identify these migrants; their faces, a day before departure, were already awash with tears. It was easy to be sentimental about this. What was the alternative? To fence the islands off, as that sardonic journalist suggested, and make them a zoo?

'Soon there will only the very young and the very old left here,' mourned one articulate islander. 'Who will know the Manihiki stories, fish the Manihiki way?'

At dusk, a bottle of New Zealand beer in hand, he regaled us with ghost stories. They lacked little in drama. The northern atolls, it seemed, seethed with shades. It was possible that they might soon displace the living. 'Wait until you see Penrhyn,' our pessimistic companion warned. He didn't elaborate. The sky filled with stars; the darkness grew deeper. The air was warm, the silence eloquent.

Most of his stories concerned beautiful women doomed by love. They all sounded like Walter Hambeuchen's lost wife.

Next day we farewelled Manihiki. Archie Pickering pointed *Akatere* toward the neighbouring island of Rakahanga, thereby demonstrating how easy it was to lose an island in the northern Cooks. There was no more than twenty-five miles between the two atolls. Half way between Manihiki and Rakahanga, both vanished. Not even the tips of their coconut trees could be seen; the ocean was suddenly a lifeless and dangerous wilderness of water. Voyagers between the atolls, caught in gusty weather, had been known to lose both and disappear forever. A party in an open sailing cutter had lately finished two thousand miles to the west, with three out of seven men surviving two killing months adrift.

Rakahanga was sultry, airless and, for some reason unappealing. The people seemed dour. They were certainly unsmiling. They took the dead seriously here too. Indeed they slept with them; they bedded on the graves of their forebears. Should they not do so, should they not remain intimate with their fretful predecessors, they might find old ghosts making their lives difficult. Bill and I decided not to sleep ashore. Our stuffy cabin seemed preferable. From the deck of *Akatere* we saw lights moving among the headstones in the island's graveyard. The place twinkled like a little town. Rakahanga's living, this night as every night, were communing with their dead. Next morning I was relieved to see sombre Rakahanga diminishing astern. There was more ocean, more and more, to underline the magnificence of the Polynesian achievement. Running at seven knots, about the speed of a Polynesian outrigger in fair weather, we pushed toward equatorial Penrhyn, the most remote island in the Cooks. Penrhyn hadn't seen a ship in four months; sometimes its inhabitants went as long as seven without a visit. Meanwhile four hungry months were enfeebling enough. Radio messages were growing more desperate daily. The island's people were out of flour, sugar, rice, soap, medicines, canned meat and tobacco. Archie Pickering handed me the helm as he lit his pipe and eyed the weather professionally. Deck passengers were at worship; their hymns and prayers lifted into the night. Perhaps the voyagers of pagan Polynesia solicited help from their deities too as they journeyed. I found it impossible to forget those firstcomers. Bill, to whom I endeavoured to explain matters, thought me obsessed. He was right. I was. Which was why I returned to it again and again. There was never a more transcendent feat in the history of human colonisation of the planet. Besides, Polynesia's past was much to be preferred to its debased present. The incriminating document I handled in Rarotonga was still on my mind.

'We'll see Penrhyn tomorrow,' Archie announced. Then, 'How much do you know about it?'

'Only what I've read,' I said.

That wasn't much either. Peruvian slavers had depopulated the place in the 19th century. None returned from the mines of Peru to tell their ghastly story. Penrhyn's last encounter with history was in World War Two. It served island-hopping US aircraft. Beside an airfield of crushed coral there were the remains of a crashed Liberator bomber, testifying to the island's ephemeral importance as a rear base in the war against Japan. The consensus was that the island had never recovered from this most recent incursion; it had been even more devastating than the Peruvian one.

Archie had a brisker judgement. 'The place is fucked,' he said.

'In what way?'

'In every way,' he said.

This intelligence was unlikely to win the hearts of *Geographic* readers.

'You heard about the ghost fire of Penrhyn?' Archie asked.

'Ghost fire?' I asked. No more occult drama, I prayed. This was supposed to be the carefree South Sea.

'When it burns, out on the lagoon, someone dies,' Archie disclosed. 'No one can explain it. It isn't natural gas or volcanic activity. It's just a light hovering over the lagoon. The Americans put out a torpedo boat to find its source; it crashed on a reef and sank. Since then no one has been keen on finding it.'

'I see,' I replied.

'I hope you don't see,' Archie answered. 'Anyway I wouldn't let it worry you. It's not as if it shows up every night. You're safe.'

'I'll take your word for it,' I said.

Next day, near dark, we cruised cautiously toward Penrhyn; the island announced itself as bobbing shoreline lights. None looked supernatural. They proved to be islanders putting out longboats to meet us. It was dark by the time they began scrambling up ropes on to the deck of *Akatere*. They were men possessed. All were crying the one word: '*Avaava!*' This, translated, meant cigarettes. Most hadn't seen one in months. Playing Father Christmas, Bill and I broke open packs and passed them around. The islanders began smoking themselves sick. They also fuelled themselves with a potent mix of beer and whisky. They called this diabolic blend 'a half and a half' in the Cooks. It was a recipe for paralysis.

Our visitors were persuaded ashore. Some deck passengers, rather than suffer another night on *Akatere*, joined them. One of this number was a mother with a sick child. Archie tried to persuade her to remain aboard *Akatere*. She remained adamant; she wanted her child ashore. Her child would surely get better ashore.

When commotion ebbed we heaved to for the night. Archie and I had a tot of whisky before going to our bunks.

'You remember what I told you about the ghost fire?'

'I can hardly forget it,' I said.

'It burned last night,' he revealed.

'And?'

'No one has yet died,' he informed me.

'That must be a relief.'

'Say that tomorrow morning,' Archie suggested.

In the morning Archie ran *Akatere* gently into the 100-square mile lagoon and parked it against a wharf with the sweetish smell of decomposing copra. Americans had blasted coral reef apart to form a pass during their wartime stay. This gave supply ships access to the lagoon and shelter from hurricane. The flaw in the new format was that it allowed sharks into the lagoon. Sharks had been the sole proprietors of Penrhyn's vast lagoon ever since. They had been known to lift savagely from the lagoon and fasten their teeth on the legs of paddling children. With predators left and right, divers found life difficult at best. Monetary return provided poor incentive to risk shark attack. Until Japan's cultured pearls drove the once coveted natural Penrhyn pearl off the market, and until oceanic ogres began to proliferate, diving here was big business. Now diving gear rotted in waterside sheds. A few hardy islanders still dived for mother of pearl. Copra was now the island's one significant saleable commodity, and even the price for that was pitiful.

There was a immense sadness about the place. It proved even

more melancholy when Archie returned from conversation with local gossips. 'The ghost fire is never wrong,' he reported.

'There was a death?'

'The baby we had aboard,' he said. 'The one whose mother wanted to get him off last night.'

Archie saw no need to enlighten us further.

Bill and I took beds ashore, in the house of the local resident. Until a trustworthy local man was found as substitute resident, Eddie represented law and order on Penrhyn. No one else was greatly interested in the job. No one in his right mind would want it. A skinny Scotsman, Eddie was an unlikely emissary of civilisation. His wife Lu, a muscular Penrhyn woman, was about twice his height and three times his girth. 'Great,' he said on our arrival at his door. 'I've been waiting half a year for someone new to drink with.'

This was unpromising.

At dinner that night we did our best to be desirable company. The residency was on the lagoon edge. In the course of too many pre-dinner drinks I put out a baited line. A minute later there was a powerful strike. I hauled in a four-foot shark. I began wishing I hadn't. The next day Bill and I were to investigate Penrhyn's lagoon; there was no point in giving premature offence to its occupants.

Dinner was rowdy. Ghosts were on the agenda here too. Eddie was insistent that his mother-in-law, some two years deceased, was a frequent visitor to the residency; he claimed to have had conversation with her within the past week. In the light of this, he had friendly advice. Should we meet up with his mother-in-law, in the course of our stay, we were not to panic; her intention was kindly, and she had a natural curiosity about house guests.

I sat quiet. Bill's eyes widened. First sharks, now shades. Then conversation took a hazardous turn. As bottles emptied Eddie became convinced that his wife was making a sexual play for Bill. The atmosphere filled with tension. I thought it tactful to take a stroll along the shore at a cautious distance from unhappy humans and patrolling sharks. My head clearing, I turned back toward the residency.

As I neared it, I heard shouts and screams. When I stepped on to the verandah I met a bizarre sight. Mrs Resident was running from room to room, screaming blue murder. It promised to become red murder. Mr Resident was in demented pursuit of his wife with a wicked cutlass in hand. He crashed it into a door. Then he sliced into a bookshelf. With lethal swings, samurai style, he set off after his wife again. Mrs Resident, despite her bulk, made good ground; her screams grew distant. Darkness was on her side too.

I slept poorly. Bill didn't sleep at all. Next morning, at breakfast, nothing was said. Mr Resident had a scar under his left eye. Had a bookshelf hit back?

We sailed across the lagoon with the island's veteran divers. They wanted to show us how they played roulette with sharks in the course of collecting mother of pearl shell. I couldn't fail to note that the men of Penrhyn were a scarred crew. An impressive number were missing limbs. I met one islander lately struck from the rear while diving off the reef. When the shark circled for a second strike, the diver was ready. He reached behind him and got a grip on the beast as it closed with his back. Then he stumbled on to the reef, shark on shoulders, and dumped it triumphantly at his feet. His blemished back confirmed the truth of his tale. Something toothy had torn strips off him.

There was a cooling breeze out on the lagoon. Three of our four companions were seasoned divers. The fourth, something of an amateur, was the local schoolteacher. Bill loaded and checked his underwater camera. He also loaded a conventional camera for me. 'If you have to get out of the water, you might get a shark shot from the boat,' he suggested.

First, before diving, there was a Polynesian prayer. A translation wasn't necessary. Whatever else it was, in current circumstances, it was bound to be a plea for our continued well-being.

We lowered ourselves gingerly over the side of the boat. My legs had never felt more vulnerable.

We snorkelled, slowly circling above brilliant shoals of tropical fish and baroque cities of coral. To my relief, no shark was on show. One diver speared and shredded a couple of the lagoon's lesser creatures. Streamers of blood drifted away.

The schoolteacher surfaced. I did too. 'What is that all about?' I asked.

'The blood will bring the sharks around,' the teacher promised. 'Don't you want to see them?'

'Naturally,' I lied.

'Just a little advice,' the teacher went on. 'If you see a shark heading for you, kick it in the nose. Not the teeth. You can lose a leg that way.'

I was beginning not to enjoy this. Personal adventure, in my view, precluded intimacy with sharks.

'There is nothing to worry about,' he insisted. 'If you went to church last Sunday, and have said your prayers since, you are perfectly safe.'

This didn't impress me either. For one thing I hadn't been seen in church the previous Sunday, nor for many Sundays before that. Too late now.

We dived again. This time the sharks took notice. Several of pale hue began circling us gracefully. Soon a dozen, then a score. Penrhyn's divers descended among them, fetching up mother of pearl by the handful and tossing it back into the boat. Floating overhead, Bill was working fast with his underwater camera, trying to frame sharks and divers in one eloquent shot.

The teacher signalled me to the surface again. Perhaps seeing the fear in my face, he again attempted to be reassuring. 'The white sharks,' he said, 'are nothing to be worried about. They very seldom attack. It's the black sharks you have to watch for. They're the worst.'

'Black sharks?' I said feebly.

'You'll see them,' my cheerful companion predicted.

Again we dived. As promised, the black sharks made a showing. Perhaps six circled beyond their white brethren, forming a menacing cordon.

Bill's pale legs were working vigorously somewhere above. He was still fastened to his lens. He didn't know it yet, but a black shark was taking an unwholesome interest in his legs, cruising toward his crutch. Bill Fortune was about to become Bill Misfortune. I found it impossible to win his attention. My shouts produced no response; his ears were underwater. I found it impossible to disguise my unhappiness. I fled back to our boat and threw myself aboard. Recalling Bill's request, I picked up a conventional camera. Triangular fins, black, white, and black and white, were flicking out of the lagoon. Then Bill looked to his rear and realised that his private parts were in peril. In the same moment he surfaced long enough to hear my shouts. He slammed into the boat, camera swinging from his neck, and scrambled to safety.

'Jesus,' he said when he recovered his breath. 'That should make one hell of a picture.'

'The divers?' I said.

'No,' he said. 'Me. Me with that monster up my arse. You did get it didn't you?'

I looked down bleakly at the unused camera. My hands were still numb.

'You mean you didn't get it?' he said.

'I didn't,' I confessed.

'Jesus,' he says. 'You'll never make a photographer.'

I wasn't inclined to disagree. It was some time before he could say a kind word to me. 'How soon can we get out of here?' he asked. That was on my mind too.

We did leave. Copra loaded, Archie Pickering pointed *Akatere* through the pass in the reef and south to Rarotonga, a 700-mile voyage. Penrhyn began to seem paradisial when we closed with a rogue storm. Tall waves, tipped with foam, tumbled down on to *Akatere*; every crash seemed likely to break the back of the vessel. We made two knots an hour when we were lucky. In those hurricane-haunted waters, slight trading vessels like *Akatere* often survived on voyager's instinct. We were a long way from regular shipping lanes, hundreds of miles from help. Prayers were loud. In this godless uproar they had to be.

Storm subsided. Nearing Rarotonga, after seven sickening days, we met thick ocean mist. We could overshoot Rarotonga or, worse, go aground on a reef. Skipper Archie wasn't daunted. He picked up a handy transistor radio, tuned it to Rarotonga's one radio station, and ingeniously began using it as direction finder (much as traditional voyagers used leaf, bird and cloud.) There was tension nevertheless. But Archie's intuition – with a little help from the 20th century – was sound. We left mist behind. The green peaks of Rarotonga soared above. The voyage was done. Other matters weren't.

There was a policeman on the wharf. He wanted Bill. He wanted me too. What had we done? The policeman was uninformative; he marched us off to a superior. At least we weren't handcuffed. It seemed we being held as witnesses to a felony. The felony? That of mine host Norm lifting a document from a guest's waste paper basket. Norm was on trial for theft. I was to testify that I saw the noxious document in his hands. Bill was to testify that he photographed the document. There was no mention of corruption. No finger was pointed at slippery Prime Minister Henry. Julian Dashwood had tactfully resigned from the Cook Island's cabinet. An infuriated Henry, caught with loot up to his elbows, was promising to sweep perfidious Europeans into the sea. Bill and I were plainly perfidious.

We were only too willing to be given our marching orders. At present pace – with Cook Island justice a slow jog – we could still be here in a year. This was emphasised when the DC-3 which flew us in, and was to fly us out, crashed in Samoa. Three dead. Our presence in the Cooks seemed more and more risky. If we hadn't been detained for the trial, there might have been five corpses.

I testified. Bill testified. It had all been arranged neatly. Hotel-keeper Norm pleaded guilty. He and his wife were packing their bags. I presumed monetary compensation had been made. Ronald Syme, the Kremlin's man in these parts, was crowing.

As the grand climax of my Cook Island sojourn I went down with food poisoning. It disguised the symptoms of hepatitis. Finally I flew home feverishly to New Zealand. Bill and I weren't sorry to have seen the last of each other.

Delirium persisted. I woke and wondered where I was. The Cook Islands had done a comprehensive demolition job: I wasn't interested in resuming work, in whittling life into narrative form; I wanted to recline under the palms and listen to surf on the reef. This was serious. Friends called and found me uninterested in literary news. This shocked them. Me too, if not as much.

Twenty-five

Some years come suddenly. Others arrive stealthily. The most startling ingredient of 1967 made itself known a year earlier. Having mailed another manuscript to London (three short novels called *The Presence of Music*), I was at a loss about what I should do with my future. The difficulty wasn't a dearth of ideas; this time I had too many entrenched in my typewriter. Two were unusually tempting. One was a novel based on a wild dolphin which swam into the Hokianga harbour and befriended the human race while Gillian and I were holidaying there ten years before. The material was literally spellbinding. It had also been worrying at me for years, not least because Patrick White had confided an interest in it too. The other idea, also with comic possibilities, also nagging at me, was a novel based on a New Zealand prison escaper named George Wilder who made a folk-hero of himself in the early 1960s. His acrobatic breakouts from prison – and his long spells at large – had New Zealand enthralled. It seemed no prison could curb him. This antipodean Jesse James had accumulated something like six hundred convictions – mostly for car theft and petty burglaries while on the run – and thirty years in sentences. That was much longer than most murderers were incarcerated. Feeling for his plight was such that people left notes on the doors of their holiday homes, telling the fugitive how to break in without smashing windows and where to find food and drink. He was held in high esteem – as 'Gentleman George' – for the thoughtful domestic touches he added to his escapes. He scrupulously washed the dishes and swept the floor before departing from an appropriated dwelling. Rumour had him sending flowers to little old ladies whose vehicles he had uplifted. His notes of apology were frequent. In the eyes of his enthusiastic audience, if not of the police, George could do no wrong. His fame was becoming international. London's *Guardian* had recently run a three-column story on the elusive desperado. It seemed the sale of movie rights couldn't be far off. There were the makings of social comedy in this. There were also literary associations. An expert bushman and hunter, George appeared to personify the 'man alone' whom literary critics identify lumbering through New Zealand literature again and again, usually in settings rich in romantic detaiI. I saw myself having a fictional feast with such a figure. The mystery was that no writer had yet been tempted to make something of the man; he was there for the taking.

Around 1967, however, I decided in favour of the dolphin story. Or my conscious self did. My subconscious had another view of the matter; my hidden half was fashioning a very different fiction. In 1966, then, I had an unusually vivid dream. I was in a prison cell, sharing it with someone I knew to be Wilder. (Was I a prisoner too, locked up with him? In that respect the dream was far from informative.) I was looking over his shoulder at a painting which sat before him. I knew it to be his painting: a landscape of sorts. There was sturdy forest and, as I remember, a river fringed with feathery New Zealand toetoe. He continued to paint with extreme concentra-tion as I watched. I couldn't see his face, but that seemed not to matter; we appeared to know each other. At that point I woke. I judged the dream interesting, But what was it about? The question left a disconcerting silence. George Wilder, at that time, couldn't have been be less on my mind. I found no palatable explanation.

In late June of 1967 I spoke at a literary luncheon, drumming up interest in *The Presence of Music*. In the course of my talk, trying to lighten it with a little humour, I said that there had to be some significance in the fact that, aside from Everest conqueror Edmund Hillary, New Zealand's one undisputed national hero was prison escaper Wilder (who while on the run had scaled a few heights himself.) What, I asked, did this say about New Zealanders? (I suggested that it meant folklore was still alive and well in New Zealand.) The sally made for some laughter; it also made an appearance in an extract from the talk published in *The Auckland Star*. Three days later my telephone rang. There was a hesitant, elderly and female voice at the other end: 'Mr Shadbolt?'

'Yes?' I said.

'I feel you should know that George is most upset about what you said about him.'

'George?' I said. 'George?' What was the woman talking about?

'George Wilder,' she said. 'He read what you said about him in the *Star*. He was extremely upset. Especially because he was in the middle of reading a book of yours. Among the Something.'

'*Among the Cinders*,' I suggested.

'That's the one. He was in the middle of reading *Among the Cinders*. Then you went and said this about him.'

I had a sick feeling. Though I didn't see that I had said anything reprehensible, I also failed to notice that George Wilder was more than a symbol of something or other, more than a plaything of a long-winded novelist looking for a lively theme; that there was a vulnerable human being confined in a joyless maximum security cell in a dismal Victorian fortress. Such an individual, sensitive to his surroundings, might see malice where none was meant. Such a man, locked up twenty-three hours a day, had reason to dwell on misuse of his name. He was entitled, if anyone was, to a mite of paranoia. There was a song about him on the New Zealand hit parade. Poet Jim Baxter, in the wake of the prison riots in 1965, during which Wilder was alleged to be a ringleader, had romantically styled him New Zealand's Spartacus. (This was pushing it. George was hardly to be seen as a gladiator rolling back the Roman Empire.) Another writer, Mike Doyle, had written a poem for him. Wilder was not only seeping into New Zealand folklore. One way and another he had become a cultural icon too. George, to his lasting credit, couldn't make much sense of this. I am not even sure that he knew what a folk-hero was. He was certainly perplexed by the people claiming to be on his side and volunteering food, drink and warm clothing when he was off on his unlawful travels.

The female voice on my phone began again. 'George,' she said, 'is going through a bad time. Joking about his situation doesn't help.'

'Please pass on my apologies,' I said. 'Is there anything I can do to help?'

'There is indeed,' she said. 'You could visit him and convey your apologies in person.'

That silenced me. 'When?' I asked.

'This Saturday,' she suggested. 'You might find it most interesting.'

I was sure I would.

'He's an artist, you know,' she added. 'Or wants to be.'

'Yes,' I said casually. 'I know.'

'You know?' she said with astonishment. 'How?'

At that point I bit back the rest of my reply. Know? How could I know? How *did* I know? Then I recalled my eccentric dream of Wilder painting in his prison cell. A hair or two rose on the back of my neck.

'I have no idea how I know,' I replied. 'I just happen to.' This was feeble. Fortunately the voice in my ear didn't pursue the matter.

'If you know he's an artist,' she said, 'then perhaps you also know that the prison authorities are refusing him paints and brushes. He's allowed pencils and crayons. That's all.'

'That,' I said, 'is preposterous.'

'But true,' she said. 'This Saturday, then?'

'This Saturday,' I promised.

I replaced the receiver, rather shaken.

Enid, George Wilder's regular visitor, was a nervous, neurotic and crippled woman of perhaps fifty. She was also a good Christian. That might have been expected. Less predictably, she was literally in love with George. Trying to protect him from the pains of prison, she became a roaring lioness. The moment the prison gate closed behind us she fell into a screaming fight with burly officials. They were attempting to confiscate some of the gifts she had brought, also a novel I intended to leave with George by way of atonement. I negotiated a truce in respect of the gifts. Finally we were escorted into the dank and dungeon-like maximum security block. Wilder and a dozen dangerous fellow long-termers, most of them convicted of murder, had been confined there since riot left the prison blazing. The place made most public urinals look elegant. Buzzers sounded as we entered; there was a crashing of cell doors. We took seats in a murky visitors' cubicle. Before us were bars and a sheet of bullet-proof glass in which a recording device was set. Everything we said would be taped and replayed to determine if anything suspicious had passed between George and his visitors. Who knew? Enid and I might be arranging George's next escape.

George finally came into view beyond glass and bars. He wasn't the sturdy figure I expected. He was also far from the daredevil escaper of the popular imagination. In poor-fitting prison denim, he had a pinched and sunless appearance. His face was bony, his eyes unnaturally bright. He was also surprisingly shy. Was this the man who, when whim took him, had the land in uproar and police and prison warders close to suicidal?

'I'm here to make apologies,' I explained.

'That's okay,' he said, and seemed to mean it.

Technically we were allowed no more than a thirty-minute visit. A compassionate warder allowed us nearer an hour. We discussed the books he had been reading. We talked about the Braille books he compiled for the sightless five days a week. Finally we got round to the touchy subject of his art work. Though I couldn't think how, I promised to try winning him paintbrushes and paints. It seemed vindictive beyond belief that he wasn't allowed to develop as a painter. What could he do with a paintbrush? Paint a hole in the wall of his cell, Monty Python style, and then leap out? Prison officials had lost their nerve after George's last escape. They would now believe anything of their celebrated guest. Nor were they ones for risks. Their most watched television programme was one called *Mission Impossible*, full of dramatic escapes. The morning after an episode screened, warders would be out checking the thickness of the prison's walls and the resilience of its bars.

I became a regular visitor. I also visited Ron Jorgenson, George's neighbour in the maximum security block. A onetime seaman and boxer, Jorgenson was a different kettle of criminal. For one thing he was serving a life sentence for murder: for a Mafia-like machine-gunning of two men who ran a backstreet grog shop. Jorgenson's role in the affair was obscure; he claimed innocence. It is possible that he was, technically; that he was an accomplice after the fact and deserving of no more than a five-year sentence. Instead he had a life term. He too wanted to do some painting. A senior official informed me that no objects were innocent in prison. Even paintbrushes. There was no telling what they might lead to. Paintings, he said, could carry coded messages. The man was mad. He was also a fancy liar. He claimed that the sun reached into the maximum security block all year; that prisoners could sunbathe in its 16 x 10 ft exercise yards in midwinter. This was rubbish. I found an architect who could prove that the exercise yards were without sun for six months of the year. But there was little I could do with the information. A new prison was to be built in Auckland. This unsightly edifice would be electronically controlled and escape-proof. It had already been dubbed the George Wilder Rest Home, reached by way of George Wilder Avenue.

In August I travelled down to Christchurch to open a student art festival. There were perhaps five hundred people present. My speech was largely about the difficulties faced by practising artists and authors in New Zealand. Pretty ho-hum stuff. To enliven it I threw in a few words about George Wilder's difficulty in winning permission to paint in prison; I used him as a playful metaphor for the condition of the artist in New Zealand.

As I spoke, a hush grew. Few stirred. The silence was soon total. Fumbling with my notes, feeling I had gone beyond my brief, I decided to sit down. After a perplexingly pregnant minute, the applause rolled in. It rolled on and on. At least I seemed to have won someone's attention.

I had. There was a journalist present. I hadn't anticipated this. Possibly he was there to pick up a routine paragraph on the festival. Instead he saw a front page story. My speech lost nothing in his telling. Next day, up and down the country, there were further headlines. Anything to do with George Wilder was news. This was the next best thing to a new escape. The Minister of Justice, poor devil, was interviewed and invited to declare himself. Why was Wilder not allowed paints and paintbrushes? The man was deeply embarrassed. Sunday newspapers wallowed in the story too. They concentrated on my relationship with George. I pretended not to find anything remarkable in it. It was widely supposed that I was stalking Wilder for literary purposes; that he was going to figure in my next novel. I wished it were true. The novel I once fancied had long evaporated; fact had erased fiction. How create a fictional, possibly comic Wilder when I saw the real thing weekly?

A fortnight later George had enough paints and brushes to last a lifetime. So had Ron Jorgenson. Their subject matter was in keeping with their characters. George painted wistful landscapes, perhaps those he remembered from his imaginative excursions through back country New Zealand. Ron painted boxers and bullfighters. Though never a bullfighter, he was once a boxer. Not surprisingly both did a competent line in still life – after all, life was mostly inert in their cells. I took two distinguished painters, Colin McCahon and Garth

Tapper, along to the prison to give George and Jorgenson tuition. With the naive belief that confession never hurt, I also encouraged George with his pen. If he was going to write, I told him, then honesty was important, a respect for truth. I quoted from Shakespeare's last lines in *King Lear*:

Speak what we feel, not what we ought to say.

There was a puzzled silence for a time.

'I'm with you,' George decided. 'So I tell the truth.'

'And not what others want you to say. Not what they want to hear.'

A few days later some crumpled documents came into my hands via a clandestine prison channel. They were from George. He had been busy. Taking heed of my proposition that honesty was important, he had gone roaring off in pursuit of elusive truth for page after page. His prose didn't ask sympathy from his readers. He didn't beg for it either. There was no account of an unhappy childhood, a miserable adolescence or a misspent youth; there was none of the self-pity, none of the long-winded alibis one hears from seasoned criminals. He had no patience with inessentials. Honesty was a serious business. First he listed the crimes for which he had been tried and sentenced. Then, in a marvellous feat of memory, he detailed the crimes for which he had never been tried. There were scores of them looking for a home, or a story. The list went on and on. In the wrong hands the narrative might have meant another hundred convictions, possibly a longer prison term.

I was left shaken. On my next prison visit George asked, 'Well, what do you think?'

'It was interesting,' I said.

'Interesting?'

'It wasn't altogether what I had in mind,' I explained. 'You've taken truth a little too literally.'

'What's that mean?'

'That I was looking for something less straightforward.'

'You want me to have another go at it?'

'Not at the moment. Perhaps you should give writing a rest and stick with your paints for a bit.'

It wasn't an auspicious week for good deeds. Failing to introduce George to the arcane ways of literature, I burned the hazardous documents in my backyard incinerator.

On a visit to Wellington I met the Secretary of Justice, Dr John Robson, a decent sort of man (a Fabian socialist, or so I was informed) in connection with George's present situation. Was there, I asked, some chance of George being confined in more wholesome circumstances than his present tomb? With a view to his winning early parole?

Robson proved a kindly man, with a twinkle. Our conversation went something like this:

Robson: Of course I want to see Wilder out of maximum security. But how can I be sure that he won't escape again? All the reports I have say that he would.

Me: Well.

Robson: Can I be sure that Wilder won't escape again? Can you be sure?

Me: Reasonably sure. But it isn't something I can discuss with George, not with warders in earshot. He has his pride. He would lose prestige – both among warders and fellow prisoners – should he be overheard promising not to escape again. He might even lose respect for himself. As you know, he's something of a performer; he doesn't want to let down his audience.

Robson (wryly): I know.

Me: If I could communicate with him privately, freely, I'm sure I could win a promise not to escape again.

Robson: You think so?

Me: I'm sure so. It's worth trying. Surely there's room for a gentleman's agreement between George and the Justice Department.

Robson (surprised and thoughtful): A gentleman's agreement?

Me: Of sorts. If George could be let out of maximum security on the understanding that freedom wasn't far away, then I'm sure he wouldn't break out again.

Robson: Hmmm. And you think you might do it?

Me: Possibly.

Robson: Let me think about it.

Back in Auckland I decided not to wait. I had a covert line of communication to George anyway. It was in the form of a retired and widely respected educationalist named Kibblewhite – a former principal of Auckland Teachers' Training College – who visited George, without hindrance, once a week. He took in printed material which George translated into Braille. He also obligingly delivered my furtive and uncensored messages. We were both, Mr Kibblewhite and I, breaking the law. Caution was necessary. Cells were searched almost daily. The system was not altogether flawless. George and Jorgenson, with a little help from outside friends, had once managed to smuggle a half-bottle of vodka into their workroom, quaffing it between bursts of Braille. Their one problem was disposing of the empty bottle. It took them two or three days to grind it into pieces small enough to flush down their toilet. No one could say they hadn't earned their tipple.

My next message to George read thus:

Possibly nothing will come of this. [The visit to Robson.] You may be on his conscience, but he is limited by his responsibility to the Justice Department. If you were to come out of maximum security, and break out again, then many of his proposed reforms of the prison system would be in jeopardy. There would be more hue and cry and clamps would go on right through the prison system with many privileges lost. In a way they're on the hook as much as you are. What we have to do is find ways of letting them off the hook. Which means you would come off the hook too. I need an undertaking that you won't attempt escape again. Give me the undertaking and I can argue your case with confidence.

Mr Kibblewhite took this message to George and returned with a verbal one. George gave me a sober promise not to escape again. The battle was half won. George came out of maximum security. He was transferred to a more easy-going prison. If he behaved himself, and refrained from squeezing through bars, he would be out in a year.

In my most lavish literary fantasies I couldn't have envisaged myself negotiating between the Justice Department and a prison escaper. It seemed I had. I also had a fireside tale for my grandchildren. George was especially generous in providing me with details of his time at large.

Was it true, I asked, that he had often washed the dishes and swept the floors after making free with someone's beach cottage?

He didn't deny it. 'I'd be a bloody fool not to,' he said. 'I didn't leave clues around.'

What about sending flowers to little old ladies?

Nope. For the same reason. He tried not to leave tracks.

So much for folklore; so much for Gentleman George.

There was, though, one piquant item. He had never been able to steal a car if there was a child's teddy bear or doll in the back seat, any evidence of children in the vehicle at all. George couldn't explain this, though a psychiatrist might.

Had he ever given himself a fright while on the loose? Well, yes, he admitted sheepishly. Looking for something edible in the glove box of a purloined car, he pulled out a human skull. He had no idea how it got there. Perhaps it was the property of a doctor, an anatomist in medical school. It was a most salutary reminder of his mortality. At all events he began to drive at a more moderate pace even with police cars close behind.

I managed to write, if less confessionally than George, in that untidy year. I pushed the manuscript of *Strangers and Journeys* along another chapter or two. It was painfully slow. Life had its familiar trip wires in place.

So had death. My loved uncle, Joe Kearon, was going downhill. There had been two heart attacks. A third would finish him. My doctor shook his head when I discussed Joe's prospects. I tried to persuade him to come and live with Gillian and me and the children at Titirangi. He stubbornly declined the offer. If Joe had been a fictional character – not my real-life bachelor uncle and surrogate father – I would admire his tenacious independence. At my desk, with my typewriter clicking, I might make it appear altogether admirable. Instead his obstinacy had me on my knees. Alas, yet again, for fiction. In the days left to us I managed to tell him how much he had meant to me; that I had always thought of myself as his son. He in turn confessed that he had many times thought of himself as my father. We were in tears as we talked.

I was loaned a beach house south of Auckland. It had the quiet I needed. At a distance from daily routine my problems might seem less mountainous. Meanwhile I went to Wellington to pick up another Katherine Mansfield award, this time for my short story 'Figures in Light' in *The Presence of Music*. It was my second such award in four years. This time, however, no spectral Mansfield put in an appearance The one rather unusual result was that the rules of the award were revised to ensure that I didn't win it a third or fourth time. The feeling was that the current rules gave me unfair advantage. This was mysterious, and certainly original. Did I have some kind of hotline to Katherine? (She telling me what to write, how to win?) The award did less for my morale than I should have liked. For one thing it reminded me that I hadn't written a short story in three years; there was reason to suspect that the prizewinning piece might be my last. It nearly was. It was all of thirty years before I published another. Appearing in more tolerant times, that earned a Mansfield award too.

Two days later, wrestling with a recalcitrant paragraph, I had a telephone call from Auckland hospital. Joe had suffered another heart attack and was unlikely to survive the day. I reached his bedside in time to share the last minutes of his life. The first of my fathers was dead. Duty wasn't. In other words it was time to finish *Strangers and Journeys*, time to make their lives seem worthwhile. No excuses now. No diversions.

I was the one with the typewriter.

Twenty-six

Summer arrived according to cantankerous custom. First storm, then peace. It was worth waiting on. I took my sons, Sean almost eight, and Brendan touching six, on a camping trip to the Bay of Islands. We pitched pup-tents on the edge of a horseshoe beach. Large fish cruised transparent sea; we pursued them excitably with rod and spear. Yachts glided on a glimmering horizon. The rocks were white with oysters: their taste tended to confirm that God's cuisine had been at its majestic best in that vicinity. We saw no one, talked to no one other than the Danish potter who functioned as caretaker of the property we camped on. It was the site of a collapsed commune: his fellow communards had called quits. Their jerry-built buildings were slowly subsiding. Shattered pottery mixed with the debris of Maori middens looked likely to drive future archaeologists to drink.

Something was going on in the outside world, and I couldn't interpret it. The batteries of my transistor radio were too weak to carry comprehensible news bulletins. It was plain, however, that the war in Vietnam, after a year or two smouldering, was blazing again. Something soon to be called the Tet offensive was in progress. Casualties were immense and mounting. The American embassy in Saigon had been stormed. American propagandists were busy trying to make the best of a bad thing. I chased the boys to bed early so I could eavesdrop on the slaughter. It became clear that the climax of the war had been reached. In the morning I woke grateful that the guns were roaring elsewhere, not near my sons; I rejoiced in the innocent sound of my impatient boys breaking open our food supplies. (Sleepy Dad was slow getting breakfast.) I hoped that they would never know anything other than peace.

The next day, but for blurred communiques from a far land, was no less exquisite. The boys gambolled at the sea's edge; I fitted them out with goggles and flippers and taught them to snorkel. Otherwise I read. Now and then, though, I looked up from my book as if the sky might begin to darken. I wasn't looking for harmless raindrops. Against my will I was meditating on the madness of my species.

I hoped the boys might remember that week with affection. The sunny week of the Tet offensive, that was, and that bewitching bay. Was it there? Though I was never happier, I already seemed to have dreamed it.

My novel *This Summer's Dolphin*, chapter after chapter, and almost without my noticing, had begun to take on a dark shade. The Vietnam war coloured it. What else? Protesters, to my surprise, overran the narrative. Where had they sprung from? I didn't recall inviting them aboard. But there they were, with banners and burning flags.

Return to Titirangi killed the lingering exhilaration of that holiday with my sons. A loud and smoky party was in progress. The household was all but unrecognisable. The twins were distressed, soon the boys too. The music was deafening, punctuated by stamping feet. Long-haired strangers scrutinised us as if we were strangers. Perhaps we were. The 1960s had begun eroding my world. It was plain that 1968 would be the last of my fifteen years of marriage.

There was a large international conference in Wellington devoted to the issues of war and peace. Having just finished *This Summer's Dolphin*, and in need of relief from domestic trauma, I decided to drive down there with friends. Among the many outside dignitaries parading across the platform were Krishna Menon of India, the Irish writer and politician Conor Cruise O'Brien, late of United Nations peacemaking in the Congo. The New Zealand government had tried and failed to silence them by denying organisers the U.S. currency needed to mount the conference and fly in outside speakers. It seemed possible that Prime Minister Holyoake wasn't responsible for this heavy-handed strategy. Labour politician Martyn Finlay told me that Holyoake continued to be equivocal about New Zealand involvement in the war. Large demonstrations – and events like this conference – helped him along. He could tell American visitors that, for domestic reasons, he was unable to provide more New Zealand troops.

Suddenly and surprisingly there was no point in the conference. Lyndon Johnson, a wrecked man, was not to stand for the US presidency again. The Tet offensive had done its worst. For a giddy moment it appeared that the war might be over. Not won. Over. Certainly the prepared speeches had to be hastily rewritten. I trashed mine and took a long walk through the Wellington of my youth; I had a deep and futile wish to begin again.

A 1960s story; it happens, more or less, to be true. Three or four citizens of the Auckland art world, merrily in tune with the times, and here left nameless, decide to go back to the land, to live in the manner of their pioneer forefathers. They pool spare cash and buy up a hundred scruffy acres and a farmhouse north of Auckland. They plan to use the property as an occasional retreat, a secular monastery. With this social experiment barely begun, their dwelling is vandalised. A caretaker looks desirable. The role might suit some indigent artist, without a reliable roof overhead.

The position falls to someone I shall call Steve. On the face of it Steve is an admirable candidate. An idiosyncratic if often pompous painter, Steve takes over the property. His benevolent sponsors at first have no complaint. Before long, however, Steve becomes overly possessive about the land. Visitors – especially the owners of the property – make him irritable. He has a garden flourishing and sheep grazing. Visitors might trample his vegetable patch and panic his livestock. Steve warns intruders away with obscenities and promises of violence. Finally he starts hurling rocks. When he runs out of rocks he discharges a shotgun.

After an anguished year the dilettante countrymen abandon their project. Though it wasn't quite the Tet offensive, and there was no body count, Steve emerges the winner. So does the decade.

With my marriage barely going through the motions I recognised myself, in coded form, within a Marilyn Duckworth short story published by *The Listener*. If I wished I could interpret it as a call for help. I began a reply but failed to finish it. It was now six years since I last saw her. I had been told that she was married again, with two more children. She might have been happy. Her short story didn't suggest it.

In the middle of 1968 I moved out of the marital dwelling and twenty miles into the forested Waitakere Ranges. I explained to the children that I wouldn't be far away. That was half true. But when I went to bed, my first day away from home, the children seemed on the far side of the moon; I was sick with grief. In the ranges, among drifts of mist, I lived and wrote in a potters' commune. Jeff Scholes, a talented potter who aspired to write, and hoped my presence might be helpful, had found a place for me in a rambling and many-windowed house overlooking Auckland. Each of us (there were five) worked quietly through the day. In the evenings there were often visitors, mostly potters. One or two musicians. One writer. There was no ideology involved in this collective. It simply provided a monastic atmosphere in which to work. I was soon addicted to the homely rhythm of the potters' life, to the preparation of the clay, the working of the clay, the biscuit firing, then the final firing. Jeff strummed a guitar while he waited on the kiln to harden his pots. On occasion he resumed one or other of his many love affairs. Most left him mournful. Currently he was grieving for the loss of a female academic. She had just flown off to England, the common fate of Jeff's women.

'There are more fish in the sea,' I tried to tell him.

He shook his head sadly and went back to his wheel. On the other hand, his pots were at their shapely best that week.

At an unfamiliar desk *Strangers and Journeys* briefly came to life again. Then it went into spin like a pot wobbling out of control on Jeff's wheel; I couldn't see where the novel was going, if anywhere. There was much to be said for the potter's life. Potters knew what they were going to finish up with. I didn't, likewise most writers I knew. That difference divided artist from craftsman. A craftsman knew, more or less, what his finished product would be. An artist, a painter or novelist, never knew; he leapt into void in the hope that something of worth might be won. I found myself thinking idly of a fictional potter. Not cheerful guitar-strumming Jeff. A man with a past. Who knew? I might live to write it. Or was that unwarranted optimism?

It turned out not to be. Those months, marooned among potters, seeded my novel *A Touch of Clay*. Otherwise there is no accounting for it.

Driving around the Bay of Plenty, I made a detour to visit Sylvia Ashton Warner for the first time in years. Her husband Keith had recently died. In the meantime she had grown even more remote from the commonplaces of existence. I might have guessed this from the tenor of her passionate personal communications. Those to me were inscrutable love songs, complete with music What was going on here? In her presence I frequently had the feeling that I was due to become an antipodean eccentric too. I had barely got my foot in her door when she announced, 'I'm so glad you've come. I've been hoping to see you.'

Hoping?

'What for?' I asked.

She leaned forward confidentially. 'I've become an alcoholic,' she disclosed.

'You?'

'What is more, I've stopped drinking as from today.'

'Good God,' I said.

'True,' she said. 'Look around.'

I looked around. It was true that there were a number of beer bottles on view in her seaside studio. Some were still full. Most were empty.

'Help yourself,' she said. 'I can't get rid of them. I can't drink them up alone.'

'Nor can I,' I pointed out. 'I have some driving to do.'

'Even better,' she said. 'You can heap them into the back of your station wagon, find somewhere to dump the empties, and drink up the rest. You'd do that for me, wouldn't you?' she added sweetly.

'Of course,' I said.

'I've always said you were my very special friend,' she reminded me. 'Please help yourself to one of those bottles. And while you're at it, open a last one for me.'

Later that day I drove home with the sound of clinking bottles in my wake, a crazed bottle merchant on the loose.

The story was to become murkier. Next day, so I learned later, Sylvia's best woman friend paid a call.

'I almost gave up drinking yesterday,' Sylvia confided.

'Really?' her friend ventured. 'And what happened?'

'Maurice Shadbolt called in and got me drunk,' Sylvia explained. 'Not content with drinking me out of house and home, he grabbed up whatever was left and carried it off.'

Twenty-seven

Life among Auckland's high western hills wasn't all work. Jeff and I sometimes ended monkish isolation by driving down to Auckland to parties, movies, musical evenings, gallery openings. All the same, I remained heartsick. I met up with a plump and ebullient painter – powerfully engaged with Biblical themes – named Michael Smither. Michael did much for my morale. We found many things in common. We had both been given a rough ride by New Zealand's critical mafia. In Michael's case the establishment didn't concede that he existed. In mine they merely wished me dead. We both had the water-worn terrain of Taranaki in common. We both had a guerilla war with God in progress. In other respects too our aspirations were similar. In my case I wished New Zealand to leap off the page; he wanted to paint it down to the last pebble. (His rock paintings, deriving from Taranaki's stony coast, are among his most memorable.) I gave him the manuscript of my new novel, *This Summer's Dolphin*. Might he, I asked, try a dustjacket in the mode of his recent religious paintings? After all, the novel was about a quasi-spiritual event, the arrival of a enigmatic dolphin in a remote New Zealand community and its effect on the humans of that community. He decided he might. After reading the novel he went one better. He enthusiastically planned a large-scale exhibition based on the book. What I didn't know, and couldn't, was that Michael was an accomplished diver and swam often with dolphins. It seemed a good and sufficient omen – for the novel, his exhibition, and our friendship.

New people impinged refreshingly on my life. At another function I found myself in animated conversation with a petite blonde woman named Beverly. A nurse of Scandinavian origin, lately parted from a difficult husband, she had a winning smile. It won me.

Then I heard a third voice near my right ear. It was not one I had heard before. Nor could it be ignored. 'Careful,' I heard it say. 'You just might finish up with this woman.'

Her? Me? We had been acquainted for fewer than ten minutes. I turned around. There was no one there.

Absurd, I told myself. An auditory illusion.

We talked a minute or two more. Did I look shaken? I was. I let Jeff drive me home.

A month after my move into the Waitakeres I had a visitor. Beverly stood at the door. She had driven twenty miles in the hope that I might be at home and in need of company. I was demonstrably at home. I was also short on company. She had the ingredients of a picnic, including a bottle of wine. We drove off to the nearest beach. Surf roared up an empty shore; spray drifted high. Sunset was as splendid.

On a spring Saturday I helped Colin McCahon hang a new exhibition. He had gone back to the landscapes of his youth, to Otago rendered in cold and monotone colours. None of the written proclamations which distinguished much of his work; no religion. Just landscape with no mark of man. Was Colin viewing death from close quarters? I was not sure we were good for each other. Yet with his busy brushes he transformed an old and battered cocktail bar in my studio, where I stored manuscripts and relaxed with friends, into a thing of joy.

That cryptic voice to the rear of my right ear proved well informed. Before 1968 was out Beverly and I were living together. We rented a sunny flat in a residential street in Parnell. Hanging curtains, on our first day of occupation, I saw a car stop on the far side of the street. It was a familiar vehicle, an ageing yellow Skoda owned by my neighbour and frequent confidante Dick Scott. We had not seen much of each other since my departure from Titirangi. Dick was soon to be seen crossing the street briskly. I was tempted to flee, to dive out the back door and hurdle a few suburban fences. Dick was surely going to remind me, in fatherly fashion, of my domestic responsibilities; to urge me to return to wife and children in Titirangi. I didn't flee. I couldn't flee. Finally, however, I shook off paralysis and opened the front door.

If Dick's mission was to win me back to the ranks of the righteous, he went about it in surprisingly sunny manner. He sidled into the flat without interesting himself in my domestic circumstances; there was no more than a nod in Beverly's direction. Then he took a chair.

'I'm here on Henry's behalf,' he announced.

I failed to understand. Henry? Henry was a mutual friend. But what the hell had he to do with my adulterous dalliance in a Parnell flat?

Dick went on, 'Henry has been having trouble with his wife.'

'Ruth?' Ruth was another mutual friend. I managed an expression of shock. I also wondered when Dick was going to get to the point.

'She's been carrying on with someone,' Dick explained.

'Ruth has?'

'She has,' he confirmed.

'I'm sorry to hear it,' I said with genuine regret. 'With who?'

'With me,' Dick said.

'You?' I said faintly.

Understanding dawned. Dick was not in the least interested in my situation or in giving me fatherly advice. Why should he be? His concerns began to look more knotty than mine.

'Henry needs your help,' Dick informed me. 'He wants you to witness him discovering Ruth in bed with me. For legal purposes of course. Henry wants a quick divorce. If you're worried, it's all very amiable.'

Those were the days when only an efficiently staged adultery would win a painless divorce. Henry was obliged to play aggrieved cuckold; I was to be a responsible observer. That night we waited for lights to be extinguished in a city flat. Then we pounced. After judging the sight disgusting, Henry and I were rewarded with champagne for our night's work.

'People are curious,' Beverly decided.

She wasn't. She trailed serenity, at least through my life.

It was also more complex than she knew. In fact, not in a piece of legal theatre, Dick and Ruth had yet to share a bed seriously. I wouldn't have guessed. People were curious.

At the year's end, in the Christmas break, my son Sean and I kept a rendezvous with Michael Smither and journeyed down the coast to Tauranga. For my dustjacket and his next exhibition Michael wanted to try his hand painting dolphins in Tauranga's marineland. He fitted himself into scuba gear and jumped into the dolphin pool. Sean and I followed. The dolphins circled Sean playfully. There was no doubt which human was their favourite. For a few bewitching minutes the classical tales about boys and dolphins came to life. Having worked out with Sean, the dolphins began posing for Michael. They looked over his shoulder to see what he was up to with waterproof crayon and white boards as he sat bubbling on the pool floor. They appeared mightily impressed. So they should. Michael was excited by the prospect of an artist communicating with fellow mammals. In the process he became a spirited sea creature himself. Would that more of life was made of such as this. We were meant to be there no more than a day. In the event we were there three. Michael's exhibition was on its way. I suspected that his images might overshadow my novel. Art had never known the like since classical times.

Back in Auckland, the Parnell flat, with Beverly waiting, seemed like home. I had done nothing to deserve such tranquillity. The idyll was too good to be true; too good to last

There was a mystery in Beverly. Since she made no attempt to conceal it, I couldn't help noticing that she was frequently in receipt of fat packages of British currency. These did much to keep us in credit with the corner grocer. In other circumstances I might have thought the money suspect, perhaps from a drug deal. That supposition didn't suit her character. I waited for her explanation, if there was to be one.

Eventually there was. One summer dusk, as we walked a beach, she began unburdening herself. I heard a story whose plot was a steal from a Henry James novel – of old world perfidy and new world innocence. Working in an English hospital, Beverly had as one of her patients an Englishman named Crabtree, many years her senior and a well-known executive in British industry. She happened to be at his bedside when he went into cardiac arrest. She professionally thumped his heart into life again, in the process breaking a rib or two. That did it. Mr Crabtree was now obsessively in love with her. Out of hospital, he pursued her with flowers, expensive clothes and jewellery and more and more money until her own marriage blew apart under his pressure. Crabtree's marriage, with a large dollop of discretion, survived. His wife, if she knew, possibly accepted the liaison. Beverly succumbed to his blandishments. As time passed, however, she became aware that Crabtree was nudging her toward his son. The man's intention was plain. He wanted to keep his doll-like acquisition in the family. How better to do this than to marry her off to his son? Understanding this, and horrified, she booked a flight home to New Zealand. But Crabtree kept her on his payroll, so to speak. Hence the packages of money with expressions of passion. There was also an English bank account in her name. Should she return to England, she would have a house and car. Presumably, however, this was conditional on her marrying Crabtree junior and resuming her intimacy with Crabtree senior.

This far she hadn't been snared. She confessed, however, to moments of weakness.

'I'm sure,' I said, and wished I could say more.

Out of steam, *Strangers and Journeys* was stationary, shunted into an obscure down-country siding. Not for the first time Michael Amato came to my rescue. It was more than six years since his death. In every one of those years I had promised myself to look at his life again – especially in late 1944 and early 1945, when he floundered through wartime Italy, first with fascist militia, then with anti-fascist partisans. We had, Michael and I, anticipated our present situation. I had given him permission to make fictional use of my life should I predecease him. He had given me permission to make use of his should he die first. Had the time come? His posthumous volume of short stories, which Ian Cross selected and I introduced, had just appeared. Something else signalled that it was time to do more with my memories of Michael. Sheena, Michael's widow, was just back from a visit to Italy. Her meeting with Michael's family had been an excruciating experience. Shocked by her informal dress, especially her skimpy bathing costume, his Italian family denounced her as a whore. Nor was financial help forthcoming. His parents and siblings weren't interested in Michael's New Zealand years. They didn't care what he had been up to there and didn't read anyway. They even remained indifferent to his now teenage son. Sheena surmised that Michael had been the black sheep of the family. Since then she had met and married an Italian doctor, the first sympathetic Italian she had met since Michael's death. Alone in Italy, Sheena fell into his arms. She now had some notion of why Michael fled Italy. Sheena and her spouse planned to live in New York. Some of my past would go with them.

More to the point, she had done much checking on Michael's past. I miraculously got some things right in my obituary and later in my memoir. I also got several things wrong. There was only one remedy. That was a novel. Even Sheena saw it now.

Strangers and Journeys was again nudged aside. As summer arrived I sifted through Michael's literary detritus. Then I began work on the novel I named *An Ear of the Dragon*. My second bite at the apple had more teeth. It also did justice to Michael. Sheena herself was never to see justice done in whole or part, and never in his native Italy. Death – a second death, this time her own – obliged her to leave Michael's life to me. She outlived him by little more than a decade.

I left Beverly in our Auckland flat and began travelling with an American photographer. This time it was for an assignment on the renaissance of the New Zealand Maori. We zig-zagged down country, visiting locations of Maori legend, hunting with Maori bushmen, netting with Maori fishermen, interviewing and photographing tribesmen both illustrious and humble. In a tiny coastal hamlet named Tikitiki, on the North Island's east coast, I stumbled on an elderly and impish Maori carver named Pine Taiapa. Lean, garrulous and rich in stories of his race, he seldom drew breath. Before the end of our first day together – a day which lasted long after midnight – we looked likely be friends for life. He not only explained what his life had been about. More marvellously, he helped me understand what mine was.

Pine's lifelong mission had been to rescue the arts and crafts of the Maori from oblivion; to preserve the narratives of his race in wood with adze and chisel. His storytelling carvings now enriched more than a hundred Maori buildings. These opulently embellished and hauntingly carved edifices – or whare whakairo – functioned as a giant book of life, love and death, a treasure house of heroic traditions and mighty forebears. Every notch, every curve, was meant to reinforce pride of tribe.

It seemed my mission was not dissimilar. *Strangers and Journeys*, the novel I had been eight years writing and two failing to finish, might be seen as my meeting house, my whare whakairo, the meeting place of *my* tribe. Pine gave me a clue to my condition. Though slow discovering it, I was a tribesman too, a Polynesian pale in colour.

I was puzzled by the absence of carvings in his spartan cottage. There wasn't a scrap of his work on show. Why?

'Giving is what art is all about,' he informed me. 'If someone admires a carving of mine, I give it away. If an artist ceases to give, he dies as an artist.'

Pine had never been affluent. Nor, on present showing, was I likely to be. After that first meeting Pine and I remained in touch. His letters were lively. He insisted that he had more to give me, more to share. I wrote a piece on Pine for the *New Zealand Listener*, calling the attention of my fellow countrymen to the fact that there was an adze-wielding giant abroad in the land, chanting the old songs of his race as he chipped. This pleased him; it pleased me even more.

My journeying ended abruptly, in Invercargill, about as far south as I could go. ('The world's last lamp post,' said Rudyard Kipling.) I called home to find how the children were. Brendan answered. He told me that the house was full of unfamiliar people. There was din in the background, the 1960s still in full swing. Brendan had to shout to make himself understood. 'Dad,' he asked, 'why aren't you here?'

An hour later I was on a plane bound for Auckland. Beverly was waiting at the airport. She now knew that I could offer no permanence; that children came first. Mr Crabtree, he of the packaged pound notes, was the clear winner on points. She bought an air ticket to England and began packing her bags. Gillian had wisely absented herself from proceedings. Beverly valiantly helped me with the children until she herself left. Then my mother lent a hand. Otherwise I was alone with four children.

Chicken after chicken fluttered home to roost. The rest of the year was no improvement. Beverly, distant in England, communicated frequently, if more and more faintly. She offered to return to New Zealand and help with the children. Did she mean it? I was never to know. As she sped to a travel agent fate halted her cruelly; she crashed her shiny new car and woke in hospital with multiple injuries. Close examination disclosed a cancerous growth. Though operable, it meant a hospital stay still longer. Soon afterward came the news she was marrying Crabtree junior. Marilyn Duckworth, now free to see me, waded into my marital mire and attempted consolation. Peace of mind, however, was still out of reach.

For sanity, with children asleep, I continued to work. The proofs of *This Summer's Dolphin* were read and corrected and sped to London and New York; warm responses followed. The final chapters of *An Ear of the Dragon* arrived with a rush. Emboldened, I stole glances at the bulky manuscript of *Strangers and Journeys*. All I needed was a little less theatre in my life.

Meanwhile *This Summer's Dolphin* was launched. Eric McCormick the country's most generous man of letters, enriched the occasion with a wry, witty speech. The launch featured Michael Smither's magnificent dolphin paintings. Several sold. Copies of the book too.

Then we staggered into the midwinter Auckland night. As usual I had a sense of loss, the kind which comes when a book has wandered off alone into the world. But this time there was worse to worry me. My unkempt existence, for example. My children too. I was a character in another novelist's novel.

With my parents baby-sitting, I sometimes managed a trip to town in search of conversation less juvenile and domestic. On one jaunt, I bought a drink for a friend of my Dunedin time: Barbara Magner, once a promising actor and lately a much-loved television journalist.

Coincidence was at work again. Barbara and I had both separately and recently been involved with Pine Taiapa. Her documentary on the life and times of the great-hearted carver had just been screened in London by the BBC.

At that time she was shakily recovering from a long-lived affair. So, for that matter, was I. I invited her out to Titirangi the following weekend. The children loved the pretty television lady Dad had brought home; she struck all the right notes on family picnics and trips to the beach. Above all she was funny, which Dad hadn't been for too long.

Sean was the first to grasp the situation.

'Is Barbara staying?' he asked.

A good question.

'With luck,' I said.

'Good,' Daniel said, and planted himself on Barbara's knee. Then thoughtful Tui climbed aboard too.

In an attempt to win sanity from my situation I gave marriage a last chance. Gillian was now in Wellington. I rented out the Titirangi house and travelled south with the children. It was soon plain, however, that no marital accord could be reached. Jim Baxter was witness to our separation agreement. He was now, to the suspicion of many, attempting to wean junkies from their perilous pastimes much as he had nursed drunkards into sobriety as an Alcoholics Anonymous troubleshooter. Most of his friends, even those who respected an enterprise based on Christian compassion, saw Jim as out of his depth. Junkies weren't to be equated with run-of-the-mill drunkards. These lost children, the nga mokai (the fatherless ones) as he styled his growing flock, had a large talent for self-deception; and an even greater aptitude for deceiving others, notably Jim. Their crash-pads, where Jim played barefoot and bearded guru, were to spawn drug dealers as deadly as any in the business. Gillian, with the best of intentions, was now on the margin of Jim's hazardous enterprise. I judged it no place for a wife and mother. Nor was it an auspicious setting for reconciliation. Jim's own marriage was wreckage. I wished he would give his own children half the affection he bestowed on his junkies. Was this fair? Possibly not. The decade was making me a dour conservative.

Through summer Barbara had chosen to keep out of my way. After a South Island holiday she arrived suddenly at our Wellington door. She needed only one look at us. The children were miserable. So was I. 'It isn't working, is it?' she said.

I couldn't argue. Three days later I aimed the car at Auckland. Her rescue successful, Barbara sat triumphant in the front seat. Back in Auckland we found a temporary residence in Titirangi not far from Arapito Road; this made change less a jolt for the children. The boys returned to their old school, the twins to kindergarten. There was also a cell-like room I could call my own. Trying to make sense of my world, I experimented with autobiography for the first time.

This helped. For much of my life I had been furnishing a mansion of personal mythology, my family lore: my whare whakairo. The exercise began early. When I visited my Welsh grandmother, in my infant years, she often took me to the cemetery to show me off to her deceased husband, an Irish master mariner, and to tidy his grave. I felt frustrated that I had never known him, that I had come along twelve years late. She caught me in the act of trying to disinter my ancestor, the better to know him, with my child's trowel. I eventually found pen and paper more suited to my scheme.

There is one thing I know. Much and perhaps even most of what I have written, these last forty years, seems to have had its beginnings before my twentieth year. As evidence I submit a short story, a winner of a school prize in or about my fourteenth year. Dramatically titled *Saved From the Hau Hau,* it took five pages to tell the story of one of the bloodiest episodes in the New Zealand wars, the Poverty Bay massacre of 1869.

In 1985, now fifty-three years old, I sat down at my desk and wrote a novel titled *Season of the Jew.* It too told the tale of the Poverty Bay massacre. Four hundred pages long, it also won a prize.

There was another curious item of schoolboy prose, artlessly titled *A Good Man.* A family saga in four pages, it told of a man convicted of theft in England and transported in chains to Norfolk Island and Tasmania. The narrative allowed him to escape to New Zealand, to make good and die a respected citizen. Though I couldn't know it then, this was my great-grandfather's story.

With domestic matters no longer urgent, Barbara and I began to welcome visitors. We even managed a party. The British novelist Anthony Burgess was one early caller. Ebullient and gnomic, he brought greetings from Patrick White in Sydney. Patrick had been a disappointment to Burgess. Until lately he had considered Patrick the greatest living writer in the English language. He seemed to have been expecting a laconic tearaway with a broad-brimmed hat, someone approximating the rugged Australian digger of legend. He hadn't foreseen an elderly, fussily feminine and asthmatic homosexual. Burgess couldn't cope with it; his antipodean idol came crashing down.

Was Burgess putting on a provocative act? Or was he as naive as he sounded? Since when was it impermissible for writers to be elderly, asthmatic and fussily feminine? Otherwise Burgess and I exchanged books and didn't come to blows. He was in New Zealand, on a side-trip from Sydney, to speak at a state-sponsored conference devoted to the arts; he had pertinent things to say, a worry to his sponsors. Governments, he told them, didn't want culture; they didn't want the arts. They wanted the *appearance* of culture; they wanted art in emasculated form. Real culture was subversive, and dangerous. Museum culture such as opera and ballet served the purpose of our political masters best. This left a reverberant silence in the conference hall. In the presence of wisdom, the organisers of the conference shuffled, clapped with reluctance, and looked at their feet.

Burgess and I must have enjoyed each other's company more than I noticed. Some weeks later I had a clipping from Sydney. It was an interview with Burgess. He informed his interviewer that I was the most promising writer he had met in Australia and New Zealand; the one writer in Australia and New Zealand unafraid of experiment. This was news to me. I concluded that Burgess was using a New Zealander's name to enrage Australians. He must have had some small success. As recently as 1996 an Australian journal was still claiming me as one of theirs. I was left to presume that Australia was running short of writers. Or did my new status derive from my discovery of convict antecedents?

The current year, 1970, moved toward its melancholy end. The twins began school in September. Along the way the boys took up rugby league. I coached their team. I was not knowledgeable about their code, having only played rugby union. But I had always thought league a faster, cleaner and more imaginative game.

The boys were hooked anyway. On the weekend I took them to senior club games and international clashes. They idolised a player named Roger Bailey whose skills with an oval ball were breathtaking. He was too original, too anarchic, for New Zealand selectors. They cruelly cropped this tall poppy from the New Zealand team. The boys were heartbroken. (They were learning that there is no justice in the world.) The following Sunday morning eight-year-old Brendan rose early and busied himself in the kitchen. The clashing of pot and pan suggested that something serious was afoot. He was certainly playing merry hell with Sunday morning.

I made a sleepy investigation. 'What's going on here?' I asked.

'Pancakes,' he explained.

'At this hour?'

'These ones are special.'

'Oh?' I said. 'How?'

'They're for Roger Bailey,' he announced.

'Roger Bailey?'

'To show we're sorry for him,' Brendan said.

That afternoon a sportswriter for the *New Zealand Herald* noted a tousle-headed youngster sprinting across Carlaw Park at the conclusion of the day's play and handing Bailey 'what appeared to be a present'. In fact it was a pancake-filled paper bag. God knows what Bailey made of the soggy gift. We didn't loiter to see. There could be the seed of a story here: 'Roger's Pancakes' perhaps.

My children were easy to love. Soon Barbara and I had the good sense to add another to our team.

A red-faced detective arrived on our doorstep, asking for George Wilder. 'I'm a great admirer of George myself,' the fellow claimed.

'Really?'

'Really.'

I didn't believe a word.

So what do you want him for?' I asked.

'A talk,' the fellow said.

I didn't believe that either. What was it now? Trouble wasn't unexpected. Six months out of prison, George was managing freedom poorly. Too many people were leaning on him, hoping his Robin Hood glamour might rub off on them. Not merely old associates in crime. Hippies too, and, no great surprise, Jim Baxter. Jim continued to insist on seeing bewildered George as an underworld saint. A week or two earlier I called on George without warning. A rather sly individual was also visiting. He shuffled off into the night when I arrived. George had a slightly furtive expression.

'Who was that?' I asked. 'The face was familiar.'

'Trevor Nash,' George told me.

'Trevor Nash? The safecracker?'

'Himself,' George confirmed.

George apart, Nash was then New Zealand's most talented felon, a specialist in blowing safes, confiscating payrolls and persuading juries of his innocence, something George seldom managed.

'Is it wise for you to be seeing him?'

'Trev's all right,' George claimed.

Trev demonstrably wasn't all right. As I fitted the pieces together later, Nash had arranged for George to pick up a vehicle crammed with stolen property. George incautiously obliged. But as soon as he approached the car, torches began flashing and men began shouting. George was in the middle of a stake out. He burst through the police cordon and sprinted into suburban Auckland, a couple of dozen constables in pursuit, and battled his way into West Auckland's familiar woodland.

171

Since I was conspicuously resident in that vicinity too, that did much to explain the detective on my doorstep. Had I been aiding and abetting the fugitive? Apparently satisfied that I hadn't, he left me alone. So did George. Besides he had enough hospitality on offer elsewhere.

It ended in court, with fluent lawyers, as such matters do.

I was a witness. I testified to the peer pressures on George since his release from prison. I also testified to hearing George say that he might be better off in prison after all.

It didn't help. George was recalled to serve his many sentences plus three years more. Nash, as party to the affair, got four years. He didn't blink an eye.

I walked away from the court with one of the lawyers involved.

'So what was that all about?' I asked.

'Jealousy,' he said.

'Jealousy?'

'Nash needs to be known as New Zealand's number one bandit. There is pride among thieves. Wilder imperils his reputation. Nash set him up.'

'Knowing he risked prison again himself?'

'He must have judged the risk worth it.'

It was too much for me. I never meddled as deeply in crime's realm again. Two or three years later George was paroled quietly. He turned up at my door with a wry smile. Newsmen were chasing him up and down the country. Busy shaking them off, he was still a little breathless. He stayed the night and in the morning went off to have breakfast with Eric and Myra McCormick. He reckoned the elderly couple the best possible cover until hue and cry died. We shook hands and I wished him luck.

'So where are you going?' I asked.

'Down country,' he said vaguely.

Folk-heroes are traditionally taciturn.

This time round he made a success of freedom. These days, or so I am told, he hunts deer and wild pig with policemen who once pursued him; his skills as a bushman remain respected. Not long ago he surfaced enigmatically in a collection of postmodern stories as a drifter on the Cote d'Azur. More recently (as recently as last week) he lived again, under an alias, in a highly successful New Zealand play. When I learned of this, my reaction was relief that someone had at last managed to preserve George on paper. I still think the Wilder story the best book I never wrote. This isn't altogether true. I wickedly gave him a cameo role in my 1980 novel *The Lovelock Version*. A 1998 reader's poll in the Auckland magazine *Metro* lately named him the country's favourite criminal. This suggests that it may be a long time before the popular imagination leaves George Wilder alone. He probably hasn't read much of what has been written about him since his heyday in the 1960s. Nor does he need to. He lived it. As for me, there are times when I have been better known as George Wilder's mate than as a novelist. I have no problem with that.

His prison companion Ron Jorgensen – he of the bullfight paintings – wasn't so lucky. Released, he went into the drug business. With arrest looming, he saw disappearance as desirable. His car was found dumped on rocks and washed by waves on a coastal highway. Nothing resembling a corpse was found.

I finished the rough draft of my autobiographical essay. It sped off in several versions, before I persuaded it to settle down and become, two decades later, a book named *One of Ben's*. My life seen with more clarity, I returned to *Strangers and Journeys* and watched it grow, rather exhilaratingly, sometimes of its own accord. My largest problem was the familiar one: money. Our situation was medium dire. To pay the bills I reviewed and wrote pieces on the Pacific for a flashy Hong Kong publication rumoured to be sponsored by the CIA. Beggars can't be choosers. For all I knew I might have written for Russian journals published under the umbrella of the KGB.

Jim Baxter at this point might have prayed for money and found angelic dollars raining down. With no divine contacts, I looked wistfully through my mail and uttered obscenities rather than prayers. In the end fate lent a compassionate ear. A note in the mail, towards the end of the year, told me that a *Reader's Digest* editor named Frank Devine, evidently a fan of my fiction, wanted to buy me a dinner. I had been down this glossy path before; riches were never there. This former world-travelling newsman for Associated Press was too stout for an angel and smoked a pipe. At the end of the dinner, his timing splendid, he challenged me to write a couple of stories for his journal. He guaranteed me US$300 for the two pieces, published or not. One on the dolphin called Opo; one on the elusive New Zealand shellfish called the toheroa. I couldn't take the man seriously. When the wine wore off the offer would be forgotten.

Still, *Strangers and Journeys* was the issue here. I needed income to see it through. News from Europe wasn't good. My first novel, *Among the Cinders*, had been doing well in Germany. At last count more than 100,000 copies had sold. This far, however, I hadn't seen a cent. My dipsomanic London agent, may God give her a hard time, remained reluctant to pay out. I learned, on the late side, that she had been drinking up the royalties of a good many authors. Things might have been worse, though it was difficult to see how. With a flash of inspiration I recalled the Devine offer. Three hundred guaranteed dollars was three hundred better than nothing. Nothing was what I currently had. I shouldered *Strangers and Journeys* aside and gave myself three days to earn the *Digest* guarantee. It wasn't worth spending longer on the two pieces. A week after I mailed them away there was a letter from Frank Devine. Within, was what looked to be a cheque for the promised three hundred dollars plus expenses. I looked again. I had missed a zero. The sum in question was three thousand dollars plus expenses. The stories had been bought. It was suggested that I might like to try a few others. Jim Baxter, at the top his form, couldn't have come up with a better miracle. I was in business again. So was *Strangers and Journeys*. Though sometimes tempted, I have never said an unkind word about *Digest* since.

Twenty-eight

'We must never leave Arapito Road again,' Brendan said as I backed our dusty car into our drive.

'No?'

'No,' he said firmly.

He wasn't the only one to have been counting the days.

'I promise,' I said. It was a promise I meant to keep. For adults as well as children the place oozed safety; we were no longer gypsies. We moved back to Arapito Road in the first week of 1971. The boys launched their Christmas canoe on the estuary. Barbara was busy establishing herself in the kitchen. I was reclaiming my work space. Change was in the wings. Barbara and I were six months away from a child of our own.

Meanwhile I turned to *Strangers and Journeys* again. Its length was even more daunting. It was something like seven hundred pages with at least another two hundred to come. I couldn't imagine a publisher taking it on. Yet it remained the book I was meant to write. 'Just the one bite at the apple,' my schoolmate Murray Halberg had promised the Olympic flame when he trotted out on to the Rome's *Stadium Olympico*. 'Just one bite.' That was my feeling too. My bite of the apple wasn't a gruelling 5000 metres. It was a manuscript ten years in the making and titled *Strangers and Journeys*,

By October the final draft was finished. There was one difficulty. While I had my head down my London agent had finally gone off on a climactic binge never to be seen again. With her had gone a large lump of my German royalties. Without an agent, and soon desperate, I decided I couldn't wait on a London publisher to come up with a contract. I handed the manuscript to the New Zealand branch of Hodder & Stoughton. The local editor, Neil Robinson, expressed

175

pleasure; the length of the manuscript didn't leave him distraught. First, however, he would have to hear what London thought. Must we wait? Yes; we must. While London deliberated, I contemplated my increasingly insolvent condition. Three stories for *Reader's Digest*, the subjects of my own choosing, saved the day. About the time my second daughter was born, Neil Robinson called.

'London says yes,' he informed me. 'We'll take it.'

It had taken five exhausting years, spread over ten, but my cup was running over. My new daughter was to take her first solo stroll in the world in the week *Strangers and Journeys* was published in London. We had named her Brigid Louise. Of all things she is now a most competent critic. She doesn't, fortunately, review her father as painstakingly as she might.

Pine Taiapa and I continued to exchange letters. He was about to carve his 103rd building. But this one was to be different. It was designed to serve urban Maori, not rural. And to serve people of several tribes, not one: all the Maori of West Auckland, my territory. Was I, Pine asked, interested in recording its beginnings? Could I pick him up and take him to Auckland for the dedication ceremony? I told Pine I would be with him in a couple of days.

It was a long and largely dark drive, most of three hundred miles, with wild-eyed cattle straddling the road. About midnight my headlights flashed over Pine's cottage. There was a hot meal waiting for me, and a bed. Ready for the trip to Auckland, Pine was all excitement. He confessed that he had lately been in a slump, ready to farewell his carving tools and forget his final building. Then a lucid dream told him that his ancestors approved of his life's work; the same dream said that for the sake of his people he mustn't stop now. This new project, as he saw it, would be a masterwork to crown his career. Leaping from one subject to the next, Pine gave me small chance to sleep. And he was at my bedside again when I woke. An hour later we were on the road north. As we travelled, Pine read from a manuscript which detailed his plan for his final whare whakairo. I recognised some of my own prose woven through his. He looked slyly sideward to see if I minded the minor plagiarism. I didn't. I was flattered. 'You will see this building grow,' he predicted. 'I will not.'

'Of course you will,' I argued.

Next day, in a scrubby field outside Auckland, the site for Pine's next and last building was blessed by a Maori clergyman. There were a dozen of us on hand for the ceremony. It was a spring day with the sun bursting through cloud. The omens were auspicious.

Afterwards I asked Pine if he wanted to be driven home to Tikitiki. He thought not. There were relatives to visit. I was never to see that amiable giant with adze and chisel again.

Death darkened the year early. Cancer claimed Pine with a rush at the beginning of the year; he was dead by the end of February. I had no message to say he was ill. Relatives tried to contact me, but by dialling the wrong number. They mentioned my name in the hope of Pine responding to it. This eventually won an unnerving rejoinder. His eyes opened feebly. 'Is Maurice dying too?' he asked.

'No,' a niece told him.

'Tell Maurice he is not allowed to die,' Pine said. 'He has too much to do.'

I got the message. Though I have had my difficulties I have also managed not to die. Death, as usual, hadn't played fair. Another friendship had been wrested from me before its meaning was seen. Thirty years later, it is now plain to me that as a novelist I remained most in debt to a weathered Maori carver; my business, like his, had been with the tales of my tribe.

Maori funerals – tangi – never fail to astonish me. Tititiki, an isolated community of a few dozen, played host to hundreds of mourners, bedding them, feeding them, entertaining them. All through a long day muddy cars spilled out mourners arriving to pay tribute to Pine, some from the furthest south of New Zealand. I thought it unlikely that I could explain what the man meant to me. I didn't try.

Twenty-nine

In June a proof copy of *Strangers and Journeys* had arrived from London. Because of a printers' strike Hodder & Stoughton allowed me only six days to read and correct some six hundred pages. At the end of my first desperate day of reading I collapsed in front of television. The small screen told me that protest boats were sailing toward the French nuclear test zone on Mururoa atoll. The aim was to shame the French and persuade them to call off their poisonous nuclear antics. Now the country's most spirited political activist, Barry Mitcalfe was prominent in the enterprise too, recruiting vessels and voyagers. He had most of the country roused. Away from the rugby field New Zealand had never been more unanimous. The anti-nuclear groundswell surprised indolent politicians. It also irritated New Zealand's cold war allies, notably Britain and the United States. It was a hint of things to come; it heralded New Zealand's renunciation of all things nuclear in the following decade. Glad of friends ready to risk their hides on my behalf, I toasted Barry with an exceptionally large whisky.

That whisky wasn't the end of it. The telephone rang at seven the next morning, soon after I had returned blearily to the proofs of *Strangers and Journeys*. It was Barry. Could I transport a Titirangi man – with provisions and marine equipment – to the port of Tauranga, where a protest boat was being manned and made ready for Mururoa? I explained my problem with the proofs of *Strangers and Journeys*, and that every minute was precious to me at the end of June; that I was busy putting ten years of my life on the line. Had it been any other week of the year I would gladly have helped. But not that week. Not with an insane deadline. That evening, feeling guilt, I surfaced fretfully from proofreading and rang Barry. I wanted to check whether he had received the provisions and equipment he needed. Instead I heard myself volunteering to crew a protest boat.

'No one expects you to,' Barry argued.

He was wrong on that score. I found that I expected myself to. Life seemed to be orchestrating a sequel to *Strangers and Journeys,* a postscript in which the world wrote itself large. It might be my one chance to be around.

Barry sailed for Mururoa two days later in a trawler called the *Boy Roel*. His was the second protest boat to leave. The first, a month earlier, was *Greenpeace III*. The vessel had been seized and the crew beaten up methodically by French commandos. That news left us with no illusion about the hazards ahead; protest voyaging was no jaunt. Barry sent me a last message. 'Make haste,' he urged. 'We can't let these bastards off the hook.' I did my best to oblige. I mailed the proofs of *Strangers and Journeys* to London and reported breathless for duty. I was assigned to *Tamure*, a 37-foot sloop with a reputation as an ocean racer. Its owner and skipper was a leathery engineer named Jim Sharp. Indignant with the way the French had savaged the crew of *Greenpeace III*, Jim had loaned his newly purchased yacht to the anti-nuclear movement. He had never taken a political stance in his life before; nor had he had much experience on the high sea. There were second thoughts in his face before we put a dozen miles to our rear. Then there was Jack Harker, our radio operator and the most improbable of voyagers. An angular and balding ex-navy man, with service under fire in the Second World War, Jack had a mystifying curriculum vitae. He distinctly wasn't the stuff of which reflexive protesters and routine banner-carriers are made. He was right-wing in every respect. He approved of apartheid in South Africa, white rule in Rhodesia. Though in favour of New Zealanders warring in Vietnam, that conflict was too much a coloured man's war for his liking. Nor did he have sympathy for the French Polynesians whose waters were befouled by nuclear testing. Most stunning of all, he also loathed protesters, especially the long-haired kind. (Fortunately my locks weren't long that day.) I pointed out that he was currently a protester, if minus long hair. Otherwise why was he here?

'To help you buggers out,' he claimed.

'That's all?' I said with some amazement.

'That's all,' he confirmed.

Didn't that, I asked, make him a protester?

There was a considerable silence.

'I'll have to think that one out,' he confessed.

'Don't take too long,' I suggested.

Jack was quiet again.

'Surely you've got some idea why you're here,' I persisted.

'To have a crack at the bloody French,' he replied.

This was alarming. Jack was missing his navy years. Unless I heard wrong, he was looking for a war.

To demonstrate his commitment he took me aside and asked how I felt about our having a revolver aboard.

I froze. 'You've got one?' I asked.

'I can arrange one,' he explained. 'No Frenchman is going to fuck about with me.'

'I don't think that's the idea,' I said. 'This is a peaceful protest.'

'Tell the French,' Jack suggested.

I decided to keep a eye on Jack and did; I felt around bunks and mattresses for a suspect bulge but found nothing. Looking back, however, I see Jack may have had an old sailor's intuition on his side. What I didn't know, what Jack couldn't either, was that the bomb-besotted French were determined to make an example of at least one protest boat to frighten off the rest. According to a document leaked to the French newspaper *Le Monde* years later, the French were already, in 1972, scheming to sink a protest boat with a bomb of the best quality. *Tamure* and its sister vessels would have been fatally in the firing line. Fortunately for the four of the *Tamure*, the French secret service didn't put its plan into operation that year. It did, however, thirteen years later. In 1985 the plan was reactivated and French frogmen sank the Greenpeace vessel *Rainbow Warrior* on the Auckland waterfront. A crewman was killed. It wasn't by chance. The intention was to behead the Greenpeace leadership. Fortunately the leaders were off at a farewell party. The bomb missed them by minutes.

The fourth in our party was our navigator, a lean, long-bearded and weathered Manxman, in his late thirties, named Jim Cottier. Jim was also cook, bottle washer and spare man, in many ways the soul of our enterprise. Vaguely hippy in appearance, a pacifist and vegetarian and distinctly a child of the 1960s, he was involved in a commune ashore, teaching delinquent teenagers seamanship and navigation. He made no secret of his ideals. Soured by the same decade, I played pessimist. But our arguments were amiable. And it wasn't long before I became a vegetarian too. Raising animals solely for slaughter – a wasteful procedure to produce protein anyway – seemed indistinguishable from all human abuse of the natural world.

Thirty

We sailed on July 17. For a time Great Barrier Island bulked to port. Then we were free of land, with just a lighthouse flashing to starboard. Soon that was gone too.

'On course for Mururoa,' Jim Cottier reported with satisfaction.

I had two-hour watches, four times daily, with occasional relief from Jim Cottier. My first stint, on our maiden night afloat, was less than exhilarating. At two, in the night's blackest hour, Jim Sharp called me to take the helm. 'Too far to port and we'll take water,' he told me. 'Too far to starboard and we'll jibe.'

He was vomiting wildly; the cockpit was already awash with bile. I had the impression that he was already losing interest in the fate of his vessel. Without another word said, he plunged into the cabin and crashed into his bunk.

The sea was seething. I became more and more aware of huge waves roaring to my rear. We weren't sailing. We were surfing. Conscious of my incompetence on the ocean, I was also aware that the lives of three unduly trusting men, deeply asleep in the cabin, now depended on me. Port? Starboard? Where the hell were they? Careering incoherently, *Tamure* was familiarising itself with every point of the compass. Unlike Jim Sharp, however, I managed to keep my dinner down.

Finally I estimated that my two hours on watch had passed; that it was time to hand the helm to Jack Harker. To establish this I shone a weak torch on my wristwatch. This was instructive. Fewer than twenty minutes had passed; I had one hour and forty minutes more at the helm. The rest was delirium. The nightmare was compounded, at 4 am, by my inability to rouse Jack Harker from slumber; my voice was a croak. Finally, swinging desperately down into the cabin, I managed to kick him in the rump. Three ill-tempered kicks did the trick. Five minutes later Jack clambered up beside me. He seemed to take five years.

'Too far to port and we'll take water,' I warned with authority. 'Too far to starboard and we'll jibe.'

With that, like Jim Sharp earlier, I disappeared in the direction of my bunk. I didn't even have the energy to shed my wet gear. Sleep wasn't rewarding. The world outside was filled with malicious waves, most of them higher than houses.

Morning was dismal. I woke on a sodden mattress. I was right. The waves were as immense as I imagined and growing no smaller. 'Jesus, Mary and Joseph,' I heard myself saying. (No Catholic, I had never before asked the Holy Family to intercede with the elements on my behalf.) The foaming swell showed no sign of shrinking. New Zealand was well out of sight; we were alone with the Pacific. Four bruised and bedraggled mariners regarded each other ruefully. We possibly shared the one thought. If the sea could wreak such havoc, what might the French navy do ? This was not a helpful thought; I attempted not to think it.

Before leaving Auckland I had promised the promoters of the expedition that I would send a daily radio report on our progress toward the test zone. After breakfast I drew Jack Harker's attention to this chore.

'A message?' he said.

'As promised,' I said. 'It's time to get started.'

'I can't do it,' he disclosed.

I was stunned. 'Why not?'

'It's against regulations.'

'Regulations? What regulations? Whose regulations?'

'Government regulations on use of the air waves. You can't just broadcast how and when you want to. Not when there's regulations. There's a fine of ten dollars for misuse of a transmitter for political purposes.'

Not sure I heard right, I struggled to keep a straight face. Here we were, aimed at the French navy, risking storm, thuggish French commandos and radioactive fallout in our modest vessel, and our radio operator was fretting about a ten dollar fine.

'I'll pay the bloody fine,' I promised.

'I can't do that,' he informed me. 'I've been given responsibility for the transmitter. I've checked with the authorities. It's for personal purposes only. No politics.'

'Bloody hell,' I said, followed by a broadside of obscenities. 'You might have told us before we started out.'

The penny dropped. I saw why he hadn't. He hadn't informed us about the infernal regulations, and his unwillingness to breach them, because he feared being left behind. Who needed a radio operator with a transmitter he was too timid to use? Desperate not to miss on a satisfying fracas, he had remained silent. (This was the same Jack who had wanted a revolver aboard, something more capable of misuse than a radio transmitter.) Otherwise it wasn't difficult to deduce that Jack's prime protest was against the constraints of New Zealand suburbia, against his colourless existence since the war. Sometimes we talked when our watches overlapped.

'People don't know what it's all about,' he confided. 'They don't know what they're missing out on.'

'War?'

'What goes with it. At least you know you're alive.'

'If not dead,' I suggested.

Though infuriating, Jack wasn't unlikable. He had his code, one literally beaten into him as a young naval rating in the 1930s. He may have been one of the last men in the New Zealand navy to have been formally scourged in front of his fellows; flogging was abolished soon after. I asked Jack what he recalled of the episode. 'Just that I wanted to kill the bastard who was laying it on,' he told me. 'The trouble was I couldn't see who.'

I made one intriguing discovery. If endangered I would prefer Jack at my side than most of my liberal or left-wing friends. The rites of courage might be reactionary, as obsolete as Alexander's warriors, but it was selfless; it kept comrades alive. Jack could be relied on to hurl himself at any French commando who tried splitting my skull. The further we voyaged the more confidence I felt in Jack's company.

Thirty-one

Running on a slender storm jib, at the edge of the Roaring Forties, *Tamure* banged on. We had to heave-to in order to eat or sleep. There was even more battering before the sea subsided. We continued to run before storm and squall and mammoth swell. To make fast time to Mururoa we kept to low latitudes, always at the mercy of driving westerlies. Everything was damp and dripping: clothes, sleeping bags, pillows. We seemed more vegetable than human, feeding the gross appetite of our craft. It lapped up our energy much as it nourished itself on wind and wave. Finally there was a conference. Jim Sharp was still suffering severe *mal de mer*. He favoured pushing north, into the trade winds and warmer weather. That would mean fighting into the wind all the way to Mururoa. It would also mean delay.

Jim Cottier was visibly dismayed. Jack Harker was too. Our skipper, however, had even more on his mind; he didn't stop there.

'I think we'll just fly the flag around Mururoa and then bugger off fast,' he announced. 'I don't fancy a hot dose of radiation up my arse.'

There was a long silence.

'Well, do any of you?' Jim Sharp asked.

'We didn't come here to blow a kiss at the French,' Jack Harker protested. 'I didn't leave home for sweet bugger all.'

'Getting in the way of a nuclear test is the point of the exercise,' Jim Cottier informed our skipper coolly.

Jim Sharp wasn't willing to be reminded.

One thing was plain. If we were to sail into the test zone, and take our chances there, it might have to be by way of mutiny. In the conventional way these things are done, we might even have to

185

overpower the skipper. In imagination anyway, we were in the province of piracy. Were mutineers still hung from the yardarm? It wasn't the high minded voyage we envisaged. It was, however the voyage we now had. The atmosphere crackled with suspicion. Laced with profanity, irritation became louder.

Having viewed it from jet plane, ocean liner and copra boat, I thought myself tolerably conversant with the third of the planet called the Pacific. This was an illusion. Intimacy came with eight hours a day at the helm, day after day, the sun to port or stars in the rigging. Conversation was often a thing of respectful whispers, though there were no eavesdroppers in the vicinity.

At the helm at night, with others asleep below, we continued such conversations solo. Jack Harker claimed to have full and frank exchanges with God. Recalling the miraculous feats of Polynesian navigators on this ocean, I suggested that his prayers might be better directed at Tangaroa, the Polynesian god of the sea.

Jim Sharp wasn't impressed by this frivolous proposal, or by tales of Polynesian navigators. 'Bullshit,' he said. He wasn't taken by Jim Cottier's altruism. That was bullshit too. As for me, he was convinced that I was secretly selling bullshit to American magazines. Otherwise why should I be aboard *Tamure*?

Jim Sharp was enjoying the voyage less and less. Even balmy trade winds, when we met them, failed to win a smile. The days passed. No day was like another. We saw whales. A lone albatross examined us and finally veered off toward Antarctica. My dreams were richly scripted, with a cast of thousands. Night after night the heaving *Tamure* shook phantoms from my subconscious. My dead returned one by one with messages I failed to decipher. They appeared to be messages of comfort, though I was less than sure. They might also have been warnings.

Jack Harker chattered idly away to Auckland on our transmitter. Personal messages flew back and forward across the Pacific. Nothing political. Nothing deserving a ten dollar fine.

There was no romance in the voyage. The ocean seemed a nullity, death itself; we were citizens of the void. I had a further fancy. If the ocean was death, then Jack Harker was its servant, a makeshift medium conveying the daily trivia of lost souls to the living. This daydream took deep root. It grew and flowered for the rest of the voyage.

Like a spiritualist medium, Jack often got things wrong: he got names wrong as he transmitted: place names, people's names, even the days of the week. Patrick White, who sent me a message of encouragement, became, unrecognisably, Pat Wright. It took me half a day to realize that the message was from a man about to receive the Nobel Prize for literature. That mightn't have impressed Jack anyway. In doubt, he invented.

Even in the spirit world no one was perfect.

Thirty-two

*T*oward the end of August *Tamure* was all but becalmed on sunlit sea. The Austral Islands, remote and rocky French possessions, had just risen from the horizon at exactly the hour, and almost the minute, that Jim Cottier predicted. He took a sun shot with his sextant and began making fresh calculations. Meanwhile Jim Sharp was at the helm of his vessel. Our first sight of French territory didn't impress him. 'We don't have to rush in,' he informed us. 'We'd be bloody fools to show them we're around.'

'We're supposed to, sooner or later,' Jim Cottier suggested.

'Better later,' Jim Sharp said stiffly.

I was trying to persuade my transistor radio to produce news from the BBC; London's coverage of the protest boats was extensive. That was how I had learned that *Boy Roel*, the second protest boat, had gone missing with Barry Mitcalfe aboard. Omens were poor. There had not been a squeak from their transmitter. Nor had there been air sightings, though pilots across the Pacific had been alerted to the possibility of a crippled vessel adrift. The BBC had nothing new either. Meanwhile Jack Harker fiddled with his transmitter, trying to fetch up our regular Auckland frequency. He was in luck. His news didn't concern the missing *Boy Roel* and its crew. It concerned me. My father, close enough to death from cancer when I left Auckland, had taken a turn for the worse. Even more dismaying, my year-old daughter Brigid was also in hospital with pneumonia. There was no prospect of my getting to their bedsides fast; I felt a numbing despair. I was now a captive of the Pacific.

That day Jack the medium was working overtime, worth every cent of a ten dollar fine. He learned that the *Boy Roel*, with all hands safe, had made landfall in American Samoa.

Then came the big news, from the reliable BBC. It put an end to my quandary about what best to do. Feeling the bite of international censure, the French had called off their test programme; there was a suggestion that atmospheric tests might be ended and replaced by underground explosions. Though this was not an attractive proposition either, at least it was success of sorts. We sat staring at each other, unable to speak.

'They must have known we were coming,' Jack Harker decided. Even Jim Sharp found a smile.

There was a late-night conference aboard *Tamure*. The vote was to push on to Tahiti and make our protest known there. Our voyage needn't be waste. When it was finished I could fly home to my father and daughter.

Five days later the peaks of Tahiti pushed above the horizon. The atmosphere began filling with the sweetish smell of tropical land. We sailed all day toward the island. It wasn't Mururoa, but it might do.

In the morning the local gendarmes sailed out to meet us. Their welcome was short on warmth. They allowed us a brief stay, as needy mariners, but threatened us with arrest should we mention nuclear testing unfavourably, especially to native Tahitians. Jim Sharp, painfully anxious to oblige, gave his word that we meant France no harm.

No harm? Now that *was* bullshit. Jim Cottier and I might have been seen gritting our teeth and biting our tongues. Jim Cottier politely informed French officials that we meant to make as much trouble as we could. He certainly was. Rebellious Jim was angrily promised a prison stay. A senior officer, however, thought better of handcuffing us. It might not read well in *Le Monde* or *The Times*.

At least our voyage was finishing on a high note. That night one of the most distinguished French residents on the island sought us out and shook our hands. 'You are doing a fine thing,' he informed us. 'You unnerve these bureaucratic bastards here.'

Jim Sharp, down on his bunk, erupted vehemently.

'Shut up,' he told the Frenchman.

'What is the matter?' our French sympathiser asked.

'No one on this boat talks about the bomb,' Jim announced. 'No one talks about the purpose of our voyage. No politics. Not any more. You hear?'

We heard. What we heard was mostly that our skipper was sick with fright. His voice was trembling. Without a truncheon waved in our direction our protest melted ingloriously away.

Our visitor was bemused. 'No politics?' he said with disbelief.

'None,' Jim Sharp repeated.

Our French ally dropped back into his dinghy, shaking his head and laughing a little. To this day he is possibly still trying to make sense of the episode; of the four New Zealand voyagers who sailed twelve hundred miles to declare themselves neutral on the subject of nuclear testing.

He tried a last word. He said, 'You must not stop now. You must keep at it. The bastards must be stopped.'

My heart agreed; not my head. I had nothing to offer which others hadn't. Though tempted to go the full distance I flew home to my father and daughter.

Thirty-three

*P*rotest boats were no longer New Zealand's story of the year. Jim Baxter had broken ranks to put literary life behind him and throw in his lot with anarchic hippies and unlettered junkies. He had established a rough and ready commune in a remote Maori village beside the fern-fringed waterway called the Wanganui River. There he hoped to woo young drug addicts from their unsavoury ways. Few of Jim's old friends could take this seriously. I was among the many who couldn't. Two or three years earlier, in Dunedin, Jim had confided in me to the effect that he was now happy to abandon bohemia and become a peaceful old man watching television in his fireside slippers. He would even, if called upon, be happy to embrace the academy and a monthly salary and kiss the feet of potential benefactors. It was, he argued, time for comfort in his life; time for security.

Three years later he was a bearded vagrant camped far from comforts. He left his followers spellbound with his denunciation of security-loving materialists. His *mea culpas* were many.

Friends had seen, or seen through, Jim's bookish masks before. But nothing to rival this one. An antipodean Socrates, he was now giddily playing the role of his life; he lacked only the hemlock which detractors and cynics would have gladly provided. Scores of disaffected young people embraced this hirsute Pied Piper as their eloquent prophet. They had never known Jim as a poet or, for that matter, as Jim. Nor would they. He now passed under the Maori name of Hemi. There was some affectation in this. Maori dwelling near his commune often found it difficult to accept him as a fellow tribesman; they didn't know what to make of this strange-talking interloper from the outer world. Hemi? So he was Hemi. So what?

191

Other Maori were less tolerant of the change he wrought in their community. His young disciples, brown or white, didn't necessarily ditch their drugs on arrival. Jim himself remained rather too attached to marijuana. In the style of prophets, he also succumbed to the wiles of the flesh, bedding female acolytes and fathering a child or two. Two of his retinue were to become murderous millionaires in the drug trade. I hesitate to make record of such matters now that Jim is seen almost solely as a saint. But truth, when we find it, comes in many colours.

Twice in the week I write this, and for the first time in years, I have encountered Jacquie Baxter, Jim's widow; she underlined the ironies in Jim's story. For Jacquie is a bona fide Maori. And she has become a talented poet and short story writer herself. She never joined his commune. She was always more concerned to see to the health of her children and grandchildren. Mysteriously, the occasion considered, we hardly mentioned Jim. Perhaps he remains too much for us.

Late in October 1972 I had a minor bout of insomnia. Careful not to wake Barbara, I slid from our bed, made a cup of tea, and then meandered into our living room. There, reflexively, I reached out for a book likely to lull me to sleep. My choice wasn't ideal. My hand had closed around, of all things, a volume titled *Pig Island Letters*. It was a sequence of poems Jim had written for me seven years earlier. I turned pages, marvelling at what a magnificent poet he had been. Been? But Jim was still with us in flamboyant form. He wasn't yet to be spoken of in the past tense. There was no reason to suspect there would not be new poems, perhaps when his guru days were done.

Turning more pages, I arrived at a poem, one of his most vivid, titled 'The Ballad Of One Tree Hill'. It was a lament on the death of a mutual friend, the printer and publisher Bob Lowry. In it Jim movingly envisaged Lowry incarcerated by death. I had read the lines often; there was nothing in the poem new to me.

Speak, Bob, though the wind has slammed the door,
From that old battered clink;
I hate to see a cobber go hungry for
Tobacco or a drink.
So tap the window, when the screws are out

Of earshot, and I
Will chuck the makings through the bars of the night
To where you never die.

Familiar or not, these lines produced a strange reaction. Tears began blurring the print. Then I found myself sobbing. I might have known Lowry well, but not *that* well, not enough to justify so immoderate a response.

What was going on here?

I returned the book to a near shelf and went to bed.

The next night, preparing for sleep, I found Barbara sitting up in bed reading. It was no ordinary bedside book. It was *Pig Island Letters*.

'Where did you get that?' I asked. Had I left it lying around.

'Off the shelf,' she said.

'But why that one?'

'It caught my eye. I haven't read Baxter for years.'

'No other reason?'

'Not that I can think of. Is something troubling you?'

'No,' I lied.

Next day I had a 4.30 appointment with Hodder & Stoughton's New Zealand editor concerning *Strangers and Journeys*. It was due to be published the following week and I was supposed to be invigorating the firm's salesmen. Racing breathless uphill to keep the appointment, already late, I found an urgent need to cross the road to a small gallery there. I had no business in the gallery. The needless detour was going to delay me even more. Nevertheless, for some reason, I crossed the road.

Within the gallery, holding court among young urban devotees, was Jim much as front page newspaper photographs now frequently showed him. Bare and grubby feet; long and greasy hair; clothing with a musty smell. Yet the wry and melancholy Baxter I knew best was still there. He embraced me.

'Are things all right now?' he asked.

He meant with our friendship. There had been an estrangement, or misunderstanding, largely to do with the demise of my marriage.

'Of course things are all right,' I told him.

'You sure?' he said rather fervently.

'I'll tell you when they're not,' I promised.

Our reunion had happened with a rush. I didn't have time to consider the nature of coincidence, of the oddity of reading *Pig Island Letters* two nights before, meeting up with him again and of my inexplicable tears. There was another conjunction. *Strangers and Journeys*, the book I was supposed to be publicising at that very moment, was the book of mine Jim had most to do with. Without Jim, the book might never have been finished.

What *was* going on? I seemed to be getting messages from all over. Finally I sprinted off to keep my appointment. Before I went we promised to try to meet again, at Titirangi, on the Sunday of Labour Day weekend.

The meeting never happened. Jim had another and larger appointment to keep on that Sunday. I waited in vain for him to arrive at Titirangi. By then his body was being moved from the morgue to the undertaker. In a poem to me, Jim had anticipated this day; he had even found room to mention

the undertaker who won't have read
Your stories or my verse – Or that a self had died
Who handled ideas like bombs.

Was that what the messages had been about? Not that the forewarnings could have helped. I couldn't have seen him sooner. His heart had been exhausted. How could I have known?

I am not a spiritualist, nor an especially dedicated student of the psychic. I would sooner leave such matters alone. But if they happened, as happen they will, then it would be spineless not to record them.

The next day I followed Jim's coffin – resident in a beaten-up tradesman's van – to a hastily dug grave in the volcanic heart of New Zealand. There were hundreds present, though mysteriously few of his literary friends.

I still hope to live long enough to make sense of the man.

Thirty-four

*A*nother intersection. Yesterday I abandoned this manuscript in mid-sentence and went into the city to see a 90-minute documentary film on Jim Baxter, no less. It was no great movie; but its subject matter was engrossing. It unveiled questions rather than answers. Talking to the camera, young John Baxter disclosed that his father had confessed loss of faith two or three weeks before his death. Had there been a spiritual death heralding the physical? I found it troubling. I prefer my own hypothesis: that coffee killed him. This isn't to joke. He had embraced caffeine as his drug of choice after he abandoned the booze. I once sat with him in a Wellington coffee bar while one of his erudite monologues rolled on, seldom changing gear and lubricated only by black coffee. At the end of the afternoon I estimated that he must have consumed twenty powerful cups of his favoured potion.

In her piece to the camera, Jacquie Baxter came up with other curiosities. Though Jim wandered Christ-like among his fellow men in cast-off attire, with never a shoe to his name, he hadn't dumped his best clothing. Not even ties and tuxedo. Everything hung mothballed in his wardrobe at home. Shoes of his size could be found there too. Why? Why hadn't he discarded his old apparel? Why, for example, hadn't he handed it to one of the needy derelicts who dogged him? A man who retained his Sunday best was not a man who had relinquished things of this world. On the other hand might he have been saving his best for the undertaker, for the day he escaped the persona he had so conscientiously created?

Still on camera, Jacquie was asked whether Jim's guru years were an act. This was a difficult question. Even in his student days Jim always had a touch of the thespian, perhaps of the mountebank. No, she answered after some thought; he wasn't posing. 'It's just that it was all so irrelevant,' she sighed. 'It's not necessary to go barefoot and long-haired into the wilderness to do good works.'

So I leave that last word to Jacquie.

Somewhere in these highly coloured proceedings – of protest boats and poets – *Strangers and Journeys* came into being. It was twice chosen New Zealand's book of the year and became a modest bestseller. American and British reviewers also had few complaints. If this was the book I was meant to write, perhaps a long intermission was in order.

Of all my years, 1973 is the one I should most like to rewrite. Some would be happier if I did. Can I risk tasting that heady brew of happiness and hell again? I still suffer puritanical spasms of guilt when an historical novel obliges me to rearrange fact in the interests of fiction. I foresaw even more remorse should I meddle carelessly with my own story.

It had been a serene and sunny Titirangi summer, with Indian summer soon on its heels. After four years together, Barbara and I were now six months married. The children, and especially baby Brigid, remained precious company. Much of the season was spent on the beach downhill from our house. We swam when tides allowed and paddled a canoe around the estuary. We steamed open cockles and mussels and netted and smoked most of the mullet in Christendom.

The boys sped off to make gifts of surplus fish to neighbours. That summer, though I didn't know it yet, would lend poignancy to my next novel. So would Titirangi and our cliff-hanging home on Arapito Road. It seemed I had never been happier. This may even have been true. Our peaceful patch of the New Zealand coast would never again know such innocent laughter. For once even my work was going well. My nuclear novel, *Danger Zone*, had begun to solidify. *A Touch of Clay*, my portrait of the 1970s, was inching into existence. It encouraged me to envisage a trilogy of the decade, with the third novel based on a Baxter-like guru. This was to prove elusive. Though dead, Jim was still far too near. There was small hope of my approaching him critically. (As will soon be seen, my life didn't stand extensive inspection either.)

So what happened?

For present purposes I shall call her Val. Flamboyantly gowned, throatily loud, she was near the end of a patchy and not particularly lucrative singing career. She had never been an international name, though not for want of ambition. She appeared at our door as an old friend of Barbara's. Currently without work in London and Sydney, she thought to see what her native land offered. As I reconstruct events, twenty-five years later, her gaze fell ravenously and covetously on our mini-paradise. She had never been shy about telling the world how she felt. Nor was she inclined to now. Her peals of pleasure rang across the estuary as she pranced into the water. At that point I should have been more perceptive. I failed to note that she wanted more than the estuary, more than our wooded retreat. She was seeing me as part of the package. She had been busy reading my novels and stories. Instinct told her correctly where my weakness was. Was I flattered by attention from a worldly woman? Reader, I was. My experience of freebooting females was limited. Barbara, though a retired television personality, didn't qualify in that respect. Her rural background was as homely as mine; we had both raked hay, raised chickens and milked cows.

One way and another I was wooed and won with shameless gusto. How did I allow it to happen? Was it because I felt – as sober family man and dedicated young writer – that I had missed out on the erotic antics of the 1960s? Might it have been because Barbara was deep in postnatal depression – a condition little acknowledged at that time – and living in long, unloving silences? At this point I am at a loss for further excuses. I just wish things had been different. Within three days I was bedded; or was it she? And if blame is to be apportioned, let music take its share. Opera had long been a dangerous indulgence of mine. To buy a ticket to my first opera I slept (or didn't sleep) through three comfortless nights on the pavement outside Auckland's old His Majesty's Theatre. Thereafter I had always been grateful to singers, male or female, who provided me with the thrilling sounds that are their stock and trade (Val's voice too lacked little in passion). In parenthesis I should add that I was in debt to that lovely Edwardian theatre which made me an opera-goer. When urban wreckers moved in on the theatre in 1988, reducing the site of my first opera to rubble, I was to be found sitting unlawfully in the path of a malicious bulldozer and being led away firmly for fingerprinting and a spell in a police cell. I owed the place that, at least. I owed opera that much too. I never dreamed that its seductive sounds might shape as a man-trap.

I digress. Let me return to 1973 and Val. How did it happen? It wasn't important. All that mattered was that in three months my marriage was dead. From a predator's point of view it was a quick and efficient strike. Months later, the family bruised, bewildered and scattered, and lawyers making thuggish sounds, I remembered our last summer together at Titirangi; and mourned. Our little beach was deserted now, and wintry. It could never be the same. It never was. Sympathetic bystanders conjectured that my work held me together through that bleak time. I wished I could share that supposition. My impression was that I deserved all the grief I got. By the end of 1973 I was barely acquainted with sanity. Misery was compounded by the death of my father. I was conscious of never having made enough effort to know him; I had been an unsatisfying son, or so I thought. Helping my mother clear away his papers, I found an unfinished note in his handwriting, addressed to a relative. It mentioned me. It informed the relative that my new book – whatever it was – had just been published in the United States. Then came the shocker. 'As you might imagine,' the note added, 'we are very proud of our boy.'

Proud?

Imagine? I couldn't imagine. I was numb.

My father proud of me, my mother too? Dear God. Why hadn't someone told me? We spend half our lifetimes looking for parental approval and, when we finally get it, there's no one at home.

At his funeral service I read Dylan Thomas's 'To My Father'. At the muddy graveside I read a short Baxter poem:

Upon the upland road
Ride easy stranger
Surrender to the sky
Your heart of anger

It felt right. So too did the song played on a tinny tape recorder by an old socialist friend of my father's. It was the ballad of Joe Hill, the Swedish bard and agitator of the IWW (the anarchist-flavoured international workers of the world), shot by firing squad in Utah. It had long been my father's favourite.

I dreamed I saw Joe Hill last night
Alive as you or me
But Joe I said
You're ten years dead
I never died said he.
The cartel bosses killed you Joe
They shot you Joe said I
Takes more than guns to kill a man
Said Joe I did not die.

In his last evening in the world my father seemed back in the 1930s, perhaps under the banners of an unemployed march, facing a phalanx of police. So far as I could determine, he was calling on his comrades to stand firm. He probably wasn't impressed by the Dylan Thomas poem. He wasn't going gentle into any bugger's good night.

The next morning he considered the world as revealed by the *New Zealand Herald*. Then he took up the *Turf Guide* to contemplate Saturday's most appealing runners. Having selected his horses and made a small monetary transaction with an obliging hospital orderly, he sighed deeply, fell forward, and was never heard from again. He had placed his last bet and that wasn't a winner either. This wasn't new. Joseph Stalin turned out a poor pick too.

Thirty-five

I had known depression before, if seldom larger than a passing mental shadow. This time it wasn't fooling around; it came with the finesse of a crash tackle on a rugby field. I went to a distinguished psychiatrist and soon saw that he had more problems than I mustered. All the same, he attempted to be helpful. 'Your problem is women,' he diagnosed accurately. He added, 'If you need me urgently, I'll be at Helen's place on Monday, Susan's on Tuesday and Mary's the rest of the week.' He wrote the names and telephone numbers down carefully, without a wisp of a smile. The rest of our appointment concerned a prescription for pills.

Left to ourselves, Barbara and I might have managed reconciliation. We almost did. Today, decades late, we agree that we should have. 'We were worth another five years of marriage,' she told me last night with a wry smile. 'Ten,' I estimated, equally melancholy.

Lawyers and pill-pushers did for us in the end. Barbara took a flat in the city and found a male companion. I made a vain attempt to shake free from the immoderate female who had triggered marital woe. I hid out in my sister's secluded cottage on Auckland's turbulent western coast. Tall surf boomed in my ears as I worked over the last, terse chapter of *A Touch of Clay*. There seemed to be something to be said for the novel.

My months in a den of potters, living the rhythm of their weeks, might not have been waste. Likewise my illness. I had pushed my sorrow into it, Barbara's too. My infant daughter was also to be found there. She was already a stranger; I was in danger of losing her most loveable years. Finally I threaded the 1970s through the manuscript. When not revising I watched lovers leaping through the surf; and suffered intolerable envy.

Then I finished. I looked down the manuscript and found nothing in need of repair. I became aware of a car being parked clumsily in front of the cottage. Dramatically garbed in black, with high leather boots and a yellow scarf drifting behind her, Val was back. Beaming, throwing her arms wide, she looked about to let loose an aria from *La Bohème*. Oh, that she were Barbara. She wasn't Barbara. Even Barbara wasn't.

Much of 1974 was dedicated to picking a path through marital wreckage. Children came and went and mostly went; the house often had the silence of a cemetery. They – the children – had loved Barbara and their little sister. Val's high notes were less to their taste. There were adult visitors too. One, Cherry Hankin, an academic brave enough to take me seriously as a writer, won my heart by telling me that, when desperate to have a copy, she had stolen *The New Zealanders* from the Montreal Public Library. That is something for an author to aim for – books worth stealing, readers ready to risk arrest. I have never had a larger literary compliment. Though I had mixed feelings about being taken seriously, I did my best to help Cherry find her way through my manuscripts.

It turned out that Cherry had recently been urged to visit a certain spiritualist medium. The visit had been rather sensational in its wealth of detail. Time after time the medium got Cherry's love life right. Time after time he uncannily came up with accurate descriptions of Cherry's dead. I did my best to remain aloof and unimpressed as Cherry finished her tale. It was plain enough to me that Cherry's new-found friend was a sly charlatan preying on suggestible women. (I remembered Sheena Amato seeking comfort from a medium after Michael's death.) To be fair, however, the fellow asked only five dollars a sitting. In 1974 it was a surprisingly modest sum for a long-distance call to the other side.

To prove my point, and expose him as a fake, I visited him incognito. He was tall, ethereal, heavily rouged and spookily homosexual. Second impressions were no better. He offered a diabolical glass of sherry and led me to a dark room.

'I have your father with me,' he announced.

'Oh, yes? I said coolly. My father been deceased for months. Most of a medium's clientele are people suffering from a recent bereavement. Hardly a risky guess.

'Your parent is most powerfully present,' the medium went on. 'He has a great deal to tell you.'

'I'm sure he has, his present situation considered.'

The medium ignored this flippancy.

'Anyway he tells me that you're a writer and that you've just finished a book partly set in the 19th century. Is that so?'

It was so. *A Touch of Clay*, despite contemporary concerns, was shaped around a 19th century pioneer journal. About five people had read the manuscript to this point. This eerie gentleman wasn't one of them. He went on, 'Your father is also telling me about your next book.'

'My next book?'

'Indeed he is. There seems to be a great deal of sea in this one.'

'There is,' I had to admit. In *Danger Zone* the Pacific was half the story.

'Meanwhile your father tells me that you've been living too long on your nerves, that you need peace and quiet.'

I couldn't argue with that either. It was possibly true of all his customers.

'He is now showing me a lake or a large and landlocked harbour. There are high hills and mountains around. Does that mean anything to you?'

There was a prickling at the back of my neck. His description of the place tallied unnervingly with Banks Peninsula, home to my pioneer ancestors and the setting of my father's boyhood years.

'Ah,' said the medium. 'I see. It's family land.'

'Possibly,' I agreed.

'Your father is now telling me that you must get it back for the family. You'll never know peace until you do.'

There was a problem in attempting to dismiss this as the work of a fraud. For one thing my father had been telling me, most of my adult life, that I must buy back the Shadbolt land on Banks Peninsula; the medium's message was disconcertingly similar.

'There's something else,' he went on.

I couldn't imagine what. The reappearance of my father was enough for one day.

'Your father says you must listen to what your mother says.'

'My mother?'

'Mothers know best,' the medium explained.

'That wasn't always his opinion,' I pointed out.

'I can't help that. I can only tell you what he tells me.'

Perhaps the man said more, but I was no longer listening. I happily dropped five dollars into his donation box as I left. At the least it was more fascinating than a session with a psychiatrist.

In the second half of 1974, Val, looking for work again, left for London. There was no reason to expect her back. My mother was relieved and wasn't slow to say so; she remained fond of Barbara and had never warmed to Val. And mothers knew best. Yes Dad, I heard.

Thirty-six

Val and I had managed a makeshift existence. She had little work, most of it scrappy. The neighbourhood was soon familiar with her Top C as she rehearsed religiously for work which never came. The outside world made no large impression on Val. When Norman Kirk died – New Zealand's most imaginative Prime Minister in decades – Val barely noticed. The world interested her only so far as it served her career. I was no better. Few events found their way through my personal murk. Even the intriguing tale that Kirk had died at the hand of the CIA failed to rouse me from drug-induced gloom. The arrest of New Zealand's best-known civil servant, William Sutch, on a charge of espionage, didn't make a great impression either. In other circumstances I should have been gripped. But circumstances weren't other. My increasingly morose condition wasn't helpful in bettering my association with Val, if we had a liaison worth the name. Even good news on the literary front failed to move me much. We had less and less in common. Nevertheless we were doomed to remain under the same roof. Doomed? Doomed. (A depressive is seldom astray in such judgements.) In late August there was a reprieve from this doleful mode of existence. Val returned to England to fetch her possessions and see what work was offering there. Her absence gave me a chance to come clean. In a letter following her to London I notified her that we couldn't go on. Or that I couldn't. My guilt was too great. So was my grief. I tried to say this gently. On the other hand there was no way of putting it painlessly.

Half a week later, in the middle of the New Zealand night, my telephone rang. It was Val on the line from London. She was sobbing. I couldn't do this to her, she argued.

I could. Sanity said I must. What I couldn't do, however, was silence those sobs. Women weeping on the far side of the world are likely to unhinge the most strong-minded male.

'Come to London,' she pleaded. 'I'll pay the fare.'

This was unlikely, considering her chronically spendthrift state, but I claimed that money wasn't the issue.

Next morning I woke thinking of London. It was sixteen years since I had last been there. There would be old friends. There would be places. There would be pubs and exhibitions and theatres. There would be agents and publishers who had never been more to me than signatures on letters.

Then, on cue, the morning mail arrived. There was a cheque within for most of a thousand solid British pounds: royalties for *Strangers and Journeys*. They meant I could go to London under my own steam, owing nothing to Val. I rang Hodders' New Zealand editor to tell him I was contemplating travel.

'I'll see what I can do,' he said.

'Like what?' I asked.

'Like launching *A Touch of Clay* in London,' he said. 'I'll ring the London office tonight.'

He did. The London office obliged. *A Touch of Clay* would be launched on the glowing summit of New Zealand House, London's tallest venue. I had left the city in 1959 with my first skinny book in my hand. I was returning with my latest to lay at London's door. The timing was fine, the symmetry impeccable. Advance reviews were judging it my best.

My jet lifted from Auckland International Airport in the first week of October 1974. As it gained height I remembered that my friendly neighbourhood medium had predicted that I would be making the acquaintance of London and New York in October. I had informed the fellow that this was preposterous on financial grounds alone. The man of mysteries proved impervious to my protest. There was no way he could have known about the thousand English pounds since I didn't either. I had a sense of things getting out of hand. What next? What was going on here?

I looked out my window and watched the last of Auckland's lights drift away. Thirty hours later the plane was circling London and landing at Heathrow. As promised, Val was at the airport, weeping copiously between stagy bursts of laughter.

'You must be tired,' she said.

'I can sleep later,' I pointed out.

'Later?' she asked with dismay.

Bed may have been high on her schedule. Sleep wasn't.

'I have something to do first,' I disclosed.

'Like what?'

'You'll see,' I promised.

I hailed a taxi and told the driver I wanted Tite Street, Chelsea.
Val saw what I had in mind. 'Tonight? Must you?'

'I must,' I confirmed.

Half an hour later the taxi was cruising along the Thames
embankment and turning into Tite Street, home to Wilde, Sargent,
Whistler and a score of other distinguished Londoners. And, once,
me. I peered down into the basement flat where Gillian and I had
lived and where I put *The New Zealanders* together – hoping, as
Katherine Mansfield once wished of her work, to make my land leap
into literature. There was a light on; there were colourful prints on
the walls and books crowded on shelves. Perhaps there was another
young writer there struggling to begin. Until that moment I hadn't
understood what I was up to either. Leaving Val puzzled and hurt
and alone, I walked away into the dusk, ambling alongside the
Thames, waiting for the magic to begin. It soon did. Suddenly, and
for some minutes, I was walking alongside my youthful self.

'You finished?' Val called impatiently.

'Let's go,' I said.

I saw myself take her arm and move off into the dusk.

Next stop was Maida Vale, the Warrington pub, a brimming pint of
Guinness and Kevin Ireland. It was fifteen years since Kevin and I
had said farewells on Sofia railway station. Those farewells, as
pictured in *One of Ben's*, had soon promised to be permanent. Kevin
had gone off to marry a voluptuous Bulgarian woman, write poetry,
and translate Bulgarian verse; he had also divorced and married
again, this time to a reliable and plain-spoken Yorkshire lass. I had
gone home to New Zealand to write novels, raise children and
divorce and remarry a couple of times myself. In most of those years
Kevin had been rescuing New Zealanders of literary bent from the
perils of London. He helped several find London publishers. He, on

the other hand, remained whimsically New Zealander. He ignored London magazines and mailed his poems off to New Zealand; they had, he modestly reasoned, little to tell England. His life seemed, after all, as reclusive as mine.

One Guinness led to another. London still fitted me like familiar slippers. Before another hour was out I was an unreformed Londoner.

The London launch of *A Touch of Clay* was decently lavish. If there were speeches, I don't recall them. Among the hundred guests there were many I wished to meet and few I didn't. Large in the first category was Dan Davin, secretary of the Oxford University Press and New Zealand's most considerable expatriate novelist. He had, it turned out, just finished reading *Clay*. He couldn't have been kinder. Nor could his review in *The Times Literary Supplement*. 'From the ashes of two lives,' he wrote, 'he [Shadbolt] manages to fan a Promethean flame, giving a light in which to look at the troubles of our times.' Even Patrick White, at his most morose, couldn't have complained.

Why do writers write?

'To be loved', the novelist Angela Carter once said to me.

That night I found enough affection to see me through me another decade. For an author more familiar with invective than praise, at least among the prima donnas of his own land, this was dizzying. I discovered myself listening to an earnest actor confess that he had kept *The New Zealanders* in a back pocket until the binding fell apart. For some reason it was an anecdote too many. In need of escape, I sidled off and found a quiet corner to light my pipe; I was followed by an actress lighting a cigarette. We recognised each other. Bridget Armstrong was a talented New Zealand actress often seen on television and the London stage. Recently, and to much praise, she had played Katherine Mansfield in a dramatised BBC documentary on the author and her work.

I congratulated her on her performance. 'You had me believing you were Katherine.' I told her.

'I believed I was too,' she disclosed.

That said, I might have moved on. I didn't.

'Your lady's looking for you,' she informed me.

Bridget's eyes had a mischievous twinkle.

'She often is,' I said.

Last seen, Val had been searching for musical expatriates who might have employment for a soprano. So far no contract had turned up.

'We have a lot to thank you for,' Bridget went on.

'Me?' I said.

'New Zealanders aren't a joke any more. They get taken seriously.'

'That's good to know.'

'How did Katherine put it? Didn't she say she wanted to make her still undiscovered country leap into the eyes of the old world?'

'That may be a trifle ambitious for me.'

Bridget knew her Mansfield; she wasn't going to let me off lightly. 'Come on,' she said. 'It must do you good to know that you're carrying on where she left off.'

'We've had our differences,' I pointed out

'So have I,' she said. 'And by the way, in case you haven't noticed, your current lady is now looking daggers.'

Val was indeed. With a few tricky sidesteps she parted me from Bridget and steered me in the direction of less perilous company. Womanly intuition may have been at work. If so, intuition was right. As she left the function, Bridget found it impossible to resist a final flirt; she surreptitiously squeezed my hand and smiled warmly as she passed. On any reading of the matter, this was unsafe. Before many more years were out, Bridget and I were to marry, if none too successfully. Kevin had the last word.

'You silly bugger,' he groaned. 'You didn't have to do that.'

'Do what?' I asked.

'Marry Katherine Mansfield,' he said.

Not many days later Val and I were on the first leg of the long journey back to New Zealand. I looked out on the Thames and its houseboats; the city was at its sunny best. How long before I saw it again? Another fifteen years? Val had been hoping that I would declare my intention of making a new life in London and helping her career along. In this she was disappointed. She heard no such declaration. She would have to find a more reliable benefactor. We flew in silence.

New York was grey with autumn. I dutifully made the acquaintance of publishers and agents past and present. They had pleasant things to say about *Clay*. There was nothing resembling a contract. Mike Bessie of Harpers, who first published *Among the Cinders*, continued to tell me that he had never cared more for any book on his lists. I may have been expected to believe this. It was even possible that he believed it. Anyway I could presume it to be a preliminary to New York's thumbs down. I could easily write the rejection letters myself. Who needed to know about a heartsick potter working on his wheel in a distant land? I had an answer. I did. Possibly it was time to ignore London and New York and settle for writing for my fellow countrymen. Writing for them was not to be thought second best. The rewards were richer, if not necessarily of a financial kind.

There were writers. John Updike entertained us in Boston, Stephen Becker in upstate Massachusetts. I found Stephen writing a foreword for a new New Zealand edition of *Among the Cinders*; he claimed he was enjoying it even more the second time round. Though his most recent novel, *The Chinese Bandit*, was as good as anything he has written, no one was now publishing Stephen's new work either. Why did we bother? What kept us going?

Angela said love. Perhaps. If so, whose?

Auckland unfurled beneath the plane. Home. I took a deep breath. London was a long way behind. Below, in the form of two lean and green islands, was what kept me going. With a little help from friends, I might soon be back in business.

Thirty-seven

Summer turned up in Titirangi again. It bore only a passing resemblance to summers past. No Barbara. No baby Brigid. Little laughter. Days of drifting rain. Melancholy also clouded such life as was lived here. Downing pills, I seemed set on keeping the chemical industry in business. Navigating through my doldrums, Val wasn't a merry sight either.

In the first days of 1975, Ian Cross, now the editor of the *New Zealand Listener,* the most respected journal in the land, rang from Wellington to ask if I would cover the Sutch spy trial for his magazine. Though I was finishing the final pages of my nuclear-powered novel *Danger Zone*, the invitation was difficult to resist. It might save me from fictional woes and another burst of depression. It was also possible that I might learn something new of New Zealand in the 1930s and of the generation which elsewhere produced spies like Philby in Britain and Alger Hiss in the United States. Had we a counterpart? There was mystery in the material. In a country with a dearth of cold war drama, we suddenly had a full-blown saga. A semi-retired government economist and lately the chairman of the New Zealand Arts Council, Sutch had been the country's most conspicuous civil servant for decades. He had lately been observed meeting KGB men in obscure Wellington locations over a period of six months or more. The storyline – enriched with stake-outs, car chases, listening posts, and furtive drops – had the ingredients of a John Le Carré novel. In some respects the unprocessed material was more arresting than any fiction Le Carré had come up with. For one thing this was literally about the man next door. (Sutch, in the 1950s, had been a near neighbour of mine. As I recall it, his blinds were never drawn.) Orthodox leftists, for whom Sutch had long been something of a hero, hastily and reflexively saw him as the victim of a frame-up. Rumour said the SIS (The New Zealand Security Intelligence Service) had been stalking him for years. But whose interests would a frame-up serve? When apprehended Sutch implausibly claimed to have been seeking information about the plight of Jews and dissident writers in the Soviet Union. Seeking information on Jews and writers on wintry Wellington street corners? And from a transparent servant of the KGB? It didn't begin to be believable. As chairman of the New Zealand Arts Council Sutch could have entertained a score of Soviet diplomats in his luxurious Wellington home without provoking suspicion. A man who loitered around murky street corners couldn't but be up to something unwholesome. His former left-wing colleagues – one of them, Martyn Finlay, currently New Zealand's Attorney General – seemed to suspect so too. All the same, Finlay had mixed feelings. He put his old comrade up for trial, so he said, 'with a heavy heart.' His heart might have been still heavier had he learned, as I had by chance, that Sutch was leading something of a double life as journalist and occasional political commentator. For example, it appears that he wrote a regular piece titled 'Letter from Washington' for the left-wing New Zealand journal *Here and Now*. Under the byline of one William McChesney Martin, it purported to be a first-hand review of US affairs. According to my informant this monthly and mostly Stalinist missive was a work of the imagination. The 'Letter from Washington' was a fiction. And William McChesney Martin? Well, he existed. He was a US Senator, a right-wing Republican. Sutch had cheekily souvenired the name and used it as a pseudonym thereafter. Why? To cover his tracks? Or because he enjoyed conspiracy? Rather amazingly, in retrospect, no one picked this up; the bona fide William McChesney Martin was never heard protesting misuse of his name. And there was never a mutter from the CIA. One might surmise that they knew all along and saw merit in leaving well alone.

That was where matters stood on the opening day of New Zealand's first spy trial. What was a novelist, a writer of fictions, doing there? I failed to persuade myself that I was necessary. Court officials apparently asked themselves the same question; they attempted to remove me from the press bench I shared with a score of card-carrying journalists. (With their indifference to fact, novelists are notoriously non-unionised.) Ian Cross talked fast to have me reinstated. A burglar in the closed shop of fact, I remained in my seat as the crisis expired and the trial began.

Witnesses for the prosecution, mostly anonymous men of the SIS alphabetically labelled, were almost endearingly bizarre. No one to rival them had ever testified in a New Zealand court. Most had English accents and martial bearing; it wasn't difficult to see them as survivors of Empire, leftovers of Britain's legions. None had a sense of humour. Their testimony was often weird. Mr Justice Beattie, trying to make sense of the proceedings in his court, eventually felt obliged to ask a question of an agent labelled Mr X; questions the prosecution was failing to ask. Mr X had given evidence concerning his observation of Dr Sutch over a five-month period from May 23, 1974 to September 1974.

What time, Mr Justice Beattie asked, had the sun set while Mr X was on watch on May 23?

About 6.30 to 6.45, answered Mr X.

And on June 20?

About the same time, said Mr X.

July 25?

The same.

September 26?

The same.

So now we knew. An intelligent schoolchild could have informed the unfortunate fellow that in the southern hemisphere the days of September were longer than the days of May; that there was a difference between winter and summer or autumn and spring. And now we knew why security operatives were better left nameless. Non-men who lived non-lives in non-seasons required no names. They knew no summer or winter, autumn or spring. They lived in the single season of the Gulag archipelagos of this world. It was more than a mental slum. It was, as persecuted and exiled Solzhenitzyn suggested, a sewer. There was no sunrise to be seen from a sewer. Just the sound of society's plumbing. Just the smell of human waste.

The increasingly dysfunctional trial stumbled on from Monday to Friday. With agents of poor mental capacity, New Zealand's SIS made an indifferent showing. As agent after agent collapsed in the witness box, the head of the SIS, a comic opera character named Brigadier Gilbert, perhaps of Gilbert and Sullivan fame, was reported to be on a heavy daily dose of valium. He had good reason to be. On the other hand Sutch didn't look healthy either. (He would be dead before many more months were gone.) There was a faint air of disdain as he looked over the crowded court. He didn't take the witness box to clear up the mystery of his meetings with Mr Rasgovorov of the KGB. His implausible written explanation did nothing to advance his cause. He had put himself on trial with so rickety a version of events. On the seventh and last day, to no one's great surprise, he was acquitted. The rest of us were left wondering what the tawdry business had been about.

It would be more than another decade before I met up with something convincingly close to the truth of the matter. Unsurprisingly, it wasn't discovered in a courtroom. It was to drift into my possession from another direction altogether.

In the week I began this chapter, trying once more to make sense of the affair, I had a propitious caller. At my front door was Hector McNeill, a retired lawyer and old student socialist colleague. Hector shared my fascination with the Sutch trial. He called whenever he turned up a nugget of new material. His timing, that midsummer day, couldn't have been better. Synchronicity had a field day.

Working through my now dog-eared report of the case for the *Listener*, Hector had suddenly found all he wanted. The truth of the affair had been looking him in the face for years. I too had dutifully recorded the material without seeing its significance. Hector himself had read through it a dozen times without shouting Eureka. Up to this point we had both surmised that Sutch was, or might have been, clumsily spying on New Zealand on behalf of the Soviet Union. It was easier to accept the defence proposition that Sutch had been involved in a rather childish escapade, an innocent intrigue. Yet it didn't make sense. Though the prosecution argued otherwise, Sutch had no secrets to interest the Soviet Union. He merely behaved as though he might have. It was not only the equivalent of a murder trial without a body; it was like a murder trial with no known victim. Both the prosecution and the defence were pushing mindless narratives. If a spy, Sutch had not been an especially devious one. He had even recorded the dates and times of his meetings with Comrade Rasgovorov in his office diary. Some modest midnight snooping by the SIS would have produced those dates and times. Might this distinguished scholar really have been stupid enough to leave a timetable for espionage lying around? Stupidity, in any case, wasn't a punishable crime.

So here we were, Hector and I, still puzzling over the affair twenty years later. Zionism – as Sutch himself had claimed – had been a major subject of discussion in the course of his nocturnal rambles with the Russian. Sutch's explanation was that he belonged to the New Zealand-Israel association and was energetically involved in that organisation – actively pro-Jewish and with a healthy knowledge of Zionism.

'There it is,' Hector said.

'There is what?' I asked.

'A Jewish connection,' he said.

It all fell into place. Bill Sutch *had* been up to no good. That was no news. But he hadn't been, as long alleged, spying on New Zealand and New Zealanders. He had been spying on Israel, if indirectly, and the Jewish community in New Zealand. In short, he had been on watch for the Kremlin, alerting the Soviet Union to the devious undertakings of Zionism in the southern hemisphere. In those cold war days Zionism was seen as a sinister enemy of the Soviet Union: such anti-semitic paranoia began with Stalin in the 1930s and was still flourishing under Brehznev in the 1970s. For the KGB – as for the SIS and CIA – all information was precious. Even the scrappy and probably irrelevant material which was all Sutch would have been in a position to provide. (Much of it, according to a former Russian career diplomat who loathed the KGB, was no more than newspaper clippings.) That material may have allowed Sutch to imagine that he was rendering some useful service to the Soviet Union; the KGB possibly used the contacts to keep Sutch on the hook and in place for some larger missions. That was the theory of the historian Keith Sinclair. All that can be said is that it was as droll a spy trial as any on record. And, just my luck, I was covering it.

In the end I rescued one item from history's rubbish bin, one which a future chronicler may find intriguing. My Titirangi neighbour Eric McCormick was a school friend and sometime student companion of Bill Sutch. He also saw something of Sutch in England in the 1930s. In 1995, the last year of his life, in conversation with me, Eric confided that Sutch once seemed to be trying to recruit him for intelligence work for the KGB. A trip to Moscow was mentioned. Eric, though his sympathies were also with the Soviets, declined the invitation. 'He was,' Eric explained breathlessly, 'always up to something with the Russians.'

With that, Eric gave in to exhaustion, slumping back on his hospital pillow. We never broached the subject again. We stepped gingerly around it until the day of his death.

Thirty-eight

*T*he Sutch trial and the subsequent *Listener* article left me depleted. Likewise my association with Val. I sensed depression on the way back. She was rehearsing *La Traviata* in Wellington. Abandoning her to Verdi, I made a leap for freedom. Safety wasn't to be found in New Zealand. I rushed through the proofs of *Danger Zone* and, trying to escape a less literary danger zone, booked a flight to London.

I slept my first night in London in Kevin and Caroline Ireland's Maida Vale studio. They had visitors. One was a rather wonderfully beautiful East European, a Czech with an enigmatic smile. Her name was Zuska. She was a photographer's agent in Soho, or so I learned from the telephone number I found in my pocket next morning. It seemed distinctly unwise to lapse into a liaison after only hours on the ground. For one thing Val, now singing her head off in Wellington, was only a twenty-four hour flight to my rear. Lapse, however, I did.

'Watch it,' Kevin warned paternally. Nevertheless I breathed a health-giving gust of freedom. It was London's warmest summer in decades; every breeze was sweet. With a cool and cosmopolitan Londoner at my side I revelled too. There was an attractively Slavic sadness in Zuska, something enhanced by high cheekbones, bleached hair, and faintly olive skin. She and her family posing as Danes, had escaped Czechoslovakia in the wake of the 1948 communist takeover. Her mother, after a perfunctory attempt at parenthood, disappeared into the world of high fashion. Her heavy-drinking father, in a fit of bravado, attempted to revisit Czechoslovakia by way of Vienna; he was picked up by that city's Russian custodians, tried, and sentenced to ten years in prison. Abandoned in London, looked after by relatives, Zuska survived a lonely adolescence. We talked of this and other things on our slow walks beside the Thames. The world grieved her. She read all the right books, saw all the approved movies, sat through the plays most praised by reviewers, and failed to find anything resembling wisdom. Life was a cheat. 'There's nothing out there,' she said of the world beyond her Chelsea window. 'People are fooling themselves if they think there is.'

Even my antipodean melancholy wasn't that panoramic. Currently Zuska had even more on her mind. She had just discovered, by way of a letter functioning as a bookmark, that her longtime English lover, a gentleman farmer, was homosexual. What, she asked me, should she do about it? Should she, after so many years, persist in the relationship? Or should she pretend that she had never read the letter? Should she just walk away?

With no word of lie I informed Zuska that I was no expert on the subject.

'But novelists write of love,' she protested.

'This one's on holiday,' I insisted.

So very soon was Zuska. She went off to vacation with her gentleman farmer after all. I urged her to avoid melancholic books when she selected her holiday reading. And especially to avoid makeshift bookmarks. That was the best I could do as a therapist. At least I left her with a smile on her face. Clattering down the steps of her apartment block, I set out to find work.

Another East European, this time a buoyant Bulgarian named Dimi Panitza, came my way. The gnomic child of an aristocratic family, always rich in gossip fresh from Stalinist Europe, Dimi was head of the Paris bureau of *Reader's Digest* and a legend in his profession. (I had a suspicion or two about Dimi also. He looked to have all the qualifications to be head of a CIA station in Europe. Who knew? In flight from the Sutch trial, I might have stumbled into something even more murky.) My past connection with Bulgaria, as an itinerant in the 1950s, cemented my friendship with Dimi. That, and the fact that we came from small countries. This meant expensive lunches and talk of work.

'Nothing political,' I insisted.

'Nothing political,' he promised.

'So what do you know about Otto Klemperer?' he asked.

217

I was mystified. 'Otto Klemperer? The conductor?'

'The conductor.'

'I have a feeling he died last year.'

'Indeed,' said Dimi. 'What else do you know?'

'That he was a great conductor. A very great conductor.'

'Excellent,' Dimi said, reaching for wine and filling my glass. 'You're my man.'

'What does that mean?'

'You've just won your first assignment. Three thousand dollars US and all expenses.'

Two days later I was in Zurich, researching Klemperer's life, interviewing his dearest friends and nearest relatives. It was an instructive assignment. For much of his life this scarred and tormented man had won music from black bouts of depression, from a lame body and an often befuddled brain. Depression had often been an ally rather than an enemy. It allowed him to withdraw, to study Beethhoven's scores, for example, with a dedication unmatched by his contemporaries. It gave him a greater repertoire than other conductors. And it gave him a lightning facility in absorbing new work.

The message was plain. Work would remain my weapon in my own fight with depression. Not a comforting panacea. A weapon. I could use it rather than let it use me. I was to owe Dimi more than he knew. Otto Klemperer too.

'So what do you know about the Danube Delta?' Dimi asked.

'Isn't it in Romania?' I asked cautiously.

'Good,' he said. 'You've got that job too.'

'Me?'

'You.'

'I know next to nothing about it,' I protested.

'You will,' Dimi promised. 'What did you know about Klemperer?'

'Not much,' I admitted.

'There you are,' he said. 'Last week you were one of the world's authorities on Klemperer. Next week you'll be a respected expert on the ecology of the delta. That's life. The same fee, by the way. $3000 plus expenses. While I think of it, what do you know about Alvar Aalto?'

'Alvar Aalto?'

'The Finnish achitect.'

'I have a feeling that I'm about to learn.'

'He's yours after Klemperer,' Dimi confirmed.

It was surprising how persuasive my empty wallet could be. Dimi's boisterous Mayfair lunches cost more than I earned in an average month.

Thirty-nine

*I*t was twenty years since I had been in a Communist country. First impressions said that things were no better. A seedy and unshaven bureaucrat in baggy trousers picked me up at the airport. He all but held his hand out for a bribe to ensure the success of my mission. I refused to oblige; I was even reluctant to buy him a drink. His immediate superiors were no improvement. Though instructed by Romanian diplomats in London to give me assistance they went into a nervous spin. An unsavoury commissar crawled from the woodwork to say that I could be an American spy. I was certainly, he said, in the pay of a known anti-Communist magazine. His aspersions on my character, as conveyed by a pretty young interpreter named Beate, became even more fanciful.

At length I could take no more. I stood. I challenged my accuser to telephone Romania's Minister of Tourism and report that he, the commissar, had refused to help the largest magazine in the world tell the story of the Danube Delta and Romanian attempts to save it from industrial pollution. Fear grew on the man's face. I recognised it. It was the fear which lubricated Communist lands.

'Go on,' I urged. 'Make a call. See what happens.'

I had never pulled rank as a writer before. It worked wonders. His expression became even more sickly.

The telephone call was made. Suddenly all Romania seemed mine for the asking: I had two scientists to help me, a tourist launch and its crew, and an interpreter. Everything I wanted. Including as much of the Danube and its delta as I needed to see.

With Romania to my rear, duty to Dimi done, I thought I might pick up on old friendships. My fifteen-year absence had taken a toll.

Friends of the 1950s were now thin on the ground. Some had died. Some had simply disappeared. Few New Zealanders remained expatriate in the conventional Mansfield manner. (And the lady herself was no longer our lone star.) In her grave at Fontainbleu she now had the antipodean readership she wished but never found in her lifetime.

An exception to prove the rule, someone still in the Mansfield mould, was the poet Fleur Adcock, sister of Marilyn Duckworth. Always aloof from her surroundings, seldom less than enigmatic, Fleur had escaped New Zealand after the collapse of a colourful love life, involving both Maurice Duggan and the boozy and wife-bashing Barry Crump. The folklorist from the bush left another victim in his wake. It was a liaison few understood. If Fleur herself did, she wasn't telling. Understandably England became her haven, far from New Zealand's bruising bohemia. There she refashioned herself as an elegant woman of letters, a crystal-voiced poet much respected by her peers. In London I looked her up in East Finchley and found her about to go into hospital. Illness wasn't her only woe. Her longtime love Maurice Duggan, after battling bone disease, tuberculosis, alcoholism and finally cancer had just died in Auckland. I brought Fleur news from his graveside. With five of his contemporaries, I had helped carry Maurice's coffin. This shouldn't have been onerous; Maurice had been wasting away through his last months and there was little of him left. But for some reason I found the coffin unnaturally heavy; so weighty, in fact, that I was afraid I was going to let it drop. I was obliged to grip my handle of the coffin awkwardly, with both hands. Worse, the metal handle began cutting into my left hand. By the time we reached the hearse – in my case, stumbling – my hand was bleeding freely, the gore colouring the sleeve of my suit. When the hearse drew away I cleaned up the hand with a handkerchief and turned to Eric McCormick, my neighbouring pallbearer.

'Did you think he was heavy?' I asked.

'Heavy?' he asked. 'Maurice?'

He looked at me strangely. I decided not to pursue the subject further, nor to distress fellow mourners. A Maori might not have had the problem. Tales of inexplicably weighty coffins are commonplace in Maori lore. Six powerful men – so such stories say – often fail to lift a coffin containing some shrivelled old grandmother reluctant to farewell this life. Had Maurice been signalling similar sentiments? If so, I was an unlikely messenger. Though we had friends in common, Maurice and I had never been intimates. Eventually I confided the episode to Fleur, by far the best person to make use of it. Sure enough, before many weeks had passed, it found a home in one of her poems.

There was more talk. Sharing memories of Maurice, we walked together in Highgate wood; picked blackberries; recited loved lines of verse, and went to theatres. This restful interval was ended by Val's rowdy arrival in London. She had just finished a season in Queensland, and had another in Tasmania. She wanted me to join her there. I said that this was now out of the question, that I was going home to New Zealand when my time in London was done. Val, however, failed to hear. She was never one to accept no as an answer.

'New Zealand?' she said.

'New Zealand,' I confirmed.

'Can't you take time out from the place?'

'I've been trying,' I pointed out.

Unsuccessfully, I might have added. At home a woeful general election was looming. A populist monster named Muldoon, by far the most repulsive candidate for high office New Zealand had known, was worming his way to power. Character assassination, red scares and racial slurs were his speciality. For the first time in the century democracy seemed under threat. Concerned citizens – conspicuous among them New Zealand's national hero Edmund Hillary – were attempting to rouse fellow countrymen to the perils inherent in a Muldoon triumph. The man was daily looking even more of a menace, vindictively promising his opponents a bad time when he took power. I had a cable from New Zealand asking if I would let my name be used by the anti-Muldoon camp. Though I imagined I had sworn off politics, I stopped short of saying no. Then I had a telephone call asking me to address a political meeting in New Zealand House. It would be the first in the building's history; the place was simmering. Again I found it impossible to cry off. Two or three hundred New Zealanders, resident temporarily in London, turned up for the meeting, which – so I learned later – was extensively publicised back in New Zealand. Did I swing any votes? I had probably done no more than have my name entered in Muldoon's black book. At least I would be in good company.

Forty

My mother wrote regularly from home. Reports of IRA bomb blasts in London made her fearful for my future. 'Watch where you walk,' she warned.

I patiently explained that I stood more risk of being levelled by a London taxi than of being minced by an Irish bomb. She was not convinced by my statistics. The sooner I was home the better, she said. She might have been even more uneasy had she known that Fleur and I were about to fly to Dublin for a quiet weekend. Quiet? Why shouldn't it be? In the course of the latest bombing campaign Dublin had remained tranquil while streets of Belfast and London were ripped apart. Dublin was out of the firing line and couldn't be safer, or so I informed my mother in a hasty note. This was to prove a monumental misjudgement.

The truth was that I had no intention of missing out on my first and perhaps last chance to visit Ireland. I wanted to walk the quays of Arklow, the waterfront where my seafaring grandfather walked, where he fitted out the sailing vessel which would carry him to New Zealand in or around 1902. Our day of departure coincided with election day in New Zealand. The flight from Heathrow was delayed two hours. Against my better judgement, I looked for a telephone, called New Zealand House and learned that Muldoon had won a devastating electoral victory. It was news I didn't need, not with the prospect of an untroubled weekend with Fleur ahead. Was the country going to be worth living in? Worth returning to? With bribes and threats Muldoon had worked on the worst of the national character to get his win. Shaken and sickened, I considered washing my hands of New Zealand. That might have pleased Val. It was a near thing.

Fleur was impatient with the airport delay. It meant we had lost two precious hours of our first day in Dublin. Inner-city pubs would be shut to customers by the time we arrived. My slump in spirits, following on the tidings from New Zealand, didn't help either. I tried to cheer her. 'I'll buy you a Guinness as soon as we've landed,' I promised. 'We can have a quick airport drink.'

'A quick airport drink?'

'To celebrate my arrival on ancestral soil.'

She smiled wanly. 'An airport drink isn't the same,' she argued.

'It's the best I can offer,' I pointed out.

Our plane landed. I picked up and parked our rental car and left Fleur installing our bags while I made use of the men's toilet. There was only one other occupant. Though I have tried to reconstruct the next minute of my life a score of times I remember only a male with a bluish suit, dark hair and perhaps olive skin. He was facing a mirror and combing his hair. There may have been something sly about the fellow; something edgy in his profile or jerky in his movements. Perhaps. I am never likely to know.

What I do recall is a powerful panic. Never before had I encountered a sensation so suffocating. Nor have I since. All I knew was that we had to move quickly. My feet, seemingly with a life of their own, were carrying me along at breakneck pace. 'What about this airport drink, then?' Fleur asked as she struggled to keep up with me.

'Let's forget it,' I said. Perhaps I was curt. 'Let's just get into the city.'

'Is there something wrong?'

'Nothing,' I claimed.

I started the car and pointed it away from the terminal. Urgency continued to prevail. For some reason I looked at my watch. It said five minutes past three. Less than a mile on I stopped the car to fasten my seat belt, something I had forgotten in my agitation. Then I accelerated away again. A minute later we met up with three police cars travelling in the reverse direction, their sirens howling and lights flashing. They all but crowded us off the road.

'Something's up,' Fleur observed.

Something was.

A little way on we met two more police vehicles moving at high speed. I parked off the roadside until the commotion had gone.

'Probably a police exercise,' I suggested.

That seemed possible. We drove sedately into Dublin. That evening, in an amiable pub in Baggot Street, we settled seriously into our Guinness. There was a discarded newspaper on a chair beside me. At first I ignored it. Then a headline leapt into view. BOMB AT DUBLIN AIRPORT, it said. Smaller type recorded that a bomb had exploded at the airport shortly after 3 pm that day. It had blown out the men's toilet and a wall of the airport bar. Several people in the bar had been injured and borne off to hospital. A body, possibly of the man planting the bomb, had been retrieved from the wreckage. It was thought to be a Protestant bomb, the first of that denomination to damage Dublin in years. It was also thought to have been brought in on our flight from London.

'Dear God,' I heard myself whisper.

Had we been a couple of minutes slower Fleur might have been among the damaged drinkers retrieved from the airport bar. The body in the shattered urinal might have been mine. It could also have been the fellow I glimpsed in the murk of the men's toilet. With no great experience and too little expertise he may even have been wiring up the bomb which killed him.

Someone was looking after us that Dublin day. Whoever it was, or whatever, it made Muldoon and his paltry politics seem immaterial. Had we halted for that airport drink I wouldn't have this tale to tell.

There must be a moral here. There is. Mothers know best.

Forty-one

Shaking off Europe in the last weeks of 1976, I flew back to New Zealand. My estranged wife Barbara and my four-year-old daughter Brigid met me at Auckland airport and drove me home to Titirangi. Tenants had gone. Expecting dirt and disorder, I found the house disarmingly spotless. It looked clean, smelled clean, and was. Even my ancient oven gleamed. And the place was coloured with freshly cut flowers. It transpired that the housework was to be seen as a gift from Barbara in lieu of a conventional welcome. It was impossible not to be touched by the gesture. There had been little sweetness and light in our lives in the years since we separated. The flowers suggested that our story might have another chapter. And that proved the case. It is marvellous what magic flowers can work.

The merciless Muldoon steamroller had left nervous friends persuaded that New Zealand no longer had a future; their gloom was a match for any melancholy of mine. At least, like a conductor named Klemperer, I could call on my work to bridge the black holes in my psyche. My situation seemed to allow for modest optimism. *Danger Zone* was winning warm reviews in New Zealand and Britain. London's *Guardian* had run a half-page feature on my work. Next morning, with sunlight rippling on the estuary, seabirds circling overhead, I read through the reviews and a mixed bag of mostly pleasant correspondence with a steaming cup of coffee in hand. It seemed that I had to ask myself a question. I might also have to provide an answer. No one else was likely to. Unless my arithmetic was faulty, I had now survived some two-thirds of my adult life. Had it been worth living? Had my narratives been necessary, my tales worth telling? There were many possible answers, not all of them comfortable, and I knew them by heart.

My fellow survivor of the Dublin bomb breezed in from London. Fleur was back to see family and friends and to take up my offer of a guided tour of the nooks and crannies of my New Zealand. She was instantly in love with Titirangi, the monster trees and mangroves, the darting kingfishers and leaping mullet. 'Only a lunatic would consider giving this up,' Fleur said firmly. That was reassuring. I may have been a depressive. I wasn't a lunatic. Every woman in my life but Barbara had seen this seascape as a rival and schemed to part me from the place. Sooner or later, and in most cases sooner, they failed. Perhaps only a poet like Fleur – or for that matter Jim Baxter – could imagine what my estuarine existence meant. Fleur was soon busy weaving the sights and sounds of Titirangi into her journal. Fleur and her journal were seldom parted. It was even discreetly on her knee when she sat to a meal. She didn't miss the humblest detail of her daily life; not even the price of a meal in her neighbourhood curry house. This was a matter of concern to her intimates past and present. They feared they were on record there too, perhaps not in flattering form. Such fear was possibly justified.

Yet one thing was sure. Unlike most writers I had known, Fleur was bound to win the applause of posterity. Possibly as a poet. Certainly as a chronicler. I envisage social historians, greedy for the grit of our 20th century lives, breaking down bookshop doors when her record of her century is polished and published. The rest of us may be trampled in the stampede.

As for me, the answer to the question seemed to be yes. Yes and yes again. It has mostly been worth it. And I had what was left of my life to make a little more of it.

Let us end this. Let it be twenty years later and one or two more. Let it, in short, be 1999. This morning's newspapers are making much of the advancing millennium. They continue to inform us that this land will shortly be the first to be brushed by the faint eastern light which will herald our next thousand years. New Zealanders are to have box seats for this weighty occasion.

Walking with Barbara after breakfast, beside the bright morning tide, I talked of my difficulty of pulling down the shutters on this manuscript. It had to come to a stop somewhere, since most things did. I also had to allow for the possibility, unlikely as it seemed, that

I might survive to resume the narrative on the far side of the millennium. Finally, and seemingly out of nowhere, I heard myself begin to argue – more vehemently than necessary – that no writer matters individually, that our successes and sorrows were insignificant. I suggested that we were no more than bricks and mortar in the house of literature, a repository for humankind's riches, an asylum for those seeking solace. Our names were unnecessary. But Homer couldn't help but be my cousin, Shakespeare and Tolstoy too. And that wasn't to acknowledge my cool and crafty half-sister Katherine. (Half here, half there. Can you hear me, kinswoman? Will you take my hand too?) Even in a sea-lapped outpost like mine we are never alone; we are one in the end. We are at our most inseparable when at our most solitary.

There was more to this morning's waterside ramble. Barbara, as has currently been her practice, was methodically testing my memory, my powers of cognition, and significant shifts of mood. For many months now my life has been shadowed by the proximity of a possibly mortal condition. It is already more than a year since a neurologist, a psychiatrist and a pair of knowledgeable GPs discerned that I had symptoms consistent with Alzheimer's Disease. (Either that or something masquerading efficiently as such.) The jury is still out on the subject. In the meantime there have been communications large and small. When the news of my condition broke – with a panicked partner of four years' standing sailing off into the security of Auckland suburbia – my postbox was awash with sympathy, good wishes, and offers of help. I had never been more grateful for the compassionate companions in my life: for Gillian and Barbara, Marilyn and Fleur, Bridget and Beverly. Even, yes, for Val. Barbara, need I say it, was first on the scene. And, not for the first time, she came to stay.

Others had more to communicate. Among them were formerly uncharitable reviewers and critics now having second thoughts. I was in the piquant and rather comic position of reading my obituaries years ahead of time. Some were surprisingly good. I must hope the next and last, which I shall unavoidably miss, are half as generous.

There is no escaping it. As the old maxim says, and even a dilettante memoirist knows, confession serves the soul best. It is also the life of the party. For once in my literary life I had no complaints to register. In short, I got a good press. 'The grand old man of New

Zealand literature, spurned by the academy but warmly judged by ordinary people,' said *The Times Literary Supplement*. 'Reviews to die for,' Bridget Armstrong would say with thespian passion. Well almost. Not quite.

As we turned for home, with a colourful flock of startled rosellas lifting overhead, Barbara said, 'You're thoughtful this morning.'

'Yes,' I agreed.

'So talk,' she suggested.

I heard myself telling her of a visit I made to an exhibition of illuminated medieval manuscripts in the British Museum. The visit left me shaken, uncomfortably close to tears. It wasn't so much the thought of anonymous monks slaving for decades on those incandescent pages. It was my discovery that I belonged to their tradition, that I was of their company; I belonged with my brothers and sisters in the fraternity of the wordsmith. And if my stories fail to survive, what does it matter? My sister Katherine's surely will.

Works by Maurice Shadbolt

Fiction

The New Zealanders (1959, revised 1993) is Maurice Shadbolt's first collection of short fiction. The subtitle, 'A Sequence of Stories', and the division of the stories into three sections, each of which takes its heading from the book's first epigraph, an excerpt from James K. Baxter's poem 'Homage to Lost Friends', highlight the collection's carefully organised structure. The first section, 'Wave Walkers', focuses on what Shadbolt has referred to as 'rural and small-town New Zealand' during the inter-war period, particularly the 1930s. The second section, 'Cloud Riders', treats urban New Zealand of the 1950s, while the third section, 'In the Blind Canyon', moves out beyond New Zealand shores. Notable amongst the stories in this collection are 'The Woman's Story', which includes what is perhaps still Shadbolt's most convincingly-realised female character, 'After the Depression', which treats for the first time some of the social and political concerns of the 1930s which would later resurface in the novel *Strangers and Journeys*, and 'Play the Fife Lowly', which shared the 1957 *Landfall* Prose Award. The settings of the stories range from the pioneer farm in 'The Woman's Story' to the various European cities of 'Maria', 'Thank you goodbye' and 'River, Girl and Onion', while the characters include male and female, Maori and

Pakeha, farmers and artists. Severally and together, the stories in *The New Zealanders* explore the need for, and emergence of, a distinct New Zealand cultural identity. In retrospect, *The New Zealanders* can be seen to signal the direction of much of Shadbolt's subsequent writing.

Summer Fires and Winter Country (1963) is Shadbolt's second collection of short stories. Again, as in *The New Zealanders*, the stories are organised to a careful pattern. The title of this collection highlights the idea oppositions, and indeed the various stories explore a number of oppositions, notably between youth and age and past and present. There is also a strong sense of return in these stories, whether it be to New Zealand, to the land, or even to the past as a source of self-discovery – which suggests that the nine stories in this collection (but perhaps particularly 'Homecoming') are a logical continuation of the sequence established in *The New Zealanders*. In many cases the stories in this collection have stood the test of time better than those of *The New Zealanders*. The opening story, 'Ben's Land', which spans four generations of Ben's tribe, including the first-person narrator's own, is particularly interesting in the light of the relationship that can be traced between the story, the novels *Among the Cinders* and *The Lovelock Version*, and Shadbolt's first volume of autobiography, *One of Ben's*. Other particularly strong stories include 'Homecoming', winner of the Katherine Mansfield Prize in 1963, 'The Room', and 'The People Before'.

Among the Cinders (1965, revised 1984) is Maurice Shadbolt's first novel. It was made into a film in 1983. The book follows Nick Flinders on a journey of maturation which takes him through New Zealand in the company of his grandfather Hubert. Through the combination of the journey and the inter-generational relationship Shadbolt addresses the male-dominated pioneer period of New Zealand's post-European history. *Among the Cinders*, which began as a playful parody of some New Zealand writing – including the work of C.K. Stead, Allen Curnow, and Ian Cross – is best read as a realist novel, and, indeed, most of the satirical passages were excised from the revised edition. The novel is short by Shadbolt's standards and the writing may appear a little dated, even näive, thirty years on; but as Shadbolt explains in the Author's Note included in the revised edition, 'it's a young man's tale'. At one point, towards the end of the novel, Nick Flinders is described as his poet brother's 'unpolished window on reality.' Nick's voice as well as his vision is indeed unpolished and näive; to polish it would be to destroy its innocence and with it the strength of Shadbolt's narrative.

The Presence of Music (1967) is a triptych of three novellas which was to be Shadbolt's last collection of new stories for almost thirty years. The three stories share common themes, particularly a concern with the position of the artist in society – in the 1950s in the first two panels of the triptych, 'The Voyagers' and 'The Presence of Music', and then in the 1960s in 'Figures in Light' (which won Shadbolt the Katherine Mansfield Prize in 1967).

This Summer's Dolphin (1969) stands apart from the historical pattern which marks almost the whole of Shadbolt's *oeuvre*. It is essentially a moral fable loosely based on the story of Opo, the mysterious dolphin whose sojourn at Opononi in New Zealand's far north in 1956 about which Shadbolt had earlier made a documentary film. This short novel focuses on a group of isolated characters – including a fisherman, a disillusioned writer, an enigmatic young girl – whose lives are temporarily brought together by their tenuous connection to Motu the dolphin, whose presence seems to offer a possibility of redemption in an otherwise hopeless world before being sacrificed on the altar of human greed or hatred.

An Ear of the Dragon (1971) attracted considerable criticism for its blatant reconstruction of the life of Renato Amato (Pietro Fratta). However, the use Shadbolt made of Amato's life is only a part of this novel. Perhaps the largest part concerns Frank Firth (posssibly a persona of the author) who, in telling the story of his friend Pietro Fratta also tells his own story, which turns out to be another version of part of New Zealand's history. The use Shadbolt makes of historical flashbacks in both stories is particularly skilful.

Strangers and Journeys (1972, revised 1990) is widely regarded as Maurice Shadbolt's major early work. It is a long and ambitious novel which took ten years to write. Essentially a work of social realism, it draws together many of the themes from his earlier fiction, particularly the story 'After the Depression' and the novel *Among the Cinders*, to draw a contrast between the lives of two fathers, Ned Livingstone and Bill Freeman, and their sons Tim and Ian. The most successful sections of the novel are those which deal with the lives of the fathers and their battles with the harsh environment and the equally harsh economic times. In the later sections, which move to the city, replicating New Zealand's rural to urban drift, the focus on the lives of the sons continues the exploration of the position of the artist in New Zealand society that had been a consistent concern in Shadbolt's earlier work.

A Touch of Clay (1974, revised 1995) was envisaged as the first part of a projected trilogy of novels about the 1970s. The setting for this novel is a West Auckland suburb overlooking an estuary, where Paul Pike, an ex-lawyer turned potter (another of the many artist figures who inhabit Shadbolt's fiction) is recovering from a breakdown. Pike's idyllic, isolated world is disrupted by a series of representative characters – a commune-leader-cum-guru figure, an environmental campaigner, the drug-dependent girl, Irene, with whom he has a disastrous affair – who are used to explore a number of the social issues which helped to characterise the 1970s, including religion, drugs, and the environment. Pike's present-time story is juxtaposed with his grandfather's nineteenth-century journals, passages of which are scattered throughout the novel and highlight once more Shadbolt's concern with history. That the stories of Pike and his grandfather begin to merge at the end when Pike takes flight suggests that this novel may be about existential and moral issues of personal responsibility as well as about New Zealand society and the parallels and contrasts between New Zealand's pioneer past and its present.

Danger Zone (1974) is the second part of Shadbolt's unfinished trilogy of the 1970s. It focuses on New Zealand's opposition to nuclear testing in the South Pacific, and is loosely based on Shadbolt's voyage to Mururoa on board the protest vessel *Tamure* in 1972. Beyond the obvious politics, the focus of *Danger Zone* – as in *A Touch of Clay* (and perhaps *This Summer's Dolphin* and *An Ear of the Dragon*, too) – is on individual relationships and responsibilities.

Figures in Light (1978) is a collection of selected (and in come cases slightly revised) stories drawn from *Summer Fires and Winter Country* and *The Presence of Music*.

The Lovelock Version (1980) is central to Shadbolt's whole body of fiction; it picks up some of the themes from earlier stories such as 'Ben's Land', the opening story of *Summer Fires and Winter Country*, his second collection of short fiction, and introduces others that he would later return to in the play *Once on Chunuk Bair*, in *Monday's Warriors*, the second novel of his New Zealand Wars trilogy, and also in his autobiographical work, *One of Ben's*. It is in some ways his finest, certainly his most exuberant novel to date, and the first novel in which he treats New Zealand's nineteenth-century colonial history in detail. Using a blend of realism and magic realism, *The Lovelock Version* presents New Zealand's postcolonial history through the stories of the three Lovelock brothers – Herman, Richard, and James – and their families. Intersecting with these three central strands, are a series of digressions which weave an extraordinary array of historical figures, locations, and events into the fictional world of the Lovelocks.

Season of the Jew (1986, revised 1997) is the first part of a loosely-linked trilogy of revisionist-historical novels, and probably Shadbolt's best-known and most popular novel. Indeed, in the 1998 *Listener* readers' poll it was voted 'favourite New Zealand book'. *Season of the Jew* marks a new stage in Shadbolt's *oeuvre*, which moves away from the metafictional treatment of nineteenth-century New Zealand history that marked his previous novel, *The Lovelock Version*, and instead treats history in a realist mode. Set in the 1860s, *Season of the Jew* tells the story of the historical Maori warrior-prophet Te Kooti Rikirangi, founder of the Ringatu faith, largely from the perspective of the composite character George Fairweather, an erstwhile army regular, a landscape painter, and a liberal-humanist whose sympathies (though he fights with the colonists) tend towards the Maori.

Monday's Warriors (1990), again set in the 1860s, retells the story of another warrior-prophet, Titokowaru – in tandem with that of the rebel Pakeha Kimball Bent, a significant historical figure himself, who provides the sympathetic perspective on historical events earlier achieved through the character of Fairweather. Kimball Bent's position in *Monday's Warriors* provides Shadbolt with a means to get much closer to Titokowaru than he could ever get to Te Kooti.

The House of Strife (1993), the final volume of the New Zealand Wars trilogy, moves backwards in time rather than forwards, to the 1840s and the early years of the New Zealand Wars. It recounts the story of Hone Heke, whose war against the colonists is perhaps even more extraordinary, though less bloody, than those of Te Kooti and Titokowaru. At one point during the course of this novel Heke is heard to lament that 'A man must have his own [story]. Otherwise he walks the world a shadow'. The person Shadbolt chooses to tell Heke's story is the wonderfully-realised Ferdinand Wildblood, alias Henry Youngman – a Victorian catchpenny novelist and plagiarist, who is in New Zealand to escape the attentions of ex-convict James Dinwiddie – who marks a fascinating progression from the narrators of the earlier volumes of the trilogy. Through Ferdinand Wildlood (who recalls events from the safe distance of forty years) Shadbolt is able to introduce a late-Victorian perspective of events as well as those of the 1840s (Hone Heke's present) and the 1990s (the author's present).

Dove on the Waters (1996) can be treated as either a collection of stories or as a novel. The title story, 'Dove on the Waters' (which won the Katherine Mansfield Prize for 1995, making Shadbolt the only writer to have won the award on three occasions), marked the author's return to the short story form after an absence of almost thirty years. That story and two others were later published as *Dove on the Waters*. The first of the three stories, the title story, tells the tale of Walter Dove, an Auckland lawyer who retreats from society supposedly to sail solo round the world. The second, 'The Venetian Bride', follows the lonely spinster Rose Lightfoot on her art-inspired journey to Venice. The third, 'The Birds of Grief Gully', focuses on the reclusive Boer war veteran Jim Bird. At first glance this might suggest a disparate group of stories, but various threads tie them together. In one way or another, the central characters of each story are hermits: Walter hiding away on his beached boat, Rose deserted and cocooned in her Auckland home, and Jim and Laurel Bird who spend fifty years living in protective isolation from their Coromandel neighbours. More significantly, all three tales are consuming stories of love: Walter's love for Alice, Rose's desperate love for the husband who abandoned her, and Jim and Laurel Bird's enduring love for one another. These unconventional love stories are skilfully held together through the constant presence of Great-Aunt Alice, her nephew the author, and the strength of their love for each other.

Selected Stories (1998) is a collection of stories, selected and introduced by Ralph Crane, which draws on all Shadbolt's published short fiction. It includes four stories from *The New Zealanders*, six stories from *Summer Fires and Winter Country*, two novellas from *The Presence of Music*, the title story from *Dove on the Waters*, and the uncollected story 'The Simple Life'.

Autobiography

One of Ben's (1993), the first volume of Shadbolt's autobiography, mixes the myths and legends of the Shadbolt tribe with those of Pakeha/postcolonial New Zealand. The book begins as a rich tapestry of stories about some of the more diverting Shadbolt ancestors: Great-grandfather Ben, a transported felon who survived the Norfolk Island and Port Arthur penal institutions to become the squire of Duvauchelle (on Banks Peninsula), and the Shadbolt family patriarch; his son Ernest, sportsman, bodyguard to George V, bush lawyer, and, in what seems to be a Shadbolt tradition, father of many children; the remarkable Aunt Sis, who nursed in Spain during the Civil War and later ruled the roost at Hokianga hospital; and Uncle Jack, who when he wasn't fighting Germans fought his way to the light-heavyweight boxing championship of the Allied forces during World War II. On his mother's side of the family there are yet more remarkable characters, including Arklow Joe Kearon (sailor, avid reader, atheist, and socialist) and his son, Uncle Joe (soldier and communist), who survived the Auckland riots of 1932. Once the past has been established, attention shifts to the author himself. In *One of Ben's* Shadbolt weaves only the stories of his early years, up to about the age of twenty-six – his days as a labourer, a newspaper reporter, a flirter with left-wing politics and (as it must have appeared to the general public at least) the quasi-bohemian lifestyle of Auckland's literary circles of the early 1950s, and his friendships with such well-known New Zealand writers as James K. Baxter and Kevin Ireland. The early years of Shadbolt's own life treated here also include the years he spent overseas, travelling and living in such countries as China, the Soviet Union, Romania, Bulgaria, Poland, Spain, and, of course, Britain. The book appropriately draws to a close with Shadbolt's return home as an established writer (following the publication of *The New Zealanders* in Britain) yet to prove himself to the satisfaction of New Zealanders.

Drama

Once on Chunuk Bair (1982) is Maurice Shadbolt's only published play. It was filmed in 1991. The action takes place during the hours between dawn and dusk on 8 August 1915, the day that New Zealand soldiers took the hill of Chunuk Bair on the Gallipoli peninsula. The play sets out to explore what is presented as the moment that New Zealand realised its identity as an independent, postcolonial nation, and everything in the play is organised to this end. Significantly, in Shadbolt's version of events it is carelessly directed 'friendly fire' from a British ship, rather than 'hostile fire' from the Turks, which ultimately does for the New Zealanders in the closing moments of the play. Despite its limited subject and its (necessarily) all male cast, *Once on Chunuk Bair* engages with a number of social and economic concerns which continue to be of relevance to contemporary New Zealand society.

Non-fiction

New Zealand: Gift of the Sea (with Brian Brake; 1963, revised 1973 and 1990) is a large-format coffee-table book which tells the story of New Zealand – from its beginnings five million years ago up to the present and perhaps beyond – through Brian Brake's magnificent pictures and Maurice Shadbolt's precise words.

The Shell Guide to New Zealand (1968, revised 1973 and 1976) is part of the international series of Shell Guides. It contains a general introduction to the country and seventeen sections which deal with fourteen specific regions as well as the four major cities. The text is complemented by photographs (mostly black and white) by Philip Temple.

Love and Legend (1976) is a collection of fifteen disparate profiles – fourteen of famous and not so famous New Zealanders, the final one of Opo the dolphin – which all originally appeared in abbreviated form in the *Reader's Digest* between 1971 and 1975.

The Reader's Digest Guide to New Zealand (with Brian Brake; 1988, revised 1993) is a large-format guide book in the form of a gazetteer which is full of useful practical information (about historical sites and other places of interest, scenic routes, local figures, and so on). The country is divided into twenty regions, each of which is thoroughly and entertainingly described by Shadbolt and photographed by Brian Brake.

Voices of Gallipoli (1988) is primarily a collection of twelve narratives in which Gallipoli veterans are allowed to tell their own stories. The origins of the book can be traced directly back to, and possibly beyond, a visit Shadbolt made to ANZAC Cove and Chunuk Bair in 1977. In the wake of that visit his consuming interest in the Gallipoli campaign of 1915 was to lead to the Chunuk Bair section of *The Lovelock Version*, the play *Once on Chunuk Bair*, a TVNZ documentary screened in 1984, and to this book – which draws on the interviews gathered for the television documentary. The veterans' narratives are supplemented by Shadbolt's own lucid account of the campaign, which provides an ideal backdrop to the individual stories.

Ralph Crane